Jim Emerton

Pigeon
Racing

My personal insights

Jim Emerton

Pigeon
Racing

My personal insights

MEREO
Cirencester

Mereo Books

1A The Wool Market Dyer Street Cirencester Gloucestershire GL7 2PR
An imprint of Memoirs Publishing www.mereobooks.com

PIGEON RACING: 978-1-86151-679-4

First published in Great Britain in 2016
by Mereo Books, an imprint of Memoirs Publishing

The address for Memoirs Publishing Group Limited can be found at
www.memoirspublishing.com

The Memoirs Publishing Group Ltd Reg. No. 7834348

The Memoirs Publishing Group supports both The Forest Stewardship Council® (FSC®) and the PEFC® leading international forest-certification organisations. Our books carrying both the FSC label and the PEFC® and are printed on FSC®-certified paper. FSC® is the only forest-certification scheme supported by the leading environmental organisations including Greenpeace. Our paper procurement policy can be found at www.memoirspublishing.com/environment

Typeset in 10/14pt Century Schoolbook
by Wiltshire Associates Publisher Services Ltd. Printed and bound in Great Britain by Printondemand-Worldwide, Peterborough PE2 6XD

My thanks and gratitude go to the influences of Mensa Special Interest Groups eg Green Scene, Elimar Pigeons, The Racing Pigeon magazine, and all the people whose paths have crossed paths with me in a rich and diverse life and who may have enjoyed my writing.

Jim Emerton

CONTENTS

ONE

—

OF PIGEONS, RAISING
AND RACING THEM

WHAT'S IN A NAME?

Pigeons tend to assume the name of the publicised or famous fancier, humans all! To my knowledge there are no homozygotically 100 per cent genetically-pure racing pigeons, ie all with the same genome. Names become popular due to the media marketing them for ego/sales and a multiplicity of reasons. Janssens and Stichelbaut, who are still famous pigeon people, did not have absolutely pure birds, although it may be perceived that they did. Fashionable strains come and go like quicksilver, yet really top pigeon men are rare, are they not?

Now it will be unearthly when the Barcelona International is won into the UK. It is possible, but improbable. The real joy is in building a family with a distinct hereditary characteristic that perform at a satisfactory level. OK, they may take your name, even though they are but a mixture. It is the humanisation element of the sport, and this is only my subjective opinion in the vast complexity of pigeon racing.

WHAT MAKES A PIGEON TICK?

Like humans, birds have basic survival needs that constitute a life cycle. Attempting to understand one may give insight into ourselves, since we are both life forms sharing the same planet. With empathy we can react and respond to the behaviours of a pigeon and perhaps to its mind, which is the essence of being - they are not soulless machines. Lady fanciers are often clever at the more sensitive aspects of communication, and Dorothy sang to each one as it sat on the perch - *O Come All Ye Faithful* perhaps?

Switch on your mind, tune in and focus on each bird in the loft - you may enjoy the relationship. All nice and soft, yet the objective is to entice the birds to race home from greater and greater distances - the good ones will give their all. This with top overall management is the quintessence of clever fanciership. A bird needs a secure, comfortable home, with quality food, water, breeding facilities, and access to nature so that it can exhibit its instincts and just be in optimal surroundings. My partner knows how to do it, and pigeons will give their all to return to his methods - as seen at Barcelona. Many good birds just lack condition when race entered, a factor which depends largely on the fancier - the man makes the bird, he is at the top of the pecking order in the food chain, and the intricate web of the sport.

PHYSICAL TYPE

To me all pigeons are beautiful. Quality racing pigeons come in a myriad of colours, shapes and sizes due to genetic diversity in their origins. My birds were mainly chequers/darks and dark velvets via breeding and race selection. I prefer darks with silky feather classed as yellow and being small or medium balanced birds with nice deep pectoral muscles and smooth and tight in the hand. An exception was Barcelona Dream - a giant of a cock bird.

If a bird becomes a champion at any distance it follows *a priori* that its genotype and phenotype are satisfactory in the reality test of racing. There are birds to score from 90 to 735 miles at Pau like my Dedication, which are rare. A good bird usually gives out to the mind's eye an essence of its quality ie in the eye of the beholder. In practical terms hard racing under optimal management will produce the desired physical type and genotype since there is no set physical type or eye type at any distance - the latter will manifest family traits and characteristics and it is fascinating to make studies of these. The greatest fancier alive knows little yet racing will put your knowledge and theory to test in the fire blade of experience.

PIGEONS

Pigeons are the end game,
They bring you joy, they bring you fame.
Gentle and without deception,
Central to my perception.
The fame of Barcelona Dream
A product of my scheme
Has set my world on fire,
Pinnacle of my desire.
All the effort I can
Has made him known in Japan.
From humble beginnings begun
I learned how to run and run.
It was the apple of my eye
When I learned how to fly.
Always on the pace,
Lover of the pigeon race.

ROOM AT THE TOP, WHERE GREATNESS AWAITS

The races are upon us, and many will enjoy reaching their chosen racing targets at different levels of competition. The secret is to enjoy what you do, whoever you are. Now on the horizon in July is the greatest race in the world. It is the complete race into the UK. I refer to the Barcelona

International in July. I promise you an unforgettable experience if you send to this race of races.

The BICC is in expansion and with the BBC will send record numbers in 2012. Gareth Watkins of the BICC will ensure excellent full media publicity to the people who send. Let it be you. Take a giant leap of faith to embrace excellence! Eventually history will realise the sheer weight of the mother of races and give full credit to you who took part in this epic test. At the end of the day it is not the politics which will prevail, it is the united spirit of the brave people who sent. Just two words left: SEND 'EM!

THE PSYCHOLOGY OF A TOP FANCIER

It's all in the mind you see, ladies and gentlemen. At the heart and root of all racing successes and pigeon-racing related activities is the mind of man - the birds being the objective reality of our desires, dreams, plans and breeding and racing systems.

The individual personality of the fancier is paramount as the essential source and requirement of success. I know this from my convoluted journey - do you?

From my analysis and introspection many character traits comprise the psyche of an expert or champion ie pure focus, dedication, ruthlessness, compassion, empathy, singularity of purpose, patience, longevity, in depth scientific/artistic insights and pragmatism. If these are suffused by possible GENIUS, and in a helpful social context, success is assured. OK, I am being analytical again and although this is a shallow reflection of a person it helps to explain in some way the complexity of the PSYCHE of a champion.

THE HARDEST RACE ROUTES INTO THE UK

My comments here are personal and not absolute or hard irrefutable fact. All routes tend to be influenced by time on the wing and distance, further impacted by environmental factors.

I clocked at distances up to 879 miles into Yorkshire from Spain, so I have some insight. Who knows a bird's experiences in its being from any race point? Studies of science and the geography and the weather en route only hint at the answers.

As an intuitive perception supported by analysis and reason, I would say Barcelona International followed by Marseilles International, and then domestic Palamos-Barcelona is the most prestigious, the final frontier of UK international racing. My feelings and the velocities tell me that NFC Pau tends to be harder than Tarbes. On the north road, Lerwick into South Wales can be hard. Continental racing into Ireland has legendary degrees of punishing difficulty, including the King's Cup. I would love to see, and it will happen, more marathon international racing into Ireland. Some arduous racing takes place into the rugged hills of Scotland to over 1000 miles. Fundamental to all routes are the unknown environmental influences of the race and the race quality of pigeon and fancier. One of my toughest races was at 138 miles – Buckingham! Do we not all live the great human mystery?

THE MIND OF THE MARATHON MAN

In my mind's eye, marathon means a distance in excess of 700 miles and can go beyond 1000 miles into the UK. If - and especially if - this is combined with the international element, it is a daunting task for the most hardened, seasoned and mentally tough mind in the UK. To achieve success at these levels takes a peculiar and special mindset, both of the fancier and pigeon. I call to mind the three Ps, perseverance, persistence and patience, for racing a marathon is a task that encourages emotions, unlike the quick, excited buzz that club sprint racing engenders, since it takes you into a mental zone which is akin to a mystical state like zen. It is an experience for the initiated.

The ultimate marathon into the UK is the Barcelona International. The mind of the marathon man will have conceived this goal; he will have planned, specialised and given long-term focus to his individual candidates. If he is successful, his place in the realms of marathon folklore is secured. A man I know who personifies the single-minded focus required is Nicholas Harvey of Taunton, Somerset (who was featured recently on Elimar). Will you become a master of the marathon? Try it – SEND 'EM.

CHASING THE RAINBOW

Sometimes in our search for success we may spend money seeking out much hyped or seemingly excellent birds or bloodlines. Commercialism in mainstream society benefits by this phenomenon and it fills hungry pockets. Some fanciers near or at a top level via almost perfected racing and breeding systems know in their wisdom that champions often begin at home! In reality all pigeon families can have the potential to produce excellence, as behind the family person's name they can be racing birds of variable innate quality.

A champion results from a fusion of its potential with the racing environment. The limiting and key factor in the equation is the total personality of the fancier; this variable applies to any human in any sport because of one's belief system. Naturally some believe in God's intervention, or that a study of eyes reveals predictability of racing/breeding performance. I am a pragmatist with a simple rule of thumb which smacks of reality to me: send 'em and see the results after liberation from the races. We are free spirits, yet may I suggest you go to some international races. Enjoy it.

INBREEDING – WHY?

In York I take an active interest in many of my birds, some of which reflect 36 years of my own breeding. There is a son and daughter of Velvet Destiny, a hen with 21 times my No.1 pair in her breeding.

It is known that my four Descamp van Hasten-based Stichelbauts used Remi of 54, Izeren Stichelbaut, the Ware Izeren, Creonne Witooger etc. For historical details (assumes correct history), please refer to the History of the Belgian Strains Vol II. With this apparent knowledge, I went brother to sister with the Iron Man and the Iron Hen. Note both of these were performance inbred birds to my two foundation Descamp van Hasten bred birds.

The key to inbreeding is to breed around performance genes inferred from the good performances of the actual racers. It is a fine feeling to look at the same birds today in 2012 and see all my performance birds at National and International level in their origin. This is a very personal and individual thing to do and I say that after more than 25 years of this practice you can your family your strain, i.e the Emerton Strain.

In terms of heterosis or hybrid vigour, I introduced two very inbred hens out of Brian Denney's Dangerman

(Stichelbaut-base) which catalysed some of my own birds. To inbreed then you persevere over many years with closely-related birds up to brother x sister, and always test the progeny in hard racing from 71 to 879 miles. Yes, I can reflect on my breeding over 36 years.

Some not closely-related birds are introduced from time to time from top birds at 700 plus miles but are absorbed back into the strain. Some inbred birds are too refined and small (may show recessive genes in the phenotype). These can be excellent for outbreeding (crossing). Others may grow into absolute specimens. Therefore, as Geoff Cooper and Deweerdt do, stick to your own and with intuition (stock sense) keep focused. Make the birds your own.

Like all lines of birds, I would suggest that fewer than 1% of mine would fly 879 miles at Barcelona International. Now, other than Rome, this is where your birds should be going.

Many of you will continue to buy birds for outcrossing, as Van Hee did, yet the pundits like Geoff Cooper and Jim Donaldson keep to their own.

To summarise then, you inbreed to performance breeders and racers and send them to International level.

CREATING YOUR OWN FAMILY

This can be a very rewarding experience and a long-term target for the dedicated fancier. It helps to specialise with the birds at your chosen race distances from sprint to marathon or even all distances. Devise an overall management plan and stick to it using related birds from up to brother and sister matings.

Logically, severe testing of all race birds in the heat of competition is essential to the goal and over many years.

From time to time a related outcross from top racers/producers may be required, whilst maintaining the overall family/hereditary characteristics of the colony. I like inbred birds, yet each bird is different. As you reap the benefits of your labour of love you may be able to run an exchange network of top breeding to your liking. A little thought and focus will help you on your way to satisfaction.

MAKING YOUNG BIRDS GROW

Young ones have an optimum growth potential. How fanciers reach this target depends upon the loft environmental conditions, the managerial input and the nutrition in relation to the genome of the birds. Growth-promoting drugs are available and should be avoided in favour of an enriched diet.

After years of research and practical experimentation I recommend the following solid and liquid foods: hopper fed GEM G10 pellets, Bamfords Premier Gold/High Protein mix, Hormoform, peanuts, brewer's yeast, Gem Ogo Oil, Red Band and hemp. Liquid feeding consists of Chevita Mycosan-T CCS, Aviform Ultimate and Rohnfried Blitzform. In my perception you will rear some corkers on this diet. Applied science is evolving in its applications and we will be able to improve on this list.

A LEAP OF FAITH

Sending to any race point is a journey into the unknown. The birds primed for the task in hand are at the cruel mercy of the elements. We may feel secure in our guesswork of the outcome, yet the beauty lies in uncertainty. Will we produce the rare champion, a strain maker to propel our name into the future? The race may test our mettle, our inner resolve, in our attempt to triumph over nature or be at one with it. In competition with our peers and rivals we have stirrings of a primal nature - will the ambitions be realised? As man conquered Everest, our highest aspiration may be Barcelona. It is a spiritual odyssey to self-realisation, a giant leap of faith into the future.

BASKET OR JUDGMENT?

In racing the key is to get your birds to the chosen race so that race reality will decide the outcome under those particular conditions. You may have been wise enough via a prior decision to nominate your leading bird with accurate decision-making from pure experience of a perceptive, thought and intuitive nature and sound stock sense. Some people develop the art, others rely on say chance. Pooling for money may hone the required skills.

There are too many variables for breeding/racing to be an exact science and much of the success is down to the personality of the fancier in juxtaposition with the intrinsic qualities of the birds. Assuming that we have some control of our pigeon destiny, then with quality judgment I recommend ambitious fanciers to persist with dogged determination until you are happy with the results - plenty of room at the top! The pioneers continue to push the boundaries of possibility, creating champions in the process.

THE NORTH/SOUTH DIVIDE

Humans tend to be prejudiced into believing or asserting that fanciers in the south or north are the best, especially in England. The motivation is often a seeking of superiority allied to the male ego! In UK racing different distances can be involved, say up to 700-plus miles in the south to over 900 in the north of England or 1000 into Scotland. We race for personal reasons from club to international levels with success dependent on many factors. Degree of difficulty may be related to time on the wing - distance and environmental conditions being some of the variables. I have lived north, south, east and west and believe me, there are quality fanciers and birds in all those quadrants. For myself, I am biased towards racing in the north of England over 700 miles and in internationals. The latter is difficult and I hope to see more participation in this onerous task. In the final analysis each race is what it is and may you derive pleasure from the activity. In the future many records will be broken and sporting icons will emerge from the heat of competition.

FIELDING

Most people frown upon their birds using local fields and in some cases this is wise practice with notable exceptions to the general practice. As a freedom lover myself and in the village of Holtby all my birds ranged as they needed to to ingest grain, minerals and some vegetable and animal supplements. From 1976 onwards very few were shot, with some predated by sparrowhawks. My birds were pin sharp and almost wild returning to the loft to nest, feed, drink and roost. Young and old walked the fields, sat on wires and sunned themselves on barns, and they were out all winter even in snow. Dorothy and I would break the ice, feed hoppers of pellets and supply all the birds' nutritional needs. At times it was bliss. Neil Bush and Nic Harvey do something similar, and for marathon races it works, and is beautiful in its simplicity. Ideally this applies to selected rural locations having checked out local conditions. In my system all ages of birds were together on deep litter in the same loft at all times - a free ranging pampered colony of pigeons. We absolutely loved it and recall those days with fond remembrance.

INTROVERT OR EXTROVERT?

These are terms created by CG Jung, the Swiss psychiatrist, and are now in general parlance. As a general observation, introversive fanciers tend to be more studious, detached and focused on long-term future goals with an enriched psychic inner life. With the right total personality in place they may be excellent long distance fliers, where great and enduring patience are prerequisites. I would expect such a character to create a strain and be singular and unique in outward presentation.

Extroversive fanciers tend to require fast results and are competitive, being people and mainstream orientated. They may do well in sprint and middle distance events, where quick excitement and rewards are the keynotes. They may seek publicity or financial rewards for their efforts and be fame driven.

All very simplistic and floats on the surface of human complexity, yet fascinating yes? Who do you think you are? Look in the mirror... and read the reports. Only takes a lifetime.

DEGREE OF DIFFICULTY

The severity of a race depends on human perception of it, and is a variable concept. We all can conjure imagery of our most difficult race points and races in the whole spectrum of racing. Some 500-mile races are in fact more easily attained than 100, depending on the race conditions. The management and the sheer quality of the bird - the beauty of racing/breeding are the unknowns, and the triumph over difficulty. It is often thought that races over 500 miles are the most difficult, and sometimes this is reality. Pigeon racing beliefs are embodied by prejudice, myth and human personality - I am no exception! In reality testing of your birds, international racing will always sort out your better birds of any named family or strain, a practice which I recommend at least once in a pigeon lifetime. In my experience of looking at the Barcelona International races into the UK, I have yet to see one without a relatively high degree of arduous, mind-bending difficulty. Have a go next year and beyond.

LEADERSHIP IN PIGEON RACING

It is a truism that there are leaders and followers in our wonderful sport. Committees are often collective meeting places for powerful egos, consisting of people seeking impact and dominance and control within our hobby. The sport needs sensible, logical and effective organisation to function in our rapid and competitive society, with the emphasis on speed, money and elitist fame. Leaders exist in many guises from authoritarian to charismatic personalities who lead by charm, inspiration and example - young John Ghent will be in this category, mark my words.

Having been a union leader of council joint comittees, I express the need for unity in the BICC and BBC in a joint objective to organise a UK Barcelona International race with excellence in it. Let us see a race without equal in the long history of the sport, one that will put our leading fanciers and birds well and truly in the international forefront of prestige pigeon racing. This is doable in 2013 with joint organisation of all the practical needs of this objective. I hope this inspires thought and action, or you reflect a little on my words, to create a new order, a new future.

THE REALITY TEST

I have made studies of most of the academic and cerebral pigeon racing theories which have been promulgated by experts and quasi-experts with belief and conviction. What really interests me are the unknowns beyond most human minds and experience - the esoteric aspects of the sport. I am poised in waiting for new discoveries, revelations and insights, the truth that real knowledge manifests to us. What gems the next 20 years will reveal in systems/personalities and performances!

Whilst this all evolves, I am very happy with empirical reality, the acceptance that hard fact results are crucial to the practical survival of the sport. It is imperative to raise the bars of excellence at every level of racing in the noble pursuit of perfection.

WINTER EXERCISE

Many fanciers, as a result of continental influences, confine their birds to lofts during the winter months, a practice which can ease management. For marathon and long-distance racing at national and international level Nic Harvey and I fly the birds on open loft all winter, being careful in foggy conditions - hens and then cocks on alternate days. With hopper feeding the race birds assume good condition, honing their instincts and living a free, almost natural life each day. At two years of age, any hardy survivors from a strict racing regime will face 710 miles at Barcelona International, with no exceptions to this practice. In this way a modern strain of endurance birds will evolve from this simple practice. We all do our best within our circumstances, do we not? Having lived with nature for years, it is lovely to be part of it.

HOMING & ORIENTATION

As far as we can perceive, the how and why of this process remain elusive to science and the fancy at large. Who can tell what a pigeon experiences within its being or the exact method or impetus that drives a pigeon to home over great distances up to and over 1000 miles against variable weather conditions? it remains the beautiful mystery! Scientific methodology as it evolves applies experiment and analysis in an attempt to resolve the enigma with examinations of sense of smell, ESP, magnetic fields, the sun, landmarks and other physical and non-physical phenomena. Having jumped birds over 500 miles into races, it is my belief that a bird may know or otherwise sense a homing impulse sitting in the transporter which may never be properly understood. Food for thought? Yes.

INSPIRATION

As humans we need to be lifted and motivated to go forward and achieve. Outstanding feats by individuals can drive us towards our goals on a psychological and spiritual level, and history is enriched by leading and classical examples of its impact.

My love of the pigeon is well known, and I recall gazing at the blue cock King of Rome in the museum at Derby. When I was a small boy Mother and I would feed the stragglers peanuts in the Wardwick Square just adjacent to the museum, and young Emerton would meditate on the charismatic Mr Hudson and his famous bird - a daydream that would ignite the fire of my imagination.

Many outstanding personalities have inspired me on a deeply-felt level and they include the Bird Man of Alcatraz, William Blake and Nelson Mandela. In the future some of you may become sources of inspiration - just go out and do it.

INTERNATIONAL RACING: THE IRISH CONNECTION

The great Irish intellectual Liam O'Comain and myself have both promoted this ideal and concept in the past. It is now time for International racing into Ireland to become a practical reality by forging a link of warm contact and understanding with the BICC. I admit my bias: I want to see marathon racing to the fanatics and pioneers in Ireland. I was offered a house to clock out of Barcelona International! I feel with optimal bird management this can be done with some regularity. Just imagine the result in the world's pigeon media - it would make some more amazing history, would it not? Now destiny is on the doorstep of the Irish fancy, eg the NFC and the BICC. Let's have some positive decisions and a determined resolve by all to initiate this type of racing for ardent fanciers into the Emerald Isle. My motto is think it, do it, so let's have a go. The birds and fanciers will enjoy lasting fame in the echelons of excellence.

THE FANCIER'S DREAM

Many people will have notions, thoughts and ambitions of happy results in the breeding and racing of pigeons at different distances. These psychic events may take the form of a daydream or a sleeping event and may be so powerful that they are life changing. The focused and wise fancier may aspire to turn things into a waking reality.

With drive and dedication, the sport is enriched by the successful who go forth and achieve against all odds - faster, further, greater. The sport can be a celebration, a living testament to those who transform dreams into real results at all levels from club to international. Young boys may be inspired by men who have embraced and cultivated their dreams. The essence is a fertile mind followed by patient and practical applications in the cauldron of pigeon racing. Perhaps you may be the person to win the next international race or clock marathon pigeons into Ireland.

SELLING PIGEONS

This is most enjoyable in practice as you expand your network of influence, perhaps in the world! Some good and published results are preferable, yet not essential for success. To be genuine the origin of the birds, I think, should be steeped in generations of related top performance bloodlines, at your preferred competitive distances and levels of competition. In racing and breeding reality very few great birds will be produced - we are yet to produce a Barcelona International winner into the UK! Good selling vehicles via media advertising are the internet/mags/stud books and word of mouth. It all adds interest, spice and money to the pigeon culture – and rewards egos!

The most valuable contribution, I see as the dissemination and expansion of top strains and bloodlines for the future benefit of the sport. Be aware and shrewd when you buy and sell - illusion and reality!

MODERN BRITISH STRAINS

In Great Britain are some outstanding world-class fanciers who dedicate their singular lives to the creation of birds with a distinct hereditary characteristic. Individuals from these groups of related birds may span performances from sprint to marathon distances up to international level, ie in excess of 700 miles - my yardstick! Let us just focus on our own stellar fanciers for a little while, detached from others, although I do like the 800-mile Dutch birds, landing on the second day out of Barcelona International - good old WOUTER JORNA.

If we look and perceive with a shrewd eye, who appears on our shores? Well there are many leading candidates such as Chris Gordon, Nick Harvey, Brian Denney, Jim Donaldson, Booth and Shipley, Neil Bush, John Tyerman, Padfield Family and many others. Wise fanciers exchange bloodlines with each other, and strains result from dedicated good management over time. I hope this article is a celebration of our own good work.

THE BIG PICTURE

In 1977 the little red hen arrived to my first club and the experience was both thrilling and intoxicating to a naive, raw and insecure novice, which described my inner self. Some of the great unknown had been flooded by a little competitive success - I had won a race with a young pigeon.

My event echoes the personal reality of many a novice in the cauldron of pigeon racing. We should remember that little seeds may germinate into a forest of giants. With dogged persistence and with great trepidation, Dorothy and I pursued our aims and objectives to improve our breeding and racing performance levels as our focus and system improved, each little stepping stone greeted with appreciation and pleasure.

Racing to me has been a history of little achievements up to the big picture, the exemplary Barcelona international race - this has been my little story.

THE SENSITIVE FANCIER

This kind of person will develop a unique and special relationship with each individual bird - they are individual avian personalities in their own right, demanding and needing delicate management and respect. An inter-reaction can take place, which can be heightened to mystical levels of knowledge and understanding. You can experience the beauty of preparing a marathon or distance candidate to its optimal level of calm and intense race fitness. At this time you may feel the happiness and joy in anticipation of a supreme race test.

The old men speak of contentment and cosy rest for the birds in the home environment on a free-ranging open loft system - an ideal state of affairs for the Barcelona International marathon as practiced by Nic Harvey and me. It may appear archaic, yet with expert feeding it is ideal. The lifestyle can be idyllic, inducing intense zen-like concentration over many years of practice.

The rush of success inspired me to poetry and was life changing. I can perhaps describe it best as an all-embracing love affair on a spiritual level, especially with chosen, sweet little hen candidates. Give it a go and find the beauty in your life with pigeons.

MODERN MYTHS

We tend to believe many things, do we not? It ain't necessarily so! Pigeon racing is a whirlpool of cherished but false beliefs.

The route that Barcelona International pigeons take is interesting and much debated, yet without an accurate tracking device to monitor the course, just how do we know in individual cases? I never knew for sure my returning birds' directions of flight.

In terms of flying systems it is often thought that exponents of separation systems such as widowhood will prevail in racing, yet many good marathon birds - and indeed birds at lesser distances - are being clocked with good effect in simple open loft, free ranging systems. A lot depends on the man or woman devising the method of action.

Many frown on inbreeding, preferring continental style outbreeding as an avenue to success, yet some of the top men in Britain practise it with a relish, for example Jim Donaldson and Brian Denney, and with good reason, ie to concentrate the best of their own birds and to be used in future outbreeding programmes.

The word 'distance' has quasi-magical connotations, but what does it mean in reality? To me a good bird performing to satisfactory levels between 500-700 miles is a distance pigeon, and it can be from any particular family or strain.

With similar analysis we can observe many other aspects of pigeon culture in pursuit of truth.

SETTING THE SOUL ON FIRE

Racing pigeons gives meaning to and is a metaphor for life. It can heighten self-awareness and realisation. I recall my first young bird race when the little red hen sat and swayed on the wires for an eternity before entering the loft to be my first winner and to galvanise the heat of my imagination.

My career has been punctuated by brainstorming moments of euphoria and some shadows of melancholy. The time I stood in the loft, transfixed, meditating deeply on the race, and saw in my mind's eye the speedy return of the gay pied hen. Stepping out into the light of external reality, she became a white vision, glowing red with the force of the sun on her. It was an experience that would resonate on a deep and profound level, and totally intoxicating to a young man on his journey.

Waiting for Barcelona Dream at 879 miles in east and north-east winds was the triumph of hope over masochism, and the significance of his arrival took years to grow and mature, to nestle into a niche of my consciousness!

There have been many lovely moments before the climax to my career when Dax My Girl arrived to be the furthest flying bird in the International result at 687 miles in 2004. It was one sunny July day when Dorothy, Jean and I sat with heady anticipation in the cottage garden. Such memories ignite my lyrical reflections today.

OBJECTIVES

I find it easier to realise your dreams in life if you have clear ambitions, targets or objectives. Mine have evolved since childhood days. A clear long-term plan is useful with breeding and racing hurdles to attain and overcome.

Realisation depends on personal circumstances, ability and temperament. You may wish to be a top prize winner, fed or national winner in time and with dedication. The essence I feel is sharp and concentrated focus over time. At the end of the day a happy result may ensue and that is a bonus, yet sometimes anticipation is better than realisation. A shrewd fancier will see that he sources or breeds birds of the right intrinsic quality for the task in hand. There is no magic formula for pigeon racing success other than a home environment and personal system which works. It may take an age before you get what you work for, which sweetens the taste of success.

SOME USEFUL MEDICATIONS

Before pairing and the main moult we reduce the count of various pests and pathogens, which are commonplace in pigeons. It is a balancing act between the immune system, stress levels and the breakout of disease symptoms. I alternate the infrequent use of Moxidectin, Harkers 3 in 1, Gambacoccid Ro, Emtryl, Ronidazole and Doxy T. If you have a virus/bacterium complex it will almost certainly run its course with some mortality. As supplements for racing I like Supersix and Blitzform. Today there is less recourse to medications and more accent on maintaining natural health and boosted immune systems. Stress, overcrowding and cross-contamination invite the pathogens to multiply and produce disease symptoms. Only fit birds will bring you fame and glory, or satisfaction.

HOW TO FORGE A CAREER IN PIGEONS

With great enthusiasm and starting at the bottom in a club, if you are good enough a long career may lurk ahead. At first good results are imperative, when others will attempt to knock you off your little perch as part of the competitive, human psyche. Good publicity leads to recognition, deserved or not deserved and aim to do something unusual or different. Many aspiring people sell birds, a nice way to make contacts. You may reach a stage, after years where enough is enough and wish to contribute back to the sport by mentoring, writing and giving birds of your strain away. With a long career in the bag, there may be changes that define the phases of your lifecycle from young ambitious man to the wise old boy. It will be a journey which tells the story of your life, of pain, pleasure and enjoyment.

BASIC OBJECTIVES OF THE SPORT

The initial essence, with love of the birds, is usually winning races. There is applied knowledge and skill to this practice and the rewards are often psychological, with recognition by peers and any associated publicity in the media. Club top prize winner is a worthy aspiration and then ambition may move you forward from there, yet you will not forget the hard, early slog to your background and the characters encountered on the way. The discerning eye can see the impact of creating a racing or breeding champion which is an example to the sport and this is a tantalising target to aim for. I emphasise the personal approach to the sport since that will dictate the level at which you and the birds function. The highest echelon of racing is at the International level from competition within a National organisation like The BICC and this is open to any bone fide members who want to have a go, well worth the effort, as it will alter your perception of racing pigeons. Objectives help to organise and motivate your efforts in life.

BASIC BLUEPRINT FOR RACING

Much can be achieved from the small back garden loft and stock loft with aviary. A nice little set up can be say 15 pairs of stock, breeding 50 YBs and racing them for pleasure, with focus on some cards. If you apply yourself you will learn as you go through trial, error and experiment, as you develop a more competitive system of management. Years can be gained via the help of a kindly mentor to teach you pigeon lore, with hardcore learning through practical experience. As good as you may become, you will depend in the races that count, on the basic ability of the bird, found via racing. Fortunate is the man with producer pairs, the golden birds of myth and legend, they do exist outside of the publicity machine. Take the yearlings out as far as you dare and see what distances suit you and the birds. Today the local clubs are cauldrons of competition and colourful characters still exchange banter and eccentricities. Over time you may find a comfort zone and enjoy a long and enduring career in birds.

BASIC UNDERSTANDING OF THE MOULT

The natural renewal of the feathers, to assist flight, body temperature and overall survival condition of the bird in nature. I like a rich diet high in oil foods and proteins as it is a stressful period in the life cycle of the bird. Our YBs are all freewheeling about, growing, resting and moulting, in fresh air and with plenty of baths, no road training is now needed. Monitor progress, as a shiny smooth, complete moult is needed with no checks and frets, watch for birds that stick in the moult as they may be ill or weak. By January the flights should be developed and observe the health of any late hatches as they are prone to invasion by diseases. Small down feathers are shed at different times of the year. In the good old days, the old boys raced natural YBs right through to the end of September to around 200 miles – today many are stopped short of this. A natural, physiological process with psychological/survival implications.

FASHIONS AND CRAZES IN PIGEONS

Some fanciers and their birds, all of mixed and various origins, hit the limelight in a wave of popularity. They become the must-have birds of the moment and many are sold until the market is almost saturated. Attached to each bird is a dream an aspiration of better and greater things. In days gone by Denney did let me have some birds from his best in 88 and 90 and I do like the performance level of Padfields Invincible at Barcelona. However, I persist with my old strain which is able to produce a few champions both breeding and racing. We stand firm in the face of temptation to buy into the popular movement, fuelled by some well publicised results.

The key to strain building is to create your own over at least 25 years of progeny testing at all levels and the secret to good results is in the care and management of the birds you breed and race. It is imperative to be advised by a top fancier, if you can't achieve success on your own. I learned from practice and trial and error and from research into the words of the good and great. Some do make the grade and today's stars become yesterday's icons and historical figures. It is wise to be careful before you part with your cash and give a lot of thought to the flying system, as the fancier makes the birds, they race on the strength of sound practice, loft and environment at the home end. The old distance men said look in the mirror. However a strain does need occasional fresh intros of high quality origin. I like the work of Dave Delea whose last intro was 1982 – now that is inbreeding, just look at his records in racing!

BASIC ARGUMENTS WITHIN THE FANCY

Wherever people meet arguments will ensue, in an attempt to show who is right and wrong. A lot of it is subjective opinion supported by a few facts. Many questions are debated; is sprint racing better than distance, who's the best at it and why? Another one is, which is the greatest bird?

Be it natural or widowhood, results stand the test of time as historical and archive documents, open to analysis and scrutiny. Mob flying, overfly, loft location, inbreeding and strain of the day are all fuel for heated debate, argument and personality led. It all makes the pigeon culture a stimulating, diverse and rich place, with the emergence of some colourful characters.

I notice a softening of attitudes towards the weather, less strain development and an influx of Barcelona International birds, although few people chance their arm at over 800 miles, with good reason. At the heart of many feelings is the bird of prey issue and there will be many arguments and developments in this field, since many people are affected seriously by it, round the loft and in training and racing. A lead may be the future recognition of domestic racing pigeons as livestock, with associated rights of protection.

BASIC NATURAL SYSTEM

This will vary from person to person, depending on circumstances and aerial predation by hawks and falcons. The key is open loft flying, all seasons, all weathers and the timing of the nest cycle to meet the demands of racing. A pure and simple way is to train the birds through actual racing and the old boys would target the 500 mile on the day race and a few people beyond that point. We still practice it now, with modern, sophisticated feeding and some periods of separation during the season to delay the moult and enhance the condition. Some birds, brought along slowly by the system can get 800 miles – all down to the fancier/system and bird. Birds on this free flying system are a joy to watch around home and bring much pleasure to the person in charge-

THE POWER AND INFLUENCE OF THE OLD STRAIN NAMES

It is amazing how history, shaped by fame and commercialism, perpetuates and cements the names of Aarden and Stichelbaut in the popular consciousness of the fancy. Now the two men have been deceased for aeons and it intrigues me why some fanciers become so luminous in the eyes of men. Image is a powerful tool, since inbred families even are of diverse, assorted origins.

I have organised inbreeding of some of my birds for 39 years and still they are not pure. A pigeon is a pigeon, all are unique individuals, yet for human reasons, the popular ones will continue to have fancier's names. The archetype of humanising birds of wide origins was Buschaert. Discerning people speak of bloodlines, or based on when selling their birds to others. Old Eric Gibson said, "They're all mongrels, Jimmy". It is a sobering reality that few birds of any origin will race with real distinction, since the champion is rare and the waking reality of dreams.

THE SPORT – A GREAT ENIGMA

The great writers, fanciers and thinkers have made bold attempts to articulate the secrets, the wisdom, the knowledge, the essence behind the fanciers and their feathered athletes and will continue to do so in a distinctly human way. With little insights that hint at truth, we delude ourselves with the arrogance of dogma, bias and belief. The great paradox is that with all the feeble power of human consciousness, the inner nature of the bird remains nebulous and poorly defined, the nature of navigation is opaque, yet we pursue the sport with intense fervour. The wonder, of pigeon racing is a true motivational force, that drives hardened men to fall in love with their humble racing pigeons. Thus records are broken, fortunes are made and the sting of fame is felt.

THOSE WERE THE DAYS

Long ago in far off 1985, I entered old Diabolos along with Denney, Peterson and stalwarts of the Strensall PRS to fly in the blue ribbon 516-mile race from Nevers in a nor-wester with a total of 2,516 birds in the Yorkshire Middle Route Federation. The old cock was on fire and shone like a diamond in the basket. Bets were taken and confidences were raised in this culmination of a heady season.

Saturday was overcast, yet a day bird was a possibility. It was the dawning of my distance career, when the cock, on silent wings, loomed low over the cottage at 8.50 pm to top the Western Section and be 6th open. He would be given the Fed's best performance of the season trophy for multiple performances. The corollary is I stopped him at 2 years, and living to 22 he would found a dynasty of good birds including Mystical Queen and Barcelona Dream to this day. Yes, GB 83S35305 was and is my favourite bird of all time. It was the right bird on the right day that created my destiny in the sport – the essential link in a long chain.

A PERCEPTION OF PURE SPEED

'Faster, higher, longer' are emotive words for the fancier. To win big sprint races takes the highest velocity of a speed bird. Looking at my archive reminds me that I cut my teeth on competitive young and old bird races. Now as a marathon man, it is long ago that I enjoyed specialist young bird races. These are the fabric of racing and some are clever at it. I had some fine moments, yet Dorothy's Courage stands out as she zoomed in flat out above the loft to win the Fed of 6,066 birds, followed by 3rd and 14th open. These were all hens and on a widowhood type system to the old natural loft. It was 89 and I can produce an image of the hen as she winged it over the loft now. The irony is that her genes are in marathon birds today. Yes, fast things are sensational and intoxicating to the mind and fundamental to the sport.

A BARCELONA DREAM THAT CAME TRUE

In 1994 Diamond Queen dropped from Pau NFC at 735 miles and lit up my mind and fired the enthusiasm. She was a lovely hen, superbly bred, and did not leave behind any good ones. Where to next, I asked myself. Now the only point that loomed large was the colossus which is Barcelona

International at 879 miles. With determination and trepidation I set out to have a concerted go at the last chance saloon, the dizzy heights of the Pyrenees. By July of '95 with six birds left from my racing and in Amtrak boxes I sent them all down to John Lyden to be marked for the Daddy of all races. Liberated a week later and surviving transit to Sandwich in cardboard boxes, I verified 3 of the surviving 6 birds. We have 2 breeding grandchildren of 2 of them now, thus their epic endurance flight ensured the survival of their genes. It takes a dream and a little lunacy to do these things and the capability of good birds. Fanciers will continue to stretch the boundaries of possibility as long as ambition and imagination work within the psyche of man.

AUTUMN AND WINTER STUDY

At this time Nick and I focus with a keen eye on pairing our 879/844 and 700-plus Barcelona bloodlines that we are breeding to maximise the potential. This will be the 40th year of inbreeding and with some outbreeding, yet concentrated breeding to marathon origins. We like nice lookers, yet the main criterion is the ancestry at all times. Breeding a top one is a rare consequence of intensive planning and cogitation. It maintains a nice buzz of interest at this time, before racing begins later. I always look out for expert books and DVDs, yet our system of action is pretty stable. Breeding and racing are like a box of chocolates -- you never know what you're gonna get next. Study of the birds is a nice distraction for the fanatic, as the years roll by and can be enlightening.

ESSENTIAL WATER

Good clean water is a must for all the birds, in the lofts, transporters and when racing home. The pigeons see it and sense it and will actively seek it in lakes, rivers and streams on duration flights home. At the old cottage my birds bathed on the edge of a pond and in the rain water on the flat roof as happy as larks.

Water is a fine medium for liquid feeding supplements and medications for the birds. A shortage of water will initiate dehydration, stress and organ damage. More will be drunk with YBs in the nest. YBs in the baskets sense it and may be drawn to the drinkers. Pigeons are often very tolerant of impure water in gutters and puddles. With top food and clean water, you are well on the way to creating condition in the team. I like my birds to take a walk on the wild side.

KEEPING COSTS DOWN

There are some ways of reducing overall costs of the sport. For very many years, in my village the birds would field and return to hoppers of layers pellets which are good and reasonable from the country store and birds will perform well on these as a base, along with hard grains and supplements. We would buy SS Swainstons' foods in bulk and share it out. When I started it was on bags of mixed corn from the pet shop. The modern, specialist mixtures are expensive, yet good grains to mix your own can be had from some farm outlets. Fresh birds can be very costly, yet good ones can be given or exchanged amongst like-minded people of friends, without losing an arm and a leg. A shrewd person may spot bargains at an entire clearance sale, as loft items and sundries. Avoid expensive supplements, unless they work and reduce your numbers of birds down to the quality via racing. Join only the organisations in which you will race. A very good way of paying off costs is to sell a few young birds each year, as many people own well-bred birds – it will ease cost worries of keeping the birds.

MY UNIQUE FEEDING SYSTEM

We give solid and liquid feeds to fuel the birds up for speed/endurance racing to 710 miles Barcelona International into Taunton, West Country. The birds have hoppers of GEM G10 pellets before them young and old and on the open loft system. Our special food mix fed on calling in is the following:

Jerry Plus, Superstar Plus, Willsbridge No.2

Mix, Yeast, Hormoform, Conditionseed, Hemp, Peanuts, Sunflower Hearts, Vydex Mvs 30, Columbine Oil, Gem Energy Oil, Ogo Oil.

To this fat/carbohydrate and protein mix we use Vydex Supersix in the water on return from the race/and build up for the water races and blitzform 2 days before basketing. We find that with hard racing, the condition of the birds by July with rest periods is excellent and first-class young are bred from the stock – all ages range the skies together for hours.

A new partnership, we aim to evolve the strain and have had 11 birds from Barcelona so far, yet we try to improve over time. At other times we use Aviform Ultimate in the water, and I used to try Bovril. The strain is versatile and some will win the sprint/middle distances. The system has flair/intuition and originality in its formulation – it works for us. At the end of the day the intrinsic ability of the birds will win through or not, if you send 'em.

TREATING THE COLONY AS ONE

With the control systems of pigeon management in vogue, let's regard the birds in the loft as one whole unit for a change. To the discerning human eye each bird is a separate entity and life form. Yet in the way the birds exercise and coexist we can see them as a single avian organism. In this sense they can be flown as a team, trained as such and then the true individuals will emerge or not emerge during race duration. Even in an inbred family they are never pure in the gene department, all being of mixed ancestral origins.

En route to our chosen race the team will all be liberated at the race points in whatever weather conditions prevail and so it is, was and will be. After a period of say 25 years you may well be wiser than the raw novice who attempted to win his first sprint race. In the colony a pecking order will prevail, akin to a human committee!!

PIGEON PHOTOGRAPHY

I like the natural-looking ones and Peter Bennet first came to me in '89 and does a great job. I do not favour the air-brushed ones which reflect a false image. The key attributes of a pigeon are beyond the lens – internal-and invisible to the camera and naked eye. However a pictorial record of your birds is good for history and thousands of birds are bought and sold on outward appearances. A family montage is a nice reminder of your key birds for reference reasons. The leading photographers will meet you at dinners and shows and some will come to your home. A pretty picture may increase your desire to buy and own that bird, and thus fortunes are made and men become famous.

PIGEON INJURIES

A pigeon appears to have an amazing pain threshold and will quickly repair itself after minor injuries. Bruised legs and wing joints tend to fix with rest and minor race injuries are frequent. Leg breaks are common collision problems and may need a sling support by the fancier to offset healing distortion if left. I do not like wing injuries – bones and tendons and muscles which may end a bird's career. Wild birds may fend very well minus a foot, or with line and bumble foot. I stitched up many a gaping crop and the birds raced again. Simple injuries by falcons tend to heal OK. Sometimes it is compassionate to cull the affected pigeon, but think first. A six-year-old bird, veteran of many races will be fortunate to escape injury and many become wing stiff due to tendon damage - always disconcerting to see a dropped wing on a favourite!

ROUND THE LOFT TRAINING

Some 39 years later we still do well letting the birds fly themselves fit around the loft, old and young, and what a joy to see. To observe the natural behaviour of a colony of pigeons is a scientist's dream and teaches you all you need to know about pigeon psychology and behaviour. If you are confident with July races in mind, no road, extra training is required and the YBs may disappear for say seven hours to come back with mud on their feet – handy for later marathons, if your area is suitable, loft flying plus the race programme obviate the need for the lazy/disabled or elderly to be hammering up the road in a van. With clever feeding you can expect to win some of the sprints as well. I hate to witness birds locked up in stuffy lofts when they can have the freedom of the skies.

THE SPECIALIST

Best to concentrate on different, certain disciplines of racing to suit your racing/ego needs. I recommend a good foundation learning curve at all distances for basic experience of variable race conditions and people encountered on the way up, to give you an insight into birds and management and as a confidence booster. A versatile family of birds will result over years of effort and all will be different individuals. I started off as a YB flier and went from there and now we value races over 700 miles and I prefer tests of over 800 miles, as the final arbiter of speed/endurance and difficulty. There are some converts to this philosophy, yet most gravitate around the 500-mile mark as a maximum, especially with the popular continental origin birds on speed motivation regimes for a quick fix. The marathon specialist must endure days of patient and perhaps anxious waiting to realise his dream- all makes for a fascinating sport overall.

PERSONALITY AND TEMPERAMENT

The top people in the sport have got where they are because of personality and temperament. They develop the right racing/breeding system with the right pigeons and make wise and intelligent decisions for the good of themselves and the sport. For distance and marathon racing, I like people to demonstrate a nice, calm relaxed and patient personality with an eye on detail and the big picture like Jim Wright who was 2nd open Pau NFC at 734 miles and the iconic Brian Denney, who is a great killer of time till the arrival of his birds. Sprint to middle distance fanciers tend to like to win and dominate race after race – this takes some keeping up.

Each bird is an individual with peculiar psychological traits and I like birds that are outstanding characters and quiet hens and cocks that doze and sleep in the transporters; the really fast sprinters look as though they are on fire. If a bird be blessed with a mind, then instinct and drive to home come into the equation. People like Mark Gilbert and the Coopers have a great desire to make a mark, and Jim Jenner is a creative genius. The global sport accepts all shades of humanity.

INSTINCT AND ACUMEN

I came alive on the edge of survival in the wilderness and faced with great difficulties in Afghanistan and an area of tribal law in Pakistan, as part of my worldly adventures. It was both thrilling and frightening to the core and the stimuli yielded great insight that serves you well. The instinctual side of the self, similar to intuition gives an instant perception of what you should take notice of. If clear thinking follows, then you may survive the threat or dangerous situation you face. With pigeons try and align your instincts with each individual bird and the colony, to gain a perception and instinctive understanding of the birds' potential, personality and some degree of predictability in type of anticipated performance at race points, particularly over distance and marathon events. The thinking man can ponder a method, a plan, yet sharp perception is instant.

A RACE OF DESTINY

The epic is on the horizon when champions are found and boys become men. Soon in the heat of the Spanish sun, winged warriors, urged on by primal instincts, will drive on through sultry air to seek a hallowed place in fame and history. Feathered athletes representing the hopes and dreams of the common man will overcome the forces of nature on huge migration flights to reach the sanctuary of the loft of their birth and their resting place. This is the race that inspires the imagination of the world of pigeon sport. A single timing in the mother of all races will linger long in memories and sweet nostalgia and may inspire you to wonder.

A SENSE OF NOSTALGIA

In those days the 500-mile winner was king and the old characters ruled the roost. We gathered on the pub veranda exchanging personalities and buying rounds of drinks on the pool winnings, acting daft and telling stories. It was the social club culture, where you tried to fathom out why certain men made winning easy. My clock was a Skymaster, and then I got all posh with an STB Quartz. The old strain names like Gits, Osmans, Barkers and Logans were popular and the back garden lofts ruled with natural pigeons fed on beans, tares and maize.

In those days we sent to every race with the same birds and right through the year from April to September. We were not so concerned about the weather and stock was sent by British Rail. Louella was the stud, with British-based birds like the Extreme Distance Family. The top dogs were the distance men, when man and woman would enjoy training with a flask.

To be honest all that competitive stuff was hard work and I prefer my life as a specialist strain builder, writer and mentor. In those days the Mecca of racing was in working men's clubs, or posh village societies. We lived with fewer sparrowhawks and falcons and allowed the birds free-range fielding. Old hand was the sage and permanganate of potash turned the water purple.

DARK ENCHANTMENT

As the sun goes down on a warm summer's evening, with the roosting crows and the biting midges, I sip another cooling drink. The doubts set in as the street lamp flickers, with emergent bats and fluttering moths. The witching hour is marked in time by the good old hen that swoops down, fresh from the twilight zone. It was Pau 735 miles and the hen would create a little dynasty of her own. I called her Dark Enchantment in memory of some magical moments. This feeling accompanies birds that fly great distances to the place of their birth and captures the essence of marathon racing.

AUTHENTIC STICHELBAUT-BASED PIGEONS

There are no pure, unadulterated Alois Stichelbaut-based birds, since the man died in 1946. Looking at archive pics and original documents, dark and black chequer birds were dominant when he raced into Belgium. As all pigeons under the mantle of one man's name the birds were of mixed origins. In 2015 certain fanciers have bred closely to the old DVH/Labeeuw and other people, where it is thought their birds were based on archetypical Stichelbaut birds. From my key four originals I inbreed today, always testing the progeny up to Barcelona International level 710-879 miles. We have some lovely dark ones in our breeding and recent introductions of a Stichelbaut nature include specimen Schlepphorst birds and a hen to come from Ponderosa UK stud, with the Frans Labeeuw birds in the genes, along with some of Vanhee origin, similar to those earlier intros by Denney, lines of which are in my strain of birds from 31 to 879 miles.

I like the small medium dark birds with great feather quality, so you can spot condition as it rises – they look like traditional distance birds, yet we can win the sprints with them. We exchange them in a network of enthusiasts over the British Isles where generosity is the key parameter. With a solid base we put certain inbred birds back in for vigour as experiments, always racing the progeny out.

WINTER SHUTDOWN OR NOT?

If possible I like our birds out on alternate days from October to March pairing time. They are flying athletes and love to be out in free air, rather than shut inside as domestic pets. Good, hard, weathered condition will result and with no rationing the birds continue to moult, grow and are contented in a wide arc around home – crucial for distance/marathon performances later. Kept separate till pairing they run into ideal condition for mating without effort or rationing. This has been my practice for nearly 40 years from sprint to marathon racing. The pleasure of watching your birds in all weathers will give you a nature fix and you learn so much of bird behaviour and your place in nature.

If at work or with serious falcon or hawk problems, or on controlled exercise regimes, you may have to reconsider the concept. Living six miles from my loft, for many, many years and with Mum helping into her 90s, I worked out the easiest system imaginable that would favour the birds. It was a walk on the wild side and little or no road training is needed for young or old on my system, as conditioning evolves through time on the wing in racing from 71 to 879 miles.

KEEPING THOSE LATE-BREDS RIGHT

We keep the July onwards birds in open aviaries, exposed to the elements for condition. All are fed a very rich diet; they are in heavy moult and will clean up soon. The stress is on with the moult and body growth, thus the birds are kept calm and given Supersix in the water. By the end of November they will be in shiny condition. They will become our breeders and some will go to my mentees in Ireland and Scotland-free of charge of course. In this way the strain is dispersed and tested in a wide playing ground. We seek another recognisable champion-that is the modus operandi.

Watch for viruses and bacteria in these late-breds, as salmonella is in many lofts. It is logical to take young off your best racers and breeders for pairing together. Always nice to breed your own good birds, rather than seeking them elsewhere, and I enjoy the creative, breeding aspects of the sport best as an outward expression of thought. Some of the best birds and fanciers are in the UK and Ireland, without being mesmerised by continentals.

THE MEANING OF RACE REALITY

The cerebral life of a young pigeon man is that of a dreamer. We set goals and aspirations to be pursued with relish and fervour. If we do it right and persist, we may have a glimpse of the rainbow over the horizon. Race reality refers to the dose of truth you feel, when the real nature of things hit you during the race. It is measured in actual race conditions that impact on the race and how you and your birds did as hard tangible results. Sporting men may become famous with what they have achieved after assessment in the real world of others and events. Without the initial desire and mind set a good race reality is not possible. Dreams may come and go in moments of inspiration, yet history can tell the true story. Take a walk on the wild side and make it happen.

REALISTIC TARGETS

Many fired by imagination, desire and dreams aim for great things. To become a great racing fancier takes time, experience, stamina and dogged persistence. The insight and knowledge needed is huge and to have it internalised belongs to the minority. However, with hard work a modicum of success can be felt early on, by setting simple targets - a few club wins here and there to progress from. After man years under the belt you may aspire to attempt great goals or press the boundaries of possibility normally beyond the scope of the novice.

For many, Barcelona is the benchmark of extreme difficulty. Despite all the Barcelona blood few people in the UK attempt it, a trend which is likely to persist. It is always an endurance race for man and bird, over a protracted period of days and nights. The bloodlines do generate a charisma, awe and appeal for sales, which the studs duly recognise. Now with the right bird in the right condition, it is a realistic target to aim at.

Ireland remains the greatest of challenges, yet a clever fancier will do it, as the years drift by.

HOURS OF DARKNESS

Racers fly when they get the urge to do so, day or night, although usually during the day. Systems have hours of darkness rules in an attempt at some control, order and an idea on fairness for competing fanciers. I have seen and heard many species of birds fly by day and night within a 24 hr cycle. Birds on the day of liberation may be timed in the hours of darkness, for example Brian's Blue - Denney at 748 miles approx, and Tarbes and Impett at 747 miles in the same race. There were five birds over 700 miles on that day of liberation, when conditions were as they were. At the time I felt that Denney would clock on the day, with his good birds and clever management.

The key to great performances is to be seen in the mirror of truth – it is the skill of the fancier in managing his birds to great feats of speed and endurance, although great birds are rare – one in a lifetime is good in relative terms. I do love to see racers drop in the twilight on warm, summer nights, to bring awe and romance and the realisation of dreams. Pure poetry.

ARMCHAIR PIGEON RACING

Nine years since I ceased to keep pigeons in the loft in my garden, I enjoy many aspects of the sport. Writing original articles is a joy, as is watching the results of the big races on the computer - the names and personalities as they emerge into prominence. I see the subtle tricks of the trade used to sell birds, to court fame and make money.

Sometimes a bird comes in to view which has the stamp of greatness and I am thinking of the dark cock of Marco Wilson – a modest man with one of the greatest marathon birds ever to grace a UK loft and up to 844 measured miles to rank with the legendary birds of the historical past. On reflection my little network of men who fly my strain are interesting characters with some success in racing from Cornwall to Scotland, Ireland and Holy Island. We live in hope of producing a great champion which is at the soul of racing pigeons – our very own, not bought from the continent. I like the reflective life of a monk - suits me.

FANCIERS THAT HAVE STOOD THE TEST OF TIME

The world of the pigeon and fancier tends to be ephemeral, transient and short-lived. I am heartened and intrigued by those who have put more than 30 years into the sport and the cultivation of their flocks. We often notice these people as they are publicised heavily in Europe and the world at large. The corollary is that many shun publicity and have excellent strains of birds. We have a perception of persistence and quality with these people - the truth is that names are made by a few good birds, after rigorous progeny testing. I think men and their ladies can be hooked on the family concept of the birds and success – it's a grand hobby. The folks tend to be of mature age, of the old school, people like Bush, Denney, Gordon, Donaldson, Van der Wegen and Denys. These are illustrious exponents of the art and science of pigeon racing and are distinguished by the strains created in the love and enjoyment of pigeon racing.

THE OBSCURE NATURE OF FAME

A person in Ethiopia was reading my work and this was significant to me. In all the places in the world where the writer's work is digested, the author remains unknown in all his complexity. We recognise and perceive an image, which may assume an identity of its own in the popular consciousness of the times.

I am intrigued by the mystery of the individual within the cult of the celebrity. Every man is an Island and I feel it is important to maintain a sense of integrity and individuality in society. People are often made famous by the media, which recognises perceived talent and originality. I believe many like a space of free air in which they function as a separate, autonomous entity, with insights this may engender.

Many go through life without knowing themselves, yet alone others. However, the fame impulse can be the beating heart of the human condition and most of us are conditioned by its influences, since humanity tends to be a social organism.

BENEFITS OF EXPERIENCE

We all start at base zero, yet some are blessed with an insight into birds and the weather, from childhood days say in the countryside, or from pigeon keeping parents. Real knowledge of breeding and racing is learned over many years by the persistent practice of those disciplines. The old master may take the young person under his wing, if you are fortunate to meet him, otherwise you will learn the hard way. After time the way forward may clear and become lucid, as a system which is repeatable is established, and there is some rational order and predictability to your efforts, a solid core of experience. You can be confident then in your experience despite the stimulus of others and their new birds to change. At this stage you know the game and can enjoy doing your own thing. It will have been a convoluted journey to reach a comfortable level of insight and wisdom.

ONE STEP BEYOND

Strange things may happen to you on your earthly journey through life and they make you wonder. In the heat and fervour of a sprint race, I was standing in the loft, shut off from the outside world in a state of heady excitement. With a mind in full gear, I visualised the gay pied hen zooming in to win the race. Stepping outside into the cold light of day, she appeared in a dazzling flash and with the sun on her she glowed red, in glorious moments of euphoria.

Then there was the time, when sitting bolt upright, my future flashed before my eyes in the form of a montage of dark chequer pigeons that I was to cultivate. I follow that profound experience, in reality some 30 years later. With travels through Afghanistan into the Himalaya and into Africa and America, I have seen some wonderful things, with moments of awe.

PIGEON RESEARCH PROJECTS

A number of areas could be investigated by the academics and the curious. How can a pigeon be jumped 4 to 500 miles in racing and return home over unknown and discovered territory? If this riddle was solved it would shed light on the navigational means, ability and process of the pigeon, and perhaps why some birds will negotiate the distance and others will not. Like all science, it would reveal a biased, human perspective on the problem. If racing ability is linked to a gene or genes, can these be examined and identified to give an insight into winning homing ability? With practising inbreeding for 39 years, what are the limits if any in a colony of racing pigeons, and is there a pattern to inheritance of certain characteristics in the birds? In terms of nutrition, is there a perfect diet for performance pigeons at various distances? What is the ideal loft space per bird in various loft types? Is there a legal supplement to beat others in producing supreme racing condition? I feel, most of these areas will be partly answered, yet they can develop thought.

THE SELECTION PROCESS

We are simple and strict in our practical approach to selection. Any yearlings will be built up in national races over the water and the residue all go to Barcelona International starting at 2 years of age. Late-breds are taken from these and picked over, along with birds of key genes. The racing proves the quality, as we do not have to cull for quality control. The procedure selects out on racing ability in practice rather than what is in our biased brains, as man can be so wrong when he thinks he knows best. The leading race in Europe is a potent, natural selector of our birds in classical Darwinian style. For stock I love birds that are closely inbred to key performance racers at our chosen distance of 700 to 879 miles. In this way our bloodlines do inspire some confidence.

CHANGES IN APPEARANCE OF MY LATE-BREDS

Some of the birds become smaller, finer and more refined. Hens and cocks may look similar with some flattening of the heads. I notice lighter iris colours and a sharper-looking head. In my strain, they appear more beautiful and delicate to me. I love these birds, packed full of Barcelona genes for outbreeding. You can expect the progeny to be bigger and more robust looking. There is no set plan to performance inheritance and it is all about progeny testing. Some families support and tolerate very extensive inbreeding and I have found some of the DVH Stichelbaut lines to be like this.

Family breeding is a fascinating series of experiments into the unknown, when reality will dawn in the nature of the breeding and racing results. Over 39 years we have put some genes into them of performance birds from others, whilst keeping the blood of the old 7 key birds. Types of birds will be those left after rigorous race testing, with no standard, exacting appearance.

RELIANCE ON "GOOD LOOKS"

We have bred some lovely lookers this year. Other than being oil paintings and pleasing to the eye, how good are they, I ask myself? The harsh reality is that a small minority will be good racers and breeders - it is the hard fact of pigeon racing! Fortunes are made on the exchange of pretty pigeons, with beauty in the eye of the beholder. In my family are some lovely birds to look at and I tend to select the late-breds well from the performance birds. My key criterion of selection is the performance of the ancestors, although good marathon birds tend to be compact and balanced in the human hand. Wise to think hard when flattered by good looks – there may be no engine in that Ferrari.

GOOD HARD LITTLE HENS

In my long career, I have flown some great hens on

widowhood and natural systems to an ancient loft. A well-seasoned little hen will perform against the odds at any conceivable distance up to 879 miles. If raced from the same family origins, where you know the ancestors, they often leave a strong influence as breeding birds like Mystical Queen, Oddball, Dots Delight, Musgrove Addiction, Insanity etc – all these are down from my No 1 pair.

It is natural wisdom to test all birds of both sexes in your loft and most marathon men go beyond the widowhood cocks syndrome and cliché – they score with the hens. Some great men, like Donaldson, Denney, Gordon and Neil Bush, have distinguished themselves with hens, and the evolution of the sport is a parade of great hens like Lancashire Rose, Storm Queen, Mystical Queen, Rennes Lass and Northern Lady. We have been blessed in the North to put our hens to the sword at great distances where 700 miles is the norm, not the exception.

IT'S WHAT'S BETWEEN THE EYES THAT COUNTS

Have you realised that the pulse and the beating heart in man and bird is the BRAIN? It determines the nature of the mind, instincts, emotions and the total psyche and personality. It is the source of any success of fancier and bird and with the right type you may do well, under the influence of a changing external world. Cultivate it, celebrate it, nurture it and squeeze the living juice from it. The brain of a champion would make a worthy study. Take a look in the mirror – what do you see? I do believe that we Westerners would benefit from a little introspection. When you look in the eye of a bird, do we not want to look within?

NOW THAT THE RACES ARE OVER...

People are looking to replace the weekly win buzz. Energies are now put into the lift given by fresh birds that catch the eye at sales – beware before parting with the dosh. Then there is the lure of club politics to follow, where egos are massaged and rules are made. We try to abide by the rules and our energies are spent in study of our own birds as they grow and moult through the winter. It should be the season of calm for all in readiness for the breeding and racing seasons.

On a practical level, any loft alterations can now be carried out. Be wary of diseases like salmonella as the birds moult – we have our birds out in the weather to give the immune system a blow. Look out for tips in the media to expand your knowledge, and keep the long-term goals in sight as times change. I have a network of contacts who trade and swap birds, which is rewarding and a few features to write. Many men will sit, ponder and dream of things that may become a reality.

DEGREE OF DIFFICULTY

Any distance can prove to be difficult in racing. I am attracted to those which test fancier and bird, as this shows in the types of birds produced and in the nature of a strain thus generated by persistent events. This is best reflected in the interiority and performance genes of the birds, although I do like the smaller sharp-looking birds. Over 500 miles on the day, against the wind is good and International races over 700 miles test the bird's navigational ability and speed/endurance faculty. In wet weather races, birds with oily, silky feather tend to shine. Good little hens in these races often leave good birds behind and I inbreed to these birds for stock. Excellent condition produced by the fancier may lessen the difficulty of the race. Too many hard races in a season and you will need a holiday and the birds a good rest.

KNOWLEDGE

The individual and specialist knowledge of the fancier is a crucial ingredient in a good or great flier, as you will NOT reach the top with just good birds. A great depth of understanding of a system and nutrition is vital to enter the birds in top race condition.

Once you have the info you need, the hardest thing is to follow it through into hard results – the objective, outward realisation of your plans and dreams. Esoteric knowledge comes with increases in distance and the Barcelona men will know the true nature of reality, since waiting in this race needs the personification of patience. It will hurt you and you will feel it to the core - memories are cultivated by hardship. It is nice to share accumulated knowledge with others, as published articles to help or stimulate others in the collective consciousness of the sport, from the mind/study relationship.

KEEPING A STRAIN OF PIGEONS ALIVE

After nearly 40 years of focus I cling to the old bloodlines which will be tested in England, Ireland, Scotland and Holy Island amongst enthusiasts. With few surviving introductions, the birds will evolve and change over time, as people reach the end of their lifecycle. It is nice to hold on to the dream that was created aeons ago.

The irony is that the UK has a culture of outbreeding any new introductions on a constant and fluid basis. Certain men, often distance specialists, inbreed as part of long term planning, as they are masters of racing, with specialist knowledge. Men like Donaldson and Denney and Denys are people I look at for a genuine inbred/outbreeding experiment to augment the basic family tree. People like these keep the quality high by strict racing regimes. Building a strain is a lasting adventure into the unknown and is a self-fulfilling exercise into existentialism.

PIGEON KEEPER OR RACER?

In my long career of 63 years in association with pigeons and birds, I have met many characters with a deep love and fondness for pigeons. My father set me off with his fancy birds and tumblers, priests, Jacobins and other beautiful, cultivated types. I know men who must have compulsions for the names of the day and collect birds to admire as crown jewel possessions – these are must-have people. Now the purist and case-hardened racing man will use his lovely birds to test his prowess and perhaps to seek fame and recognition in true competitive racing. The champion will aim to perfect an overall system where results will be the parameter of excellence, not the joy of keeping a loft of nice birds. I find many of the keepers to be warmly sentimental and kindly, whereas the great racing men are tough-minded and goal-orientated. Perhaps I am a fusion of the two traits, as I do love my strain.

THE ONLY WAY WE CAN PROGRESS

My partner and I have put some top birds together in the

aviaries for breeding of versatile performance genes. We have made nice progress with results up to 710 miles. Our birds are finding their way into the lofts of contacts and friends. The way forward – the race is on to find another producer pair and a further racing champion, as our last was lost in training.

These goals represent ways in which we can progress and are single-minded fixations to keep us motivated. The lesson we learn is not to be satisfied with what is achieved, as it keeps the job going. Our birds are pretty, yet they become beautiful after they have performed. The sport in general will continue to progress as long as standards are high on the agenda. As an organisational model and template, we can learn a lot from how The Barcelona International Race is run and managed in Europe as a whole, for the eventual liberation of all the convoy to destinations as far as Poland.

COMPETITIVE ONEUPMANSHIP

There are thousands of fanciers going all out to be top dogs and rule the roost by racing their birds. This is the quintessence of the sport and is linked with many human emotions, which we all feel from time to time. The successful fancier will face the sting of criticism and the warmth of praise. They are all exemplified by their humanity.

My insight tells me, with the hindsight of wisdom, that if you focus on the birds, then things may happen for you over many years of objective dedication. In a sense, a love of the birds may transcend all your positive experiences in the sport, especially the sentiments associated with old favourites or the ideas behind a personal strain. The "I want to be better than you" syndrome endures at every level and runs through the commercial world of publicity and adverts. It is the competitive fuel of society at large. A few wise old owls find a degree of aloofness from its sting and enjoy a little integrity. The icons of the sport follow a blueprint and stick to their guns. The sport has a distinctly human face.

KEEPING BIRDS FRESH FOR THE BIG EVENTS

To maintain the reserves in our birds, we give as few races as possible with weeks of rest at home before the target race. They are out daily to do their thing and see the basket as little as possible, so as not to overstress them and trigger viral invasions. With a gradual build up in distances and time on the racing wing, serious muscle is formed and our feeding forms the essential fat and glycogen reserves in the internal organs.

The conditioning of a super marathon pigeon is both art and science and the will of the fancier with his chosen candidates. Paired in March and raced dry, the sole objective is form for July. The approach is the opposite to the road work/motivation ethos of the sprinter. Many steady distance birds are culled or burned out by May-I like the slow burners.

HOW I WOULD TACKLE BARCELONA INTO
IRELAND/SCOTLAND

People are cogitating this awesome concept – it can be done! I would rear around 60 YBs, all from proven 7 to 900 mile bloodlines, and fly them on open loft in all weathers if practicable. Education in races up to 200 miles would build them up nicely and on a marathon feeding regime – top quality, all they can eat. Flown out all winter I would gradually increase the yearling distances to the 350/450 mark depending on availability of the races. Then the residue would be lifted to 5 to 600 miles as 2 yr olds. I would study the potential of each bird along the way.

At 3 years of age, and with close planning and organisation, all birds would be lifted from the 500-mile distance mark to the Barcelona race in excess of 8-900 miles. With steady and careful management, a bird of real stamina and navigational ability can break from the convoy and arrive home in race time. A guide to my feeding is under my unique feeding system. The mental demands on the fancier are large, and it will change your life forever.

THE NATURE OF MY WRITING

The whole purpose is to project what I see is the truth of my own experiences, combined with knowledge gleaned from cultural studies of the arts and sciences. Writing is a way of life and my personal contribution back to the birds and subjects to which I have devoted a lifetime. It is most rewarding when people find it all interesting or enlightening, although some of the ideas are poetic or philosophical.

My unusual travel experiences in life lend some originality and creativity to the work, which is my own. I like to reflect special feelings and insights into the racing pigeon, as their study has shaped my life. Educated on the great writers like Blake, Kafka, Dostoevsky and Sartre, I hope I have a fraction of their collective wisdom and penetrating insight. MENSA has opened up a sea of writing possibilities in specialist newsletters and magazines and I do indulge myself in this activity. Thanks to all who take an interest in my publications and highly personalised writings.

SIMPLICITY IS GENIUS!

To the purist, the essence of pigeon racing is pure and simple. Make the system as easy and predictable as possible to practice – I like a minimal approach to it. You do not have to be complex to win, as it is the birds that should be doing the work for you. Many people work too hard with the birds, as I used to – it stresses both you and the birds and then you pack up for the season.

With the minimum work in training, we enter birds in the race programme to bring on gradual condition. If possible we feed to appetite on open loft, as it is complex to have controlled feeding and exercise regimes. In terms of sprint or distance – find the birds out by sending them – a simple formula and recipe. An actual race will show the truth or not of all your plans, dreams, thoughts and theories. A strain is built on years and years of actual performance birds to your lofts. The easier you make the job, the more contented you will feel with a long season. In a lifetime you may count the champions on one hand.

BENEFITS OF TESTING A FAMILY OVER MANY YEARS

With nearly 40 years of race testing at all levels of distance and weather, I have drawn some conclusions. The generations of some proven birds inspire confidence in the bloodlines – you believe there is some potential there in some of the birds. The sobering reality is that few great birds will be bred; each one is different, and a family is not pure for producing good racers at any specific distance – ie to think that all my birds are distance birds is a fallacy and a nonsense. You will find a minority of good birds from any fancier, when put to the test. All our birds are tested and other than the genes, you never are sure of a good one until you race it or breed from it. When I get some birds in for outbreeding, it is always a case of testing the unknown and when you have a good breeder it becomes the exception and an aristocrat in your loft. I always base my breeding around these, irrespective of outward appearance.

LOOKING FOR AN INBRED FOR OUTBREEDING

There are some good marathon men about who keep a family of birds alive. In doing what they have done all the birds are tested and they are masters at and perfectionists in their quest for quality. Some individual birds of sound genes I have experimented with are from Donaldson, Denney, Denys and T. Robinson, whilst maintaining the core inbred element of the strain. It is an ongoing leap of faith and a shot in the dark to produce another performance champion. These are rare from birds of any origin and produced by good management. I like inbred birds to the main performances of the flier and then you have potential to play with. We are now consolidating and concentrating on what we have, as the cliché 'the other man's grass is always greener' can apply. If you persist with the basic plan, then results may happen.

PIGEON PHOTOGRAPHY

We like to see nice pretty pictures of key birds, the champions, the strains of the day, for their aesthetic beauty and as historical records of external appearance. They are a huge selling point for those with commercial interests and business aspirations. My favourite photographer is Peter Bennet and my 1990 Squills montage was done by this man in a professional and quiet manner.

I like raw, natural photos that help to exhibit the true appearance of the bird. Many people can see through the pretence of airbrushed, adulterated pictures – I like the real thing. Nice to see the visual progression of your strain over many years and to visualise the champions of yesterday in moments of nostalgia. It's amazing the impact of mobiles and computers on visual imagery today. They are great reminders of the birds of yesteryear, from times of good racing.

THE IMPORTANCE OF RESULTS

Results are the hardcore of every sporting endeavour and value judgements are made on them. Beyond the dreams, personalities and minds of men they remain as concrete evidence and the subject of scrutiny. The record side of it is hotly debated and contested, as far as the Guinness Book of Records. There are some great performances by fancier and bird at all distances and velocities. I do like to judge a fancier on the perceived, total impact in all areas of the pigeon culture; results in racing are part of that total.

Without doubt Mark Gilbert is gaining a right set of good, actual race results. Results if proven to be accurate and valid can stand on their own as objective evidence, beyond what we may think of the birds and the humans who flew them. I say good luck to you if you enjoy it and give a little back in return. I need to see my efforts improve at Barcelona, since we base a strain on it.

NATIONALITIES OF PIGEONS

There are some good birds and many bad in most countries. It is a fact that the contemporary racer is a mixture of diverse origins, often from many countries in the world. I have introduced birds from Belgium, Holland, Scotland, Germany and England etc over the years. It is how they have reacted to my breeding and racing system, with results that have made me decide on their value and not a bias towards the country of origin. Any birds will prevail or not prevail in the distances that you race, although I like a versatile background with some sprinters in the make-up. I stretched birds of 600-mile origins out to 879 miles through the basket. Michael Feeney has some 1000-mile bloodlines – I expect some of the progeny to sprint. Denney and I found this out through the distances in the programme.

Whatever the nationality of origin, every bird born is a distinct individual. I would like to read about Japanese, Russian, Canadian and Swedish birds to see how they perform and the characters that race them!

SUCCESS WITH DIFFERENT FAMILIES AND STRAINS

There is no one strain that is superior to others, since they are all of mixed origins. The essence of success is in the hands of the fancier who races them. The birds are diverse and of mixed genetic origins. People like Gilbert and Denney have used birds of many origins. I do like to experiment with birds of great breeding potential, yet our top stock hen was given to us from my old breeding. If you fly well a really good producer for you can light up your results and have a profound influence on a strain you may create. Bearing in mind the influence of loft, home and racing the fancier creates a strain to take his name, which will all be individual birds, yet perhaps with similar traits and some inbreeding. A good fancier will be able to have success with many types of racing pigeon, due to the condition he creates.

THE GREAT STRAINS OF TODAY

There are men who against all odds have battled on for years to do great things through guts and balls with birds of their breeding and racing. The essence is the mastery they demonstrate to the art, craft and science of distance racing. They are British and as good as any in the world at their chosen distances. Others find it hard to emulate their results and charisma, even after obtaining birds from them. In a society that celebrates and denigrates the famous, I bring you Neil Bush, Chris Gordon, Brian Denney and Jim Donaldson, who persist in dropping birds over 700 miles. Marco Wilson and Trevor Robinson raised the bar at 800-mile plus flying at Barcelona into England - I still fancy that some will try and negotiate the Pyrenees on their way to the roost. My favourite bird of the modern era is the champion Marco Wilson cock – I have two children for outbreeding and we like the Polish 1000 milers.

TRENDS IN PIGEON SALES

Although no pure birds bred by Aarden exist, the name is promulgated by commercial publicity. All racing pigeons today are of diverse and assorted origins, in the evolution of the types we see today. Some popular human names, as references survive for very many years such as Stichelbaut, Janssen, Vandenabeele and Busschaert. We hear very little of Logan, Osman, Gits and Barker now. It is adverts, articles, publicity and the spoken word that generate fame in the popular pigeon consciousness of the day.

I have put 39 years of inbreeding into my strain, housed at people's lofts and they are still impure. The modern, Continental trend is to exchange birds amongst enthusiasts and friends from the good birds of the day and I have indulged in this practice. A good bird is the result of the person who tests it out in practical breeding and racing and I follow a strict policy in this regard. Whatever the trend and whatever the name of the origin, very few racing and breeding champions are bred and sold - It is a sobering reality of the sport. Men of dreams search for the elusive champion and thus fashions and trends are born and we all become excited once more. Be shrewd in your purchases.

WHAT WE DO NOT SEE

Assuming that racing quality is in part dictated by the inner workings of the pigeon as a result of DNA and genes, then at the moment we are blind to something profound. I would love science to isolate some genes that are linked to say long distance ability and name them. Until this happens in horses and pigeons, this complex world is concealed. Knowing something of my strain, I am most impressed by real breeders and racers, since great looking pigeons can be hopeless on both accounts. I regard this fact as being illuminating and very important for the novice to know, especially when looking at sales ads which work on your mind and senses. The Ferrari parked in the road might be without an engine! When a pigeon proves itself, I am satisfied that it is right inside and the DNA is good for purpose. It is all I need to see.

THE HUMAN ELEMENT IN PIGEON RACING

Good bloodlines of great origin abound at every distance that may interest you. With a shrewd eye they are easy to obtain and people love to covert them, to have, hold and collect them. Enthusiasm tends to be ephemeral and transient and thus thousands of birds change hands like quicksilver. Rare is the fancier today who endures over aeons of chronological time and creates a strain of distinct birds, when outbreeding tends to be the modus operandi. Birds and man are mutually dependent on each other in a form of symbiosis. Believe me, the key element in the equation is the person flying the pigeons. Man will fly and create the champion from selective breeding and racing; pigeons are easy to find, but good practitioners – fanciers of real knowledge like Jim Biss – are rare. Personalities make the sport prosper and thrive around the globe, especially if they breed good producers.

INTEGRITY AND TRUST

Even with a DNA certificate, a bird may not always be what you think it is. It pays to be wise and shrewd when deciding about birds and pigeons. In your own colony where you have tested and bred every bird, you can know a little of the background of the birds, especially reared in single pair flights. There are certain people who can be trusted to a large degree and they are often strain makers with a champion or two from back garden lofts, especially where money is not the modus vivendi and operandi.

No matter what the analysis is, your racing and breeding will prove the real value of the birds in the hands of the purist. I like the principle of exchanging birds of good breeding between apparent friends, yet still testing them all, as the basket is a superior judge to man, who tends to pick on good looks and bias. My partner and I value any bird in the clock at Barcelona International – a house rule.

WINTER RATIONING??

This often takes place with cheaper food and less of it and the birds kept in like pets. We do not follow this practice, as the birds are growing body and feather throughout the winter in the UK. We season them with a good mixture, pellets and Supersix in the water, hens out one day, cocks the next. I like good bodily and instinctual condition every day from October to March and then no rationing is needed for the hens to lay in March and April. I do not buy cheap barley, yet this is used often in pellets - a superior food for pigeons. I came across pellet feeding in the 60s and it is common food now, as are peanuts popularised by Eddie Newcombe.

Winter nutrition, and lots of it, should be balanced and plentiful. I build up the reserves in the racers during the winter and muscle is matured through racing as the fat level declines – no thin birds with us, unless they have just raced hard. My article is geared towards the distance and marathon men and is best suited to types of natural system in the traditional style, which has never died.

PREPARING THE BIRDS FOR BREEDING

Many birds will carry worms, canker-producing trichomonads and some bacterial pathogens. Against these and to reduce the count we treat after racing and before pairing. On completion we liquid feed with Supersix - a very active product. I like G10S pellets, a high protein mix and matrix for egg production and squab rearing. The basic feed can be enhanced with Hormoform, peanuts and seed. I find this feeding to be optimal for several rounds of young, which will grow like mushrooms. Birds that have been out all winter will be in better condition than prisoners, which must have access to aviaries. I put the bowls into the stock pairs on December 5th and the racers paired as love mates in March. All simple, clear and straightforward – basic husbandries needed.

WRITTEN PEDIGREES

I have spent hours writing them out and will have made errors. They are only as good as the person creating them, are they not? From a genuine man, there is often some accuracy on the breeding side, yet errors on the ring codes and script are frequent. Just what is there to believe, with money and reputations at stake? Pedigrees are an expression of the human element – accuracy, attention to detail and honesty. I do like scanning them and once saw a bird whose parents were two hens. Like pictures of birds they are parts of the sport and worth a shrewd and cautious look. A man with his personal strain of good birds is worth a look and his peds. may reflect his hard work in producing the colony. When buying birds, proceed with caution.

GETTING STARTED WITH PIGEONS

On establishing a nice, big, airy, dry spacious loft and perhaps a separate stock loft, it is time to source some birds. My way now would be to befriend a top man at your chosen distance and communicate closely with him. If genuine enough, he may see a spark of potential in you, mentor you, or breed say 5 pairs of late-breds from his best performance birds. Actual results will be the arbiter of selection, not the appearance of the birds.

Breed like mad off these birds and race all the progeny

as far as you can in the local club to gain experience yourself. With success you can get more and more ambitious with racing, then see what you can do. I started with gifts from peers, and having an eye for a good one I went to Louella and rang the Ponderosa, as the studs do have some top ones of great bloodlines.

With experience you learn how to trade and swap good birds and who's who in the sport to be dealing with. Some of my seven originals I did pick on handling, the rest were bought on trust of John and Michael Massarella and Ponderosa. With time I got to know some great fanciers to source my rare outbreeding experiments on the inbreeding programme. Your racing will produce the types you need.

REAPING WHAT YOU SOW

Without getting biblical or too rural, I have a belief that fanciers who plan well ahead harvest the treasures of their hard work. Next year's 2 year olds are this year's yearlings. It is key to having new candidates evolving that you can select by racing them. The ones you spot with potential are cultivated for later and for marathon racing it is often the plodding, slowest birds in the build-up shorter races. A degree of single-minded singularity will reward you and a champion may be born.

It may be wise to start at the bottom of the ladder and progress in a linear direction towards more ambitious race targets. If you find a producer pair or two and then improve the system, some good ones will emerge. Pigeon racing is a step in the dark into the minefield of the unknown.

FOCUS ON PRACTICAL PIGEON RACING

Actual hard results are the evidence of sound racing practice. To do this, the job has been done correctly and consistent good results mean that you, the birds and your system are working. Failures would warrant an analysis of where improvements can be made, eg in housing, feeding, breeding and planning. The only way to prove the ability of racers is to send them to the race points, at your chosen distances and 7 to 800 miles is normally the racing peak of distance in the UK. Increases in distances often compound the degree of difficulty, where stamina and navigational ability come into the equation – those that do it, have it.

It's wise to put your mind and theories to the test and then study the remaining birds – how do they appear to be on surface observation? The residue can be bred from, as inbreds, outbreds or any other breds, as performance breeding genetics is not an exacting or predictable science. Performance levels are highly dependent on the prowess of the fancier. It is a bold thing to do to send every old bird beyond 500 miles, and there is no standard physical type for a distance pigeon – I have bred small, medium and large. The inside of a bird is key.

COOL, CALCULATED RISK

Thoughtful planning years ahead with individual birds is a concentrated and risky stratagem. We lay down a blueprint of operation and aim to execute the races that we have thought about. Often there is no fluke to success, as the top fanciers have a well-oiled system of practice. It's wise to go thought first followed by action. If you have made the right decisions, then in time good results should come your way.

Potentially, the further the distance of the race point the greater the calculated risk. The highest risk is normally in the Barcelona International, which is a great test of the skill and resolve of the fancier and the abilities of the bird; these elements are connected. Liberating pigeons, at any distance, is risky, with the natural elements to face. If the sport was safe and predictable, it would be of little interest.

MODERN MYTHS OF PIGEON RACING

I believe what I have learned to be true from my own experiences, which may not be the popular conventions of the day. A bird may be versatile at different distances and its racing abilities are brought out by the fancier who races it. Birds are sold as sprint, middle distance and distance, as marketing tools – few will achieve great things in race reality. The truth is that all are individuals, like the fanciers who fly them.

There is a popular belief that young birds need racing to make good birds later – a few nice tosses up to say 100 miles can do the trick. Some of my best racers have been inbred over generations and good ones may be inbred or outbred – all are different from one another. Selection theories are plentiful, yet it is always the race that proves if you were right or wrong; a good bird performs that way. Birds flown on a type of darkness system may grow into good old birds. I find that tic beans can be a valuable food source in a mixture and pellets, once frowned upon are now popular, due to G10S.

I find the best way to reality-check a belief or myth is to test it out in your own breeding and racing system – what happens will have the ring of personal truth to it. Trends project the idea of the superiority of a particular strain name, but the real world tells me that champions are rare, from birds of any origin. Wise perhaps to think in a creative and original manner and find out for yourself - you may hit on something new.

LEARNING FROM FERAL PIGEONS

Wild-living birds have much to teach us with their habits and behaviours. Their survival skills are large, breeding around the year and being omnivorous, eating anything from chips to bacon butties. When fielding they will flight out from the towns to the countryside in rain, fog, wind and snow, and I love to see them do so. The instinctual, primal urge to survive is great and our good racers demonstrate similar life traits, since we fly them on open loft.

The main colour of ferals is dark chequer and there will be good evolutionary, survival reasons for this on a genetic level. The immune system in some of the rural ferals is sky high and sparrowhawks have difficulty catching them, due to their alertness and avoidance tactics. The sharpest doves I observed out rough shooting were Stock Doves - not woodies - with rapid acceleration and jinking.

The countryside is the university of instincts and perceptual skills, the boy's adventure playground. In my old loft at Holtby, ferals and the odd crow came in and out and sparrows in the 70s and 80s - we were like hillbillies.

SERIOUS JUDGEMENT OF A PIGEON

Choosing a good one under your system is very simple. If it breeds good ones then all is fine, and likewise if it races to your satisfaction. Any other qualities, traits, dreams and opinions may have helped in the process, but until proven are all at the human level.

We send all our birds over 700 miles irrespective of our judgements before the race, or how good we think they are. You want birds to perform at your distance and send them and see feels like a good way to start. I do judge late-breds out of the top racers to be worth breeding from, especially if they are pretty, balanced birds with silky feather. There are certain more racy types, as a show homer will not race marathons. Type will be similar in closely-related birds, yet the inner abilities will be variable and individual. It is wise to concentrate on performance birds only.

THE GREAT UNKNOWNS OF PIGEON RACING

We have some lovely birds of good origins and few good ones and rare champions. Why? In marathon racing this is how it is, a fact which we can only speculate over. My conclusion is that the good ones had the inner qualities that we need, qualities cannot be seen, only inferred. The successful ones have it and have prevailed under race reality conditions. You can look at a bird until you go dizzy and will never know it.

The mystery of racing remains, hence the fascination with the sport. As close you can get to the essence of the game is to race all your birds out and study the remainder - the sport is about the racing not just the keeping of beautiful, well-bred birds.

WHEN TO STOP A RACER

Young birds can be stopped after 100 miles with impunity. These can be grown on, moulted and allowed to mature into promising yearlings. I would stop yearlings at the 450-mile mark and then rest them for the season. Keep older birds going while they exhibit race power and ability, although some of my best birds were stocked for breeding in the height of their careers. If you stop the best, they will found a strain for you, where real esoteric knowledge is learned. Our good hen with 3 times Barcelona International to her name is scheduled to go again as a 5yr old. She is a big hen with lots of stamina, being a gdtr. of Joe's Delight - Tarbes 720-plus miles. Stopping is a test of the acumen and foresight of the fancier and happens between the eyes.

RACING DIFFERENCES BETWEEN DISTANCE AND MARATHON RACING

I regard distance as being between 500 and 700 miles, with marathon coming in over 700 miles. There are many pigeons that will race 500 to 600 miles on the day of liberation and some against the wind. It is lovely to see them drop in the twilight with the local lights on, if there are any. If conditioned well, some of these will get up the next day to be timed over the 700 mark, yet this is normally a skill of the specialist, with esoteric feeding knowledge.

Distance pigeons will be nice and buoyant in the hand and well rested before the event and may come from many sources, people and families. Marathon birds of real quality are rare, sent loaded with body and fat reserves for what is a migration which may take over a week to the home loft. They exhibit rare qualities of navigation and endurance and are always worth breeding from. In our strain we concentrate our breeding around perceived good marathon genes and then at least our breeders will have some tested ancestors. We have yet to produce the perfect pigeon – it is a distant dream.

PROGRESS ON MY MENTORING

All the lads take pleasure from the birds, which is the main thing. Nick continues to refine the strain by race testing out to Barcelona. My man in Scotland is assembling a race team for the extreme distance and Chris Booth is building for the NFC races. Michael Feeney is starting out with a stud, on Facebook and later as a website under the name of Safe Haven lofts. These lads are all keen in various aspects of the sport from marathons to articles. I enjoy making a positive contribution to their impact in the sport. We source and exchange birds of excellent origins from as far as Poland. I like the personality aspect of it all as kindred spirits. We seek another racing champion as the ultimate goal of our collective enterprises and I am keen on the Irish BICC connection.

SUBTLE DIFFERENCES BETWEEN 750 AND 850-MILE RACING

The difficulty of these distances is compounded by the Barcelona International race. No one has ever timed in this over 800 miles on the 2nd day into the UK and Ireland - the challenge remains an onerous one. The Padfields manage 757 miles very well. I consider that Vince a racing genius, with huge insight and rare knowledge into racing management and the preparation to tackle the marathon distance with birds of mixed origins. It would enhance our knowledge if he were to consent to an interview via Dave or a third party-original knowledge in print!

Around 800 miles most birds have stopped to rest, forage and perhaps to stray. A rare minority of any breeding will press on beyond the 850 mark. Some reasons for this may be in reduced energy reserves, poor navigational ability and inner resolve to home, as pigeons are not the best migratory birds in the world.

In my mind's eye the champion bird of the last few years is the Marco Wilson Dark Cock - BICC, 844 miles, 3rd day in difficult conditions. My bias is evident, yet the old lad has a string of Tarbes performances over 700 miles and is sire of an 844-mile hen. Dreamers and oddballs – the pioneers – will continue to race on the edge of possibility and to challenge probability.

LIMITATIONS OF THE RACING PIGEON

Pigeons are not the furthest-flying migratory birds in the world by any means. In the UK, few will crack on over 800 miles in race time, yet 748 miles has been achieved on the day of liberation, when the old school thought that 500 miles was a long way. Fuel them up with fats and supplements and they still need to rest, drink and forage en route. Many birds feed on the wing, or fly at night. With over 100 miles an hour a possibility, some racers can sure speed on home.

There is a race each year which will show the navigational and homing potential of pigeons – the Barcelona International in July. It tests all the theories and answers all the questions, believe me. At distances over 700 miles, many racers do it in stages over weeks and are sometimes much faster the next year. Each individual bird has a performance potential and the clever fancier discovers this in practice. There is a strong link between the bird and the limitations of the human flying it.

HOW HUMBLE BIRDS BECOME RACING CHAMPIONS

A bird is born with a racing potential, which is in part

influenced by genes. Some of these may be performance related in terms of racing and could be isolated, analysed and coded. In a racing career a pigeon with its inner potential comes under many environmental influences, including the personal impact of the fancier and his total management regime, including the loft and the intricacies of his racing system. On liberation the bird is influenced by raw nature in many guises such as weather, possible predation and assorted risks en route to base loft.

To become a racing champion in the eyes of man, all the facets of the diamond need to sparkle as a brilliant whole, so that the bird realises its innate potential in racing. The expert fancier has the esoteric knowledge to assist the production of optimal condition. I take a holistic approach and attempt to influence the entire being of the bird on a physiological and psychological level. There is much more to pigeons than our current literature suggests and it can be studied from many human perspectives. In reality the limitation is human consciousness – this hints at both psychology and philosophy and language, as aids to an incomplete understanding of the humble pigeon.

ESSENTIAL SPIRITUAL ASPECTS OF PIGEON RACING

The relationship between man and his birds is both deeply felt and profound. In the endless search for results, the spiritual aspect can be the catalyst that fires a loft to greatness. This sensitive relationship can be absent where hardened men treat the birds as objects and machines, in neglect of the fact that each bird is a sentient being. Being quiet and kind with your birds creates a tangible contentment in the loft. The little old boy sat with his corn tin in the rose garden knew this well. Modern society with rampant materialism and a scientific bias neglects the spirit and soul of man to his peril, which accounts for much mental disorder. The essence is peace and harmony in the loft.

Race condition is to be found in a bird with an optimal level of physiological and psychological functioning. Men of rare talent cultivate these essentials through devotion to and love of the birds. I like a monasterial approach to the sport.

PUTTING THEORY INTO PRACTICE

The pigeon racing sport is laden with theorists and theories and it is verbal oil for the culture. Personalities and characters thrive on all the emotion, opinion and speculation. These days and with due insight, I concentrate on how to get the birds home from the really long races. This race reality tells me all I need to know about the birds and the system in action.

A system starts from an acute understanding of the needs of the birds, which you translate into management conducive to the conditioning of the birds. Once the loft and surroundings are OK, I work on the interior psychology and physiology of the bird, to create optimal condition for the target race. Are the birds content? Are they fuelled up for the task? Are you going to send them? How do you react if you fail to clock? At this stage reputations are on the line.

It's wise in the early days to keep a low profile and keep plugging away until you may do well. A producer pair can change a racing career. I reiterate that your best-looking bird in the loft may be the worst – I put breeding first, looks second. The formation of a strain will take years of related breeding.

THE REALMS OF POSSIBILITY

We are now reaching the normal limits of the abilities of racing pigeons. Speed is very dependent on wind direction and velocity and is fostered by motivation and condition. Some of the extremes of possibility, which may excite certain specialists in the UK, are 800 miles on the day of lib at Tarbes NFC, 400 miles on the day for a YB, and 600-plus miles on the day for a yearling. The magical 800 miles on the second day out of Barcelona International into the UK has yet to be achieved – possible, yet very difficult. All these are on the outer edge of possibility – they require clever management, excellent birds and favourable flying conditions. These sorts of races may attract oddballs, dreamers and compulsive optimists with lofty ambitions. Birds and men will need to be highly individual and people like these are treasures indeed. They are all within the realms of possibility, yet not probability. Interesting to contemplate and discuss.

RACING VERSATILITY OF SOME PIGEONS

Brian Denney and I flew in the same clubs - it was a very active time. Some of our birds, before we became out and out marathon specialists, would score in the sprints and through to Pau NFC at beyond the 700-mile mark, such as my Dark Dedication. Birds of this ilk have good natural ability and condition over many weeks. In recent times our birds Musgrove Addiction and Obsession won in shorter races and were clocked from Barcelona International at 710 miles. The birds I mention here are all from my early work, when every race was a challenge. The corollary is that some birds are sprinters or marathon birds only. A clever flying system will prove the capability of each bird as it races to your loft – this is the time to judge the value of each bird. The fun is in the performance of each bird in the strain that you create for yourself.

KNOWING EACH BIRD

Like people, pigeons are all individuals and you should aim to recognise each one without recourse to paperwork or records. This will test your mental powers and perception. Study each one and try to detail some of the ancestry in your mind. In meditation I can reflect on some of mine over 39 years. The process is intensified if all your birds are types of chequer or blue.

When flying out and returning from races, see if you can recognise each bird in flight, rather than as a flock. Favourites will come to mind very easily and champions will be known. Every bird will be a mixture of origins from any given name of a fancier. I like nice, calm, quiet birds that reserve energy and fall asleep in the basket. They all have a distinct personality and I wonder what they sense about us?

IRELAND BEYOND 500 MILES

Racing beyond 500 miles into Ireland involves a radical change in outlook and the establishment of dedicated, specialist marathon flying systems. People are yet to make a breakthrough in the BICC. It needs one or two rugged individualists to break from the sprint-middle convention and test all their birds out in races beyond the 500-mile mark.

A few dreamers and optimists led by Michael Feeney are

going to chance their arm at this practical possibility. It will take more than just marathon genes and the birds must be sent with huge reserves of energy and glycogen to navigate the trip from the Pyrenees. I would build up the time on the wing in racing to send 3 yr olds in blown-up peak condition and then wait and wait. The first birds will be champions and the men who race them will make international news in the pigeon and mainstream media. I have assembled birds out there for the purpose and the next few years may realise a dream for some with the fire of ambition.

TALKING UP THE BIG RACES

There is plenty of excited chatter, hype and verbal personality exchange before the business end of competition. Here the characters and personalities come out to play, which I often enjoy as the sport is intrinsically human. Some of the challenges, like the Irish Barcelona one, are bound to fire emotions and the imagination.

The reality is that the remaining goals and targets in the sport will take years of concerted preparation and dedication to achieve. For this purpose I like a slow-burning, controlled, long-term enthusiasm. The major races demand a spiritual and psychological input of a high order, with the scarcity of really good birds for these events. Feelings and reputations may be on the line and you may need to recover from disappointments and chance your arm again and again – the big marathon races are a leap of faith. Some years I sent all my birds to Pau 735 miles and waited over a week. I feel that great patience is an essential quality in the psyche – Jim Wright and Brian Denney are the personifications of this trait.

THINGS TO THINK ABOUT

Well-bred birds are easy to find, yet are they of real value? In my long career, I gave most thought to developing my prowess as a fancier. How can we aim to perfect the breeding and flying system? What are the logical steps to take, and how we can practise them? What are the races and distances of real significance?

I like to question all aspects of the sport, people and pigeons to see what is significant to me. A healthy dose of obsessive perfectionism helps, especially if you set out on the convoluted path to form a strain. It is a journey both of the spirit and in practice, where steady improvements can be realised over many, protracted years. The essence is to enjoy the process whilst it is lived.

LADS IN THE NORTH

My career was against a backcloth of exceptional men who flew Pau at beyond 700 miles. To put this into perspective, it is nearly impossible for an international race to be won over 700 miles into the UK. There are obvious and evident reasons for this and flying distance in relation to the shorter fliers springs to mind. Many birds will not sprint much beyond the 500-mile mark to be capable of a 700-mile-plus outright win. As migrating birds go the humble pigeon falls short on out and out distance capability, with some exceptions. Stepping it up to 800-plus miles makes Barcelona a big, big challenge, when some of the birds will do 700 miles with relative ease.

I dedicate these notes to Gordon, Bush, Denney, Donaldson, Kay, Riley and other select northern stalwarts who make a stand in this very difficult discipline of racing – heroes all.

IMPROVING AND EVOLVING THE
MODERN RACING PIGEON

With competitive advances in nutrition and systems in place, the sport does produce some rare, outstanding pigeons. If they are evolving on a genetic basis, eg mutations, in terms of performance levels, I imagine it to be a very slow process. In terms of the future, a serious push from Ireland and Scotland may see targets in marathon racing being realised, as all the difficulties with the limited natural abilities of the birds are worked on from the preparation and breeding aspects.

Speed is in part dependent on system, which will see some improvement in some sprinters. Some men will be driven by new goals and challenges, and I perceive a change in approach and mindset in some of these at the present time. Overall, apart from some obvious exceptions, most racing pigeons are limited by type and their ability to store reserves of energy and associated stamina levels. 7 to 800 miles seems to be a guide to the normal limit for a decent marathon pigeon in today's racing, with some homing exceptions and over 500 miles into Ireland is exceptional now. The next 10 years will see some strong attempts to set new boundaries in time, distance and location.

A RECIPE FOR SUCCESS

The art, craft and science of pigeon racing are a discipline that can be learned. With an eye on the future, start at the lesser distances and persist and persist until you develop a winning system in your area. Aim to equal the results of your peers before becoming more ambitious. You will have failures, and this is where self-belief kicks in. Befriend a top man at your distance and negotiate for a round of late-breds off his key performance birds and learn from him – at this stage you listen to the master, since he holds the reasons why he got to the top.

Housing should be spacious, light and airy, or diseases will take hold and kill some of your birds – they hit us all, the great, good and the small. At stage 1 have an eye on strain building, which will impassion you for a lifetime and long after the race results have ceased to be quite so important. The main ingredient of success is your personality and then the quality of the birds you breed. Your returns from races over 800 miles will be few, whoever you are.

WHEN THE REALITY KICKS IN

There are some races that are so difficult as to be on the edge of possibility. If people attempt these then they will become acutely aware of what serious racing is all about. Only specialist preparation of rare birds will suffice, in optimal condition. The knowledge and dedication required is of the highest order and the people will be famous in the pigeon media. These are the races of optimists and oddballs. If people achieve these high aspirations it will cause shock waves in the fancy. I refer to BICC clocking over 500-800 miles into Ireland and Barcelona BICC into Scotland.

In the next 10 years men will try to improve on the natural limitations of the racing pigeon. There are initiatives to attempt these race disciplines, yet I would recommend caution as I perceive great difficulties with distance, location, weather and the sheer organisation of it all. Having said that, there are BICC trophies in place for any adventurous spirits who achieve such targets.

A PERSONALISED SYSTEM

We talk of natural, widowhood and other so called systems, yet in practice they are peculiar to the individual person, loft and location. No 2 systems are the same in reality, eg Nick operates a system based on my old one, yet it is unique to him. There is our understanding of a named system like celibate, and then we fly the birds to a personal interpretation of it. This falls back on the personality of the fancier to get the performance levels of the birds to the maximum. A magic formula for success does not exist, as you have to find your own way and a superstrain of birds, where all are good racers, does not exist. The reality and acid test is that with success at your race points comes the effectiveness of your breeding and racing system. The conclusion is that all birds are unique along with the people and systems in practice. This sounds philosophical and existential, yet is true.

ROOM AT THE TOP

In the push and shove of competitive racing, new personalities will evolve and emerge, along with fashions in birds to excite our attention. As some of the old guard come and go, a few will live long in the memories of today. These will have done unusual things or given much publicity. They act as barometers of the health and popularity of the sport and now there is a wealth of information on these people in the media. I prefer books and hard copy as internet sites can crash, with the loss of original material.

I have a hunch that the next real champion may emerge in Ireland, and I have invested a lot of thought into this possibility. A small number send to Barcelona, yet the sport is flooded with birds bred around birds that have raced it. In this race is a great deal of scope and room at the top for the serious aspirant.

Who will it be to make more history? I bet it will be a bird of mixed origins that emerges into the limelight. Marketed by name all racing pigeons are from a diverse gene pool.

THE MAGIC FORMULA FOR SUCCESS

All the answers you need lie between the eyes. People look for a rapid solution to get results. In fact there is no one standard recipe. I will suggest that if your birds are content at home, in secure, comfortable surroundings and are kept fit and healthy by you, then they are ready to go to the races. It is not enough to obtain well-bred stock: they must be brought into optimal condition before sending them.

It is imperative to focus on the complete wellbeing of the birds, then they may perform for you, if they are any good. Find a system that suits your needs and is effective for you, then it will be your magic formula for success. Pigeon racing is all about individual people and their birds, not a standard formula. I will help anyone with tips and advice, yet the way forward is personal to them. My methods work for me, yet good birds are rare and champions seldom.

PROFILE OF A CHAMPION

The personality of a champion is complex, yet certain traits are conducive to creating one. I like to see a strong sense of originality, creative thinking and independence from mainstream conventions. With a powerful focus and dedicated objectivity, this perfectionist pursues goals and results with passion and fervour. Little fish are sweet and starting at base level, this person will aspire to the top or greatness. On the way to this self-realisation, some great or unusual results may be achieved. At or near the top this person may contribute to knowledge or act as a mentor or philanthropist. Often charismatic people they may transcend the sport or activity that has generated so much interest for them, so that they become a focus of interest for others or a role model. Two people who spring to mind in the sporting sphere are Ayrton Senna and Ronnie O'Sullivan - both touched by the hand of genius.

COMMON DISTANCE PROBLEMS

Many start at home with a lack of focus and persistence by the fancier. In reality few birds will hit the ceiling in the greater distances, no matter how much you put faith into the stock birds. The absolutely essential thing to do is send the birds to the races in the first place to prove their worth and to judge capability by doing this. Many birds will not repeat the performance. Treasure the breeders and persist with them over many years and avoid the impulse to keep changing birds and the system, especially after good results. It will not be a quick fix type of racing and to do well may take years and years and a strain takes a good 25 years of solid breeding and racing. It is not easy to condition the birds with limited home exercise and I hate birds closed in stuffy lofts. If you fear your reputation is at risk it may deter you from sending to 5 to 700 miles. All these problems can be overcome by the PERSONALITY of the fancier.

THE DAWN AWAKENS - A NEW BEGINNING

I have been impressed by the intellect and ambition of Michael Feeney with his Barcelona aspirations in Ireland. An influential man, he will inspire many people with his creative ideas focused on pigeons and marathon racing. We hope to race together as Feeney and Emerton. Our well-defined objectives are laden with challenge and difficulty and this is the motivation we need. It will be a long term project and it remains on the edge of possibility. My role has been the sourcing of quality bred birds and systems advisor. It is one of many creative projects, which I find stimulating. Michael is as honest as they come, with factual flair, a keen intellect and will enjoy his journey facing the challenges of dedicated marathon racing and the cultivation of capable bloodlines for this purpose.

SALES

There are some good genes out there and nice-looking birds, but beware! Few birds are really good in reality as racers and breeders. I prefer to give birds away or exchange them with the marathonists of the day. However we all start somewhere, and if you pick the right ones at the studs, you may prosper. The selection is down to the brain of the fancier in relation to the bird on offer – a highly subjective process. Wise to spot the sales publicity tricks, enhanced photos and hype, designed to make a killing. Fortunately there are some quality birds around and the reality test is what you breed and race from them. Be shrewd and watch your money before you part with it. I went to Louella with an idea of what I wanted and got it, a fortunate step indeed. It is essential to go to the right people in the first place and

I learned in the souks and bazaars of the world, where they specialise in English tourists.

A PIGEON BUSINESS

In my younger days, money was hard won and with my parent's business prowess, I later branched out into pigeon sales. To be pure in this regard, a family of birds with some real results is de rigueur. I enjoyed the human aspect of sales, the visitors and characters and exported to China in the 80s. Keeping an eye on the money sharpens the mind, alerts the senses and is a mainstream thing to do. People buy with desire and a dream and under popular, cultural influences of the times - the media has an impact on the minds of men. Sales are about persuasion and supplying a demand.

The sobering truth and harsh reality is that few great champions are bred and raced in the vast numbers bought and sold. Many birds are acquired under the illusion of quality and potential – frequently a psychological phenomenon in the mind of the fancier. In the theatre of dreams of the sport, pigeons evolve around hopes, aspirations and ambitions and these generate business and commercialism.

THE STRAIN MAKER

This for a fancier is in the highest echelon of achievement. A good 25 years should be devoted to related birds from a gene pool that produces some great individuals. The life cycle of a man can be expressed in the continuous task of progeny testing of birds of his breeding. With no fixed patterns of inheritance, despite the theory of genetics, the yearly grind of racing will prove the worth of the birds or not.

At marathon distances over 700 miles, you will breed and race a few good ones that become key, named birds of distinction. Men who have created good strains are in demand and we know they are purists. It takes a compulsive focus and enduring focus to do this-people like Bush, Gordon, Denney, Donaldson and Delea have done it. The opposite is to keep getting in fresh birds to put on a racing regime. Long-term enthusiasm called for here.

JAN AARDEN PHENOMENON

The interest in this name is a collective, cultural phenomenon. As he passed away very many years ago, there are no pure, direct birds from this fancier, although some of the diluted genome may exist, as fanciers have come and gone who support the name of Aarden. All racers are of diverse origins - I include mine with 39 years of close family breeding - a pedantic point which is true. Under the generalised umbrella of the name are some good birds as is the case with Stichelbaut. It is the fame and charisma of the fancier's name that sells the birds in the open market place. If you can, introduce birds direct from the noted champions of the day – my outbreeds have come from Denney, Donaldson, Wright, Wilson, Robinson, Denys, Schlepphorst and Hanby to add to the base foundation of 7 birds post 1976. The racers have been outbred or inbred – all are tested to this day. Naming a strain is the humanisation of the birds and will continue, especially in the commercial world.

LOGICAL STEPS OF THE GOOD FANCIER

People do not get to the top by chance. They plot and plan their way forward in a well-conceived stratagem. Armed with good information and perhaps insight, they develop a system that can be applied in practice with good impact, so that results are generated. An effective system is one that can be repeated year in year out. This type of thought process requires a single-minded approach from the individual. I do find that many of the great marathon men are strong on individuality and sometimes eccentricity and I love people with innovative and creative ideas, like Michael Feeney with his rare bloodlines and establishing a distance/marathon stud in Ireland. Since this type of racing is so difficult in Ireland, most fanciers have opted for sprint-middle distance disciplines. Top marathon performances over there will be most unorthodox and ignite world news. It is worth the long shot, for the bold ambitious fancier and what quality birds they will be.

THE GRAND AND BEAUTIFUL DESIGN

Many years ago, I visualised a network of men who would dedicate themselves, with free will, to the cultivation of marathon pigeons. With BICC connections in Scotland, England and Ireland some leading players are emerging to have their days in the sun. All individuals, they are important elements in the grand design and the core of the apple is marathon birds and their performance. I have sourced some lovely birds for us all and we work on the continued cultivation of mine. All free to pursue their innermost dreams, the birds they evolve will be an avian expression of their personality. They are men of desire and ambition. We are like monks attending to the bees in a monastery garden and I do like the spiritual aspect of the devotion required. Some of the men on the chessboard are Feeney, Harvey, Ghent, Booth and Little. A new racing champion will emerge from this association. We welcome all enthusiasts who hear the same tune.

TEMPERAMENT OF THE MARATHON PERSONALITY

Marathons place great demands on the psyche of the individual – they drive you mad! Allow up to 10 days' waiting time from Barcelona International – the birds have difficult terrain to navigate. It is demanding on mood, resolve, patience and persistence, as in the old days we wildfowlers dug hides in the mud flats of the Wash. Light the fuse and enter the zone for a long, long time. If you persist and plan every minute of the day around the race, then perhaps you will be rewarded.

I think the endurance level of stamina and concentration puts off many, as you need to be very target orientated. The planning is the years ahead variety, around every bird in the loft and the race point will always have you at its mercy, as it is greater than yourself, no matter that you try to conquer it. The lads in Ireland will learn the essence of difficulty on the road to possible glory. The most patient men, with control can realise their dreams in the Formula 1 of pigeon racing. Take a leap of faith, feel the rush of realisation of the arrival from great distance - an intense psychological phenomenon.

THE TRUE VALUE OF A PIGEON

They may raise thousands of pounds and be coveted and

valued in material terms. This is mainstream market forces in action, and fuels the international world of pigeon racing. Having sold birds myself, I came to alter my philosophy on pigeons. I believe the real value of a bird lies in its racing and breeding potential and at my chosen distance and race point for it. This is a pedantic and purist approach to the intrinsic value of a racing pigeon. In this i place the emphasis on an approach to the actual bird rather than the money generated – unorthodox yet crucial in my philosophy towards marathon pigeon racing.

In a long career, I have bred many good ones, and a few rare champions, yet the satisfaction lies in the creation of a strain of some quality, related individuals. In an aesthetic sense the good ones always look beautiful.

PUTTING THE HOURS IN

Looking back over 40 years of evolution with related bloodlines, a network of enthusiasts shows a human face in my life and we are all experimenting with the birds, yet waiting for another champion to emerge out of Barcelona International. My exchange mechanism for birds is going well amongst people with marathon aspirations. We hope some of these men will excel in pure racing. All will express their individual personalities in various ways peculiar to themselves. We ask a lot of the humble pigeon, as they are not the best of migratory birds – 800 miles stretches the species right out. In spite of this, dedicated souls become obsessed by the beauty, grace and power and the mystery of navigation.

CULTIVATING GREAT MARATHON CONDITION

The inner nature of the bird is influenced by the external world it inhabits. The expert fancier with his esoteric knowledge plays a tune with his birds to create optimal racing condition. With open loft, in and out of the natural elements and advanced feeding techniques. My feeding system, using assorted foods with liquid feeding of supplements, is unique. People are trying to replicate the system I created and evolved, and it will always be an interpretation, because of the personal, human element – the system is an outward expression of the personality of the fancier. Most pigeons are on the limit at 800 miles for Barcelona. For the UK it takes a great bird, sent in top condition, like the Marco Wilson cock, to do something truly remarkable. Steps to condition can be under the control of the mind and hand of the fancier-your marathon future begins in the back garden.

HARD ENDURANCE PIGEONS

Long-term, continuous, competitive racing from 500 to 879 miles up to Barcelona International level and in all weathers will produce some birds of great navigational ability and solid character. In my strain and with inbreeding to performance birds many small-medium dark chequer birds have contributed to my career. Going very close indeed as a continuous entity, some of the birds are prolific breeders when outbred and every one must be tested right out. After 40 years my partners and contacts are in this process that will continue.

The modern lure is Barcelona into Ireland in race time. All individuals these folk will shape a destiny out of birds and dedication. We are seeking another champion to add to the genome. On perception, the good birds may radiate an aura about themselves, like charisma in people. A bird may mature into a good racer with years of time on the wing experience and you will recognise them in race reality. I reflect on the birds I raced and bred with admiration and affection.

OUTBREEDING INBRED PIGEONS

With specialism, some great birds may be raced from this breeding process. Inbred birds may race well too; the formula is to race all the progeny and see how good they are in race reality. With outbreeding an increase in size and vigour may result on appearance and testing, although I prefer small to medium, compact pigeons. I do believe that the real value of a bird lies within it and is partly dictated by the genome inherited by the ancestors. Good ones are all a nice type, and radiate individuality of character and external appearance when perceived by the human brain. My networks of enthusiasts are poised to experiment with types of breeding system, yet i still inbreed my strain after 40 years. The untrained eye will see them as peas in a pod, yet all are different.

Always nice to reflect on the key birds that you have evolved over time, you stamp your personality on them, and they can be recognised by others as being distinct. I outbreed inbreds to inbreds of different performance origins.

THE RIGHT DECISIONS

An eye and mind for the right bird is very significant in strain building. Knowledge and focus – a perception of quality and potential are important. In 76 I matched 2 birds up out of the pens, with value judgements on feather texture, balance and the total impression in my mind, having studied the evolutionary history of the strain origins and a montage advertised by Louella. The image was of the DVH Stichelbaut-based birds from Descamps Van Hasten. I felt that they were the birds for me and would be successful for me. With strict progeny testing, the originals with two more from inbred, related birds have left descendants that are raced out to Barcelona International some 40 years later, with inbreeding back to my 7 foundation birds-these origins are documented on the internet.

The decision to inbreed around real performance birds has been good, with some outbreeding of inbred pigeons in the strain creation. Today top-class UK and Ireland Barcelona marathon performers are rare, especially in excess of 800 miles, ie within 3 to 4 days - yet to be a Barcelona bird into the UK on the second day over 800 miles! Have a go in the race of all races – it is mind bending.

METICULOUS RECORDS

Never perfect in reality, it is important to keep, pedantic and accurate records in the recording of the creation of a strain. Over 40 years I have tried to maintain this principle, and the evolution using my 7 foundation birds is well documented on Google. Some indication of key, prepotent birds may be seen, yet it is the total ancestry that is of highest significance. The apples may have fallen from the tree 50 years later for example – when I got the DVH in 76 they were already in bred for generations. It is fastidious, hard work, yet leaves behind the history of the human who created a group of birds with distinct hereditary characteristics.

This type of activity is often undertaken by academic, scientific and intellectual types who may be visionary in conscious perception. Gerhard Schlepphorst personifies these traits – I have bought in 28 of his Stichelbaut-based birds, and the standard phenotype is beautiful. We will progeny test them all. A strain is the outward expression of the psyche of man. Nice to reflect back on birds that shaped the strain. There are often many errors in the recording of pedigrees-we do try.

TRIBUTE TO A GREAT ENGLISH BARCELONA PIGEON

After the epic performances of Flange of Biss and Padfield's Invincible from Barcelona International there emerged a wonderful champion cock. Dark in colour and with multiple performances at Tarbes NFC in excess of 700 miles, he won the Northern Section in the BICC at 844 miles to be 12th open on the 3rd day. I interviewed Marco Wilson and Cath on the exemplary achievement of this great bird in such hard conditions. A nice, genuine man, Marco gave me two offspring, and one to my racing partner Michael Feeney in Ireland. The genes are secure and progeny will be raced out to Barcelona.

From time to time over 25 years some great 800-mile marathon birds emerge after Riley's Duchess and Barcelona Dream. The genes of these birds are used by purist marathon men who join the Barcelona International dream - men of vision and imagination who seek a name in history, and triumph over great difficulty.

A QUALITY PIGEON

Looks can be deceptive, yet inbred birds of your own creative breeding programme can be beautiful in the eye of the beholder. I fell in love with my dark chequers 40 years ago. Balanced, silky birds with shiny, sparkling, coloured eyes are an aesthete's delight. They inspire a career in racing and breeding. From a batch of late-breds I like to select the quality looking ones. However, my concept of a good one has evolved and changed. We have a simple race reality test for a bird as follows – the breeder must produce a Barcelona International timer and the racer must fly it as often as possible. These are tough and fanatical criteria to set, yet the strain building philosophy works well in our biased perspective. Always consider the apparent breeding origin of the bird, be wary of the flattering beauty!

TAME PIGEONS

The Iron Hen, my very first section winner from Clermont, would fly down the garden and sit on my head, as I walked about. She was dam of my top stock cock Dark Destiny. Generations of nice, pretty, quiet birds are down from that hen hatched in 77 - she was an uncrossed DVH Stichelbaut. I hate wild, highly-strung birds, yet like them to live a free semi-wild life.

Quiet, introverted pigeons are often best for beyond 500 miles, since they rest and conserve energy better and are more inward and interior as beings, in an anthropomorphic sense from the human perspective. Tame birds will sharpen and liven up on liberation from great distances, as the brain/survival instinct mode kicks in. The essence is harmony between man and the flock, in a safe environment, to look for that edge in racing and homing ability from great distances. We use any race under 700 miles as preparation only, yet enjoy studying form on the way with nice tame birds.

A BIG TEAM OF PIGEONS

With a cottage garden loft, and my racing regime, my team was small by the end of the year. A big flock of birds whizzing about informs me of a sprint-middle distance set up, a real marathon man always has a small team – it is an eloquent expression for obvious reasons. Beyond 7 to 800 miles selects for stamina and solo navigational ability, not group, flock flying. First place at Barcelona is a remote possibility, as one in race time is a triumph over difficulty. My modern strain is forged on these birds, yet they still sprint as individuals within the family – our feeding philosophy produces some good ones at all distances, as hard results have shown. Good men tend to have several good birds due to the system – wise men make the right choices. I am always coaxing my chaps to progeny test each bird in the season. In a team of birds of say 20 to 30 a champion may exist.

FINDING A DISTANCE PIGEON

Top pigeons are uncommon, yet many make-believe ones are sold on the commercial scene. I have invested in a few well-bred birds to see the reality of their results. It is easy, develop a system that generates condition to fly 4 to 500 miles as yearlings and then send them all to over 700 miles as 2 yr olds. Any birds in race time will be distance birds, irrespective of looks, handling and origin. I have maintained this fastidious approach for 23 years in the evolution of my strain, and hope that my mates will continue the rigorous selection philosophy and practice.

Good birds over 700 miles are MARATHON birds. This is a purist approach - proof of the pudding, shit or bust racing. You can create personal theories in relation to the birds in admiration of the good ones - my approach is empirical and existential. Not for all this approach, which is tinged with a modicum of madness. You will treasure the good ones you evolve and the rare champion. There are some geniuses of the modern game like Jim Donaldson, Vince Padfield and Marco Wilson - bags of nails all.

APPLES THAT FALL FAR FROM THE TREE

We were looking at some of the historical ancestors of our strain, and some great names loom up from the distant past, the genes and shadows of which are relevant in 2016. You guess about the breeding value of the birds from the past, yet they are there. Some are famous, others not, yet the truth is that all performing birds of today are of mixed, diverse origins. What a mixture these modern named birds are in reality – the truth behind the illusion of commercial hype. Tracing what we know of Alois Stichelbaut, DVH, Emiel Denys and birds like Woodsider and Lancashire Rose - all in my strain - is absorbing. Given all this complexity, and to the purist, the love of the game lies in good to great performances of modern birds that can hack Barcelona International, since you know these have stamina and sound navigational ability. I feel the mystery in the history of each good bird. Birds as good as the Marco Wilson cock are very, very rare, and not as famous as they should be - extremists are a minority group.

ONE LOFT RACING

One loft races are popular social events, where birds are raced from different sources under one management regime. It can be lucrative, fun, risky and commercial. I will not enter any birds in these events, since it would be a departure from the purist principles that I have cultivated and cogitated over for 25 years or so. These are that that my birds must be bred to race Barcelona International, now in various locations at different distances beyond 700 miles into UK and Ireland.

The benchmark of difficulty is my parameter and criterion for inculcation into the strain. We are a motley crew of mad monks, illuminated by a shared dream... It is an extension of the old, traditional values, of the old sage, pipe in mouth, corn tin in hand, sunning himself in his deckchair in his rose garden. That is how the iconic birds in folklore and history were raced. My friends share mutual aspirations of excellence, to continue the dedicated work of our sporting ancestors like Alois Stichelbaut, who left us in 1946, for his vision to fall into the grasp of Michael Descamps-DVH.

MY VALENTINE'S DAY

I will be dreaming, thinking and talking about pigeons and the last 38 years of our relationship. With two racing partners in Ireland and sleeping partners in the UK, things are buzzing at every level. I tend to source new birds and advise on systems and science. We are all playing with my strain and each man is trying to forge an identity in the sport; the dedicated work continues between the monks in the monastery of racing pigeons.

I am keen to see the results of our classy new birds - there may be a good one in them. The strain will evolve again as the egos of the keepers make an impact. The key racing man has been Sir Nicholas Harvey of Taunton - a practical racing man with great empathy - modestly setting about his Barcelona strain. My bulbs are flourishing in the garden where I meditate on a daily basis, as I did in the 1950s at Skendleby in the Lincolnshire Wolds, where I had my first flying out racers, mainly strags. I am looking forward to July - we need a second day bird from Barcelona into the West Country. My pal plans to send from Cornwall, so watch out.

OLD SYCAMORE COTTAGE, HOLTBY - THE GENESIS

In 1976 we moved there from Southampton for 30 years to develop my career and strain surrounded by trees, open fields and sparrowhawks. Mother and I lived like spartan hillbillies, as the plantation, orchard and gardens grew wild – it was ecological bliss, with stoats and pheasants in the butterfly garden and a loft of free-range pigeons.

The man to beat in the formative years was Denney, who at Tarbes emerged as a great flier with his own strain of mixtures. From this romantic, ideal setting our personal histories were cemented by some special racing performances that have stood the test of time. My mother and i were not materialistic, with intellectual and artistic traits that were allowed to grow and mature under the guiding hand of nature. Now I reflect with sweet nostalgia on the days when the sun shone and the birds raced with distinction to the home they loved. My main work now is to inspire others to reach for the stars, to touch them for a single moment, as destiny unfolds.

RESULTS COUNT

The essence of the nature of the racing game is hard results; we are never satisfied with ours, which is a motivational source. We need more champions to come from the strain – there will be some.

How do I judge a pigeon man? He has to meet my criteria, as follows. He has made a lasting contribution to the collective good of the sport and has developed a good strain of birds over 25 years-plus at all distances to beyond 700 miles. One way is to mentor novices to get results and donate trophies – a kind of ego-altruism. Psychologically if you are happy with a career in birds then it is the result that counts in the end. Personally I would sacrifice all my firsts for one champion out of Barcelona.

Racing is hard grind, and I do prefer my creative writing and mentoring the neophytes and initiates – some of them appreciate it in a genuine sense. I am aware of the Janus face of humanity.

KNOWLEDGE AND LEARNING

The top men in the game all have advanced esoteric info in their heads and at their fingertips. Mine was created from academic study and insights from breeding and racing practices. In 40 years some intuitive leaps have helped me to create a unique breeding and racing system. Others attempt to replicate it, and may become quite close, yet it remains mine.

The Zsolt Talaber books are great, as was Schraag, since good applied science is there to help the intelligent fancier. I use a fusion of the wild open loft with quality solid and liquid feeding, which with the man all optimise and maximise race condition that is crucial for marathon flying from Spain.

What works is a fusion of all we think and do with our key genes and inner potential of the birds. The desire has always been to improve the strain - after 40 years some steady progress is made.

THE TOTAL BEING OF EACH BIRD

Pigeons are sentient, complex creatures in an intimate relationship with man. How do they tick, and respond to our understanding and empathy? The men of old were right with their love of the home concepts of distance racing. A hen may flirt with you and race her heart out - stroke them on the nest and feed peanuts to each one. Today I apply science and personal insight to supply all the physiological and psychological needs of the blood, heart, brain, lungs and psyche. A bird in great form will need navigational ability, individual solo flight, speed and endurance – some are hatched with it. A quiet, if not silent approach is key, with calm handling by the master.

ADVANCED NUTRITION FOR PIGEONS

I have created a real cocktail of feeds for our racers and breeders. As a base are G10 pellets in the hoppers for all birds, with Matrix in containers. We mix Versela Laga Gerry Plus with Superstar Plus, and add Wilsbridge No 2, peanuts, sunflower hearts, Hormoform, tovo, hemp, brewer's yeast, seed and oil mixtures. In the water is Vydex Supersix or Blitzform on certain days before basketing - stock in aviaries, old and young racers on open loft. We have won from 31 to 879 miles with the same strain on similar methods. The young are perfect and we have had 15 birds from Barcelona International over the years. No rationing and starving of the birds, no breakdown, is countenanced. A build up regime in racing prepares the birds for 710 plus miles and further. Then it's down to the race and the pigeon.

RACERS NEED REST

I like four weeks or so loft rest at home before a marathon flight of over 700 miles. Before this and in steady increases in race distance a nice fly of up to 500 miles will be under the birds' belt. They will have fuelled up on my unique feeding system and will be laden with fuel and fat reserves in the internal organs – glycogen in the liver etc. A short toss of around 100 miles in the week before basketing will add the final tuning element to the condition. Exercise at home then, with no stressful basket/road training. The birds are then calmly caught for basketing and marking.

Time on the wing for build-up preparation is essential, with birds left at home certain weekends from the race programme – BICC/BBC/NFC. The birds are blown up with air/muscle and fat reserves for Barcelona, where stamina is key. We are not expecting to win this race as no UK person has done it - the essence is the majesty and awesome challenge of the Pyrenees and Spain in the greatest race on Planet Earth.

FEEDING PELLETS

I saw the value of layers pellets for pigeons in 1963, and we had fed them at Skendleby to poultry in 1956. In 1976 when I started my pigeon racing career at Holtby, York, we fed hoppers of layers' pellets ad lib to all birds at all times, along with my unique feeding mixtures. They are cheap, good science and effective nutrition from sprint to marathon racing at over 800 miles Barcelona. My racing partner uses G10S, which are very effective as part of the overall feeding concept. I have used many types of pellets and all you need in reality are cheap layers for all ages of birds. Save money, be wise and get some – they are as near to perfect as you can get. See my unique feeding system below. They are easily digested and absorb water, ideal for returning stressed out birds and before racing – I never starve birds, ever! Since the 1970s many people have caught on to pellets and peanuts as great food sources for pigeons.

FEEDING STOCK HENS

We give them a complete diet of pellets and our own mixture. Liquid feeds are Vydex Supersix and Rohnfried Blitzform. When rearing I like Matrix, some peanuts, yeast, Hormoform, Tovo, seed, hemp and sunflower hearts mixed with oils to moisten the yeast powder. The base mixture is high protein, which we replace with Gerry Plus and Superstar Plus for racing, with no keeping birds hungry ever. This is fed to young and old, all flying out together on open loft. The young will have 3 tosses to 100 miles, yearlings to Saintes NFC, older birds to Barcelona International on the same weekend. A very simple system, where effort is made by the birds, not the fancier. The progeny testing produces some good ones and proves your breeding plans and racing prowess under race reality conditions - it is what it is.

MY UNIQUE FEEDING SYSTEM

- We give solid and liquid feeds to fuel the birds up for speed/endurance racing to 710 miles Barcelona Int. into Taunton, West Country.

- The birds have hoppers of GEM G1O pellets before them young and old and on the open loft system.

- Our special food mix fed on calling in is the following: Gerry Plus, Superstar Plus, Willsbridge No.2 Mix, Yeast, Hormoform, Conditionseed, hemp, peanuts, sunflower hearts, Vydex Mvs 30, Columbine Oil, Gem Energy Oil, Ogo Oil.

- To this fat, carbohydrate and protein mix we use Vydex Supersix in the water on return from the race, and build up for the water races and Blitzform 2 days before basketing.

- At other times we use Aviform Ultimate in the water, and I used to try Bovril.

We find that with hard racing, the condition of the birds by July with rest periods is excellent and first-class young are bred from the stock – all ages range the skies together for hours. As a new partnership we aim to evolve the strain and have had 11 birds from Barcelona International so far, yet try to improve over time. The strain is versatile and some will win the sprint/middle distances. The system has flair/intuition and originality in its formulation – it works for us. At the end of the day the intrinsic ability of the birds will win through or not if you send em.

THE BAND OF BARCELONA BROTHERS

I have been inspired to write this as a tribute to and celebration of the wonderful feeling of kinship that the advocates and enthusiasts share in their support and dedication to the Barcelona objective. Friendships are being fostered throughout the UK in the spirit of endeavour. Some of these will be life changing and will endure the passage of time. I think these relationships are fired by the hardship of the task and the sheer endurance required of the Barcelona vigil.

The race is gathering momentum, established by early pioneers in the BICC, and we are seeing a renaissance of popular interest in the race where myths and legends are cemented in pigeon folklore. Who will light the torch of recognition in 2013? Will it be Goddard, Kay, Gilbert or Harvey, or other aspiring stalwarts of the queen of races? Just who is set to make UK history?

WIND & DRAG

In reality we can but reason and guess regarding a pigeon's return from the race point unless an accurate tracking device is fitted, with imagery on a computer screen. Naturally there will be clever and informed opinions which may or may not reflect external reality!

Three performances I rate regardless of the wind and drag cliché are: Flange by Biss 778 miles Barcelona International on the second day, Padfield's Invincible 2nd BICC Barcelona 750 miles on the 2nd day and Riley's Duchess 2nd BICC Barcelona over 850 miles on the 3rd day.

If you look at the first 20 BICC Perpignan birds of 2013 all are from east or central England, giving me the thought that the drag can be of consequence to the result even if the wind appears to favour the west of England and Wales. An interesting concept for good fanciers north, south, east and west to ponder, yes? In my own racing and with Nic Harvey in the west, we aim for the greatest possible difficulty, yet can go to only 710 measured miles at Barcelona International. We make the best of our positional geography, which is the modus operandi.

WHEN THE STICHELBAUTS CAME TO SYCAMORE COTTAGE

When we moved from Southampton in 1976, I met my mentor in racing pigeons, Jack Ross of Holtby. On a race day his birds homed over Sycamore Cottage, the home of Mum, Dad and myself. Kind Jack took me in his care and set me off with racing birds and got me into the clubs.

I saw an advert from Louella for Stichelbauts and from the image knew they were my future. The matched pair selected from the sales pens was GB 76 J90513 and GB76J90079. They were lovely, small dark chequers and I hit the jackpot with them instantly. They bred The Iron Man and Iron Hen, 4th and 1st sect Clermont 350 miles. As brother and sister, when paired together they bred in September my No 1 Stock Cock Dark Destiny and his brother No 2. I had inbred already-inbred birds with immediate super performances. At this time we were hungry to win club and fed races, with time and dedication we made good progress with many firsts and prizes.

Two more uncrossed DVH Stichelbauts were sent up by the great John Massarella. These were GB 81V60171, Dreadnought, and GB 80V84859, Delilah. These 4 birds, based on Belgian sprinters, all became prepotent producers under my evolving, ruthless, racing regime. In the early creative formation of my strain I used 3 more birds as follows; Belge 4415080/76 direct Emiel Denys, which bred the no 1 stock hen Daughter. of Darkness when paired to GB76J83650 LOUELLA (extreme distance family) and NL 85 695044. I persisted with relentless ardour, producing key racer producers from the No.1 pair like Diabolos GB 83S35305 - my greatest ever racing pigeon.

Over 40 years and rare intros from Stichelbaut-based Denney and Hanby birds and the great Jim Donaldson, Scottish genius, my birds won from 71 to 879 miles in the BICC Barcelona International. The strain is thriving, as my partner and I have extended the sprint winning lines to sending every bird of my origin 710 measured miles at Barcelona. Now with partners in Ireland we aim to crack Barcelona at around 850 miles - a noble ambition for little me and the birds I fell for 40 years ago - a true versatile strain of birds guided by the hand of a simple man.

Louella did a lovely visual image promotion of the strain, and from a hunch within I proclaimed them to be the birds for me. Of a nice small balanced type, they oozed streamlined elegance, feather quality and racing ability on phenotype. Reading the publicity literature, the DVH birds were great stock in the hands of Belgian masters like Denys, Van Hee and many other iconic fanciers in the world. I had to have some, and struck a rich vein of success with my selections. I found that mine inbred from the off - I had learned the rudiments from my father Jim in '57 with bantams. I persevered with them and believed in my abilities with the birds, gradually getting more and more competitive and expanding the stock and racing from 71 to 879 miles with my evolving, hard-bitten strain of warriors.

I loved the dark chequers so much that I had a vision that my future would be formed around these birds in the form of a prophetic, life-enhancing presentiment, which became my Dark Destiny No 1 stock and many more. I saw these in a pictorial montage in my head. Loyal to my own personal dream, I was relentless in the impossible pursuit of perfection with these birds, since we made them perform like magic. My intuitive vision is so powerful with the birds that 40 years on I have sourced close relatives of the originals.

You may say I am a dedicated follower of my own fashion, in an aloof and introverted way. Now many others are reaping the benefits of the initiatives I took 40 years ago - I love to be individual in a rather intellectual, conceptual and abstract way - the strain is an outward expression of my personality

IN THE BEGINNING

In 1954 I caught a pencil-blue young bird, a rubbered straggler. It fired my naive wonder and curiosity, and after reporting it we realised the little cock belonged to an Irish fancier called Eugene. My old Dad explained pigeon racing to me and the dye was cast. I love all birds, and little Charlie Fantail was my favourite pet bird, at five years old. Many moons would pass on the journey to the sage, when the pages would open and a light would shine on my life in pigeons. Now in the twilight of my career, I reflect, with silent and sweet nostalgia, on the wonderful and beautiful birds that have raced with distinction to the home of their birth. I cling on to one dream in pigeon racing and that is the winning of the BICC Belief Trophy into Ireland from Barcelona International - it will be done.

REMEMBERING PIGEON PERCY

In the 60s and at Alvaston Derby, I would go on a trolley bus to Derby. I bought peanuts from the market to sit on a park bench and feed the strags and ferals in the Riverside Gardens. Fascinated by the racers, I caught the old mealy cock with peanuts and the violet-eyed med. Ch. cock. As vagrants snored on the summer lawns, alive with lice and fleas, I met one of the redoubtable pigeon eccentrics of the town. Celebrated in the local paper, he was known as a grand old personality of pigeons. I was fascinated by the man and most intrigued, since he would spin his head like a performing Birmingham Roller pigeon. We all knew him in Alvaston and Derby the endurance tippler men, the roller men and the racing men, who shared the love of their feathered friends. Hudson flew the legendary King of Rome into Derby, and I gazed upon the blue cock's stuffed body on many occasions, laying the foundations of my lifelong dreams. Old Percy died an old man, yet left his imprint behind.

TWO

—

A PIGEON FANCIER AT HOME AND ABROAD

PIGEON MAN IN SKENDLEBY

As a child, for five almost feral years, I lived in this beautiful village which time had almost forgotten. Sunk in the gentle countryside of the Lincolnshire Wolds, its images were wrapped in sweet nostalgia, matured by time. I loved my rambling childhood as an adventurous spirit, playing a tune in the boy's adventure tale.

Our three acres were ornamented by a large orchard, grass and shrubs and dominated by an impressive yew tree and a *Juglans nigra* walnut. Wild geese grazed the pasture and our banty cocks crowed in dominant defiance while the turkeys and geese grew nervous as Christmas neared. The land was enriched by Chinese pheasants as a stray banty hen produced her twelve chicks from the womb of a dry hedge and a young cuckoo called loudly to its parent slave, a little hedge sparrow.

Hour after hour, head raised, I would gaze into the sky as my roller pigeons spun through warm summer air. Befriending farm boys, we learned the country lesson of the gun, and scaled the inner sanctum of the church belfry in excited admiration of the huge bells, the jackdaws' nests and the nesting feral pigeons. Oh for the glowing euphoria of times past, when a spirit flowed free in the sun, the wind and the rain and the roof was the sky!

PIGEON MAN IN LONDON

In pursuit of knowledge I left my rural pursuit, my precious pigeons, behind. It was a heartfelt sacrifice to become a student at the Royal Botanic Gardens, Kew. My dream in its grand illusion was shattered by the sobering reality of concrete and the anonymous crowds of humanity that oozed from every pore of London.

With some spiritual alienation I found solace in my academic studies, where I flourished in a monastery-like cloister. I found some lift in musical concerts staged by the popular bands of the time and witnessed the voodoo god of rock, the sublime genius of shaman Jimi Hendrix. Little love affairs arrived with ephemeral frequency and dissolved in the rain of incompatibility.

Surrounded by solid and inanimate features, I longed for the comforting embrace of raw nature. London sharpened my wits and opened my naive little eyes to the realities of human nature. I have not forgotten the university of life and walk in free everyday country air and relish my escape to freedom – read spiritual.

PIGEON MAN IN THE GARDENS

As a man in love with the big outdoors, I have relished my time in the real world of nature. My years at the Royal Botanic Gardens Kew were punctuated by rare characters from different corners of the world, and I was brainwashed by botanical Latin, which echoes today. The glasshouses flourished under many microclimates, home to unique floral collections, dedicated plantsmen and species of horrific cockroaches that stirred you into instinctual wakefulness.

The dark side was that I longed for fields, woods and hedgerows and flocks of wild birds, and to embrace the raw power of wilderness. Subsequent years saw more cloistered academia, until MENSA became a friendly academic ceiling, allowing free expression to the flow of creativity. Now I satiate my senses in nature reserves, with visits to distinguished gardens like Bodnant in Wales, cypress gardens in Florida and Monets in Giverny. In my floral cottage retreat I am absorbed in mindful transcendence by bees, butterflies and a backcloth of plant specimens. I love the truth and direct impact of nature.

PIGEON MAN ON THE ISLE OF WIGHT

The compulsive draw to us bright young things from Kew Gardens was the famous festival of 1970. Alan, Mick and I, who were neophytes of the psychedelic subculture, set forth in great enthusiasm, crammed and laden with survival needs in a mini-van fashioned by Issigonis. Speeding along to the coast we charmed the attention of two young chicks - as they were then called - who kept us in sweet companionship in Lymington car park. The island was electrified by the teaming masses of music freaks, in a huge musical and wild organism. The locals were mortified as the human source of the music celebration took shape on sun charged fields. I recall the trembling effects of sunstroke, and eating 'oggies' (pasties) fresh from the South West. Although a drugs fest, we were loaded with the perpetual sounds of days and days of music as the stars of the day, including the Who, performed. This band is noted for the mystical genius of Pete Townshend on guitar, the sublimely manic antics of Keith Moon on drums, and Roger Daltrey, fuelled by testosterone, as lead singer. However a mesmeric shaman called Jimi Hendrix caused the crowd to erupt in spontaneous worship. They had witnessed a twilight performance in the exalted career of the greatest guitar genius who lived on planet earth. Nothing sounds like Voodoo Child. Two great forces of nature including Janis Joplin took performance art into a cosmic dimension.

PIGEON MAN IN SWEDEN

1971 was the genesis of my extensive travels, which contributed towards a real and lasting education of life apart from the cloistered world of academia, with its formal and conventional brain washing. A cool and charming Kew student called Tony captivated my imagination with his persuasive techniques, so we set off from London in a miniscule Minivan on a quasi-migration to Sweden.

After pausing in Valenciennes and being captivated by fireflies as we savoured the rugged outdoors in Belgium, we sped along the German autobahns tasting the exhilaration of sweet freedom. We were amazed by the reality that a little projectile held together as foreign speedsters flashed by us. Sweden was populated by tall blonde folk who radiated good looks, especially under psychedelic disco lights in pulsating night clubs. Tony and I baked on a beach in intense and dazzling sunlight as my skin started to shed in a painful ecdysis. We savoured the strawberries in the two sisters' garden, but no delights were in store for my friend, whose amorous objectives failed him.

PIGEON MAN IN MOROCCO

In my early travel days my anticipation soared as I joined Camp Africa at Asilah. It was a heady revelation sharing the primitive, authentic mud hut with a kind and seasoned old man of the world, as seen from naive and juvenile eyes. An exciting voyage of intense self-discovery ensued as we ventured far and wide into a new world. In Fez we saw the intricate work of skilled craftsmen in brass, wood and gold and the singular expertise of Tuareg nomads, the products of aeons of cultural time. The sights, the sounds, the smells were an opiate to the senses.

In Rabat, at the ancient tannery you could almost smell the vivid colours used by barefooted workers who toiled in the heat to produce the soft, high quality leather for demanding Western taste. An evening in the pink city of Marrakesh lit up our narrow little eyes with jugglers, charmers, dealers and a plethora of colourful characters.

Escaping the intensity and heavy city atmosphere we arrived in the Rif mountains, breathing deep the pure air and scenic splendour. I found myself tasting hot sweet mint tea, a custom shared with friendly Berber people. As fit young lads emerged from a rocky pool they held a cicada to my ear which buzzed in peculiar and dramatic resonance. In the Kasbah I learned of the ritualistic and cunning sales effrontery as witty salesmen bargained out a living. It was an experience that would shape my little psyche.

PIGEON MAN IN TURKEY

What a wonderful and enduring experience it was to encounter this mind-blowing country into the deep east and in sight of Odessa and the Russian border. The Blue Mosque of Istanbul with its inner sanctum in shiny blue, surrounded by elegant minarets - a feast of beauty for an aesthete's eye. We devoured the delicious chocolate mousses tinged with green pistachios at that famous meeting place of travellers and hippies, the Pudding Club. We traversed the ancient Bosphorus in contemplation of the East meets West connection. I found the people to be generous and friendly, and the traders in the countryside left their precious goods out into the sultry night, under the warmth of human trust.

Witnessing the tourist trap of Troy of literary fame, we journeyed into the Goreme Valley to behold a lunar and rocky landscape with fanciful fairy columns and troglodytic cave dwelling individuals. The scenes challenged perception in weird formations. We languished in the cool springs of the calcite pools of Cappodocia, reflecting on the earth's magnificence. In Dalyan we bathed in a pungent coating, feeling purified by the silky mud as it cleansed our skins, later to relish the bodily embarrassment of steaming hot Turkish baths in the Hamman tradition. In all, a sojourn which fired my imagination.

PIGEON MAN IN MALTA

Little birds caged for their intrinsic and fragile beauty sing for their freedom from bougainvillea-clad balconies, from a different perspective of cruelty in Malta. The speedy racing pigeons whirling round the sultry evening sky, above roof-topped lofts to be expertly called down by the urgency of whistles. We ventured into the summer night to relish the heady perfection of Simon's cocktails in Sliema. In the morning after a euphoric evening we responded to the street fish trader crying *lampuki, lampuki!*

The sun-drenched beaches of Melieha Bay, home of the charismatic and great Eddie Newcombe, gave champion racing significance to our sojourn here. We rested in the tropical Barraka gardens, where a colony of cats led by a huge matriarch pursued a free and instinctual life away from the madding crowd. We spied the graceful yachts as they floated serenely out of Valetta harbour, as an old local described a resort to rabbits in a pot in World War II. These are some sweet memories of the Maltese connection.

PIGEON MAN IN GIBRALTAR

In reality I came face to face with the Rock of Gibraltar of popular consciousness. We were surrounded, enveloped by dewy mist, by the impressive forms of barbary apes or macaques. As humanoid as evolutionary theory would insist, I remain unconvinced of the truth of man's origins. They certainly were sentient creatures who gave animation to the morning atmosphere. We became aware of the military connection, and of the fractious dispute in sovereignty between England and Spain, which bubbles in the human cauldron today. On a lighter, materialistic note we searched the crowded streets in pursuit of cheap whiskey, motivated in our pockets by bargains. A Russian influence in the form of a hospital ship lay in calm dominance offshore, conducting eye operations for the needy.

PIGEON MAN IN JERSEY

Our transit vehicle, a new hovercraft, drew us near to the island with one of its state-of-the-art engines on song. We had arrived at the land of Jersey Royal potatoes, whose real claim to fame is not their sweet earthy flavour but the premium paid for early gathering. There were many scars, remnants of the German occupation during in a hideous and needless war – an outward manifestation of the will to power by inflated national egos.

The delicate pink carnations of a show parade portrayed a warmer sentiment, further enhanced by the intricate and elaborate work of the House of Shells. A tall, dark, witty coach driver spun us round a traffic island as a promised trip round the island of Jersey. His remarkable and wickedly infectious humour remained strong, as aping the call of a randy bull he called in a herd of female cows to ardent applause. We had the benefit as his psyche scintillated on a local pub crawl.

Taking in the optional excursion around the celebrity and millionaire haunts to bask in the wake of collective esteem, we gravitated to the zoological collection of Gerald Durrell. With its rare captives appealing to my ecological sensibilities we marvelled at the spectacled bears, the white Asiatic tigers and the prehistoric-looking fruit bats of dark mythology.

PIGEON MAN IN JAMAICA

With the sound of the song 'Airport' buzzing in my mind, we arrived in the land of hurricanes, banana plantations and blue mountain coffee. I loved the cool nonchalance of the locals, where chronological time paled into insignificance. Jean and I sealed our romance with a kiss in a pristine and cool pool whilst climbing the severity of the slopes of Dunn's river falls. In lush and verdant foliage we explored the gardens, where in sight of iridescent sunbirds and butterflies that coloured a gentle breeze, I was offered ganja by a handsome security man in a smart uniform.

At night we wandered into the depths of Ocho Rios, where our physical and cultural differences created a communication gap with the locals. Later we bathed in the warm and shallow waters of Negril, where a relaxing aloe vera massage was a tempting distraction. Taking tea in a plantation grand house, we were disturbed by recollections of the former murderous lady owner who had exercised her reign of terror in times past. In the setting sun we gazed with intense focus on streaming white egrets as they cut the sky to their nightly roost on paths determined by historical time. Fearing our immediate safety, we avoided the street atmosphere of downtown Kingston, and absorbed rhythmic music from Rasta souls in Montego Bay. These are pure and lasting images of Jamaica.

PIGEON MAN IN THE MEDITERRANEAN

The clear and soft light was a visual medium for artistic greats like Matisse and Chagall,
and I find myself inspired by the genus loci of the beautiful French Mediterranean.

We felt uplifted as we strolled arm in arm, a romantic unity along the Promenade des Anglais at Nice, the ambience ruined somewhat by a jumbo jet which hung low over the sea.
Under a sapphire-blue sky we experienced the sensory delights of Antibes and Juan les Pins, the stylish villas, their elegance framed by dramatic green conifer trees. The roof of one bore the hallmark of John Wayne in the form of a 10-gallon cowboy hat, notable for its quaint eccentricity.

Our feelgood factor persisted as we searched the coastal waves in pursuit of misty craft and buoyant sea birds lifted by warm thermals. It was tempting to feel the embrace of cosy euphoria under such sophistication. We paused a little in Cannes to feel the impact of the stars who gave the film festival its cultural significance. In all I hold gentle and ethereal thoughts of our little visit into another world.

PIGEON MAN IN ISRAEL

Beside the wailing wall, strange men in black whisper praise and subservience to the godhead of their fantasy, each note placed with reverence in walls of cold stone. the silence is shattered by yet another exploding bomb, a symbol of aggressive unrest detonated by the ego of men. A poster of John Travolta welcomes you in true Western style to the holy church of nativity, its spiritual past celebrated in gold.

Old Jerusalem, ancient factions of troubled and war-weary souls who echo loudly from monuments of the past. Then to Jad Vashem, the hall of names that give ghoulish permanence to the pain and anguish of the holocaust.

The biblical gardens of Gethsemane; not the luxuriant paradise of bookish legend but arid rocks baking in an unforgiving heat. Dark glowing eyes of beautiful maidens as they humanise the past and the presence and yield hope to human suffering.

PIGEON MAN IN ROMANIA

Furtively changing money in an exciting black-market currency drew my attention to the influence of the dominant Russian Mafia. The oppressive heat of the scorching sun reminded me of the acute risks to fearless and foolhardy travellers. The jostling queues for bread in a land of some impoverishment reinforced my notion of social need and deprivation.

We were drawn by acres of sunflower heads as they searched skyward for solar sustenance. In a dusty village, dancing bears tormented by cruel masters performed in abject misery for human delight. Ruthless and cunning gypsy con artists seduced gullible tourists as they liberated them from their money. The supermarket shelves were void of produce, apart from stark jars of preserves shrouded in dust. An old lady, face craggy with time and dressed in peasant garb, sold us her wizened apricots for pence. A land of material poverty then, where we were spiritually enriched. It made us contemplate and reason the contribution and place of man on earth.

PIGEON MAN IN TENERIFE

In the land of the canaries where only budgerigars exist, we savoured the unusual and distinctive attractions. With the blistering sun scorching down from a pure blue sky, we felt naked, stripped of our Englishness, as we endured the exposure with the native people on the alien black, volcanic sand of an island.

When it was time, and in sweet relief, we sailed in cool sea air, in escape from the beach of torment. A thuggish local took a peculiar dislike to my symbol of Englishness, a travel bag, and taunted me almost to the point of violent remonstration. In safer climes we enjoyed the brilliant array of exotic parrotlike birds in the Loro Parque of Santa de la Cruz, as they represented the nucleus of an international conservation collection. A cockatoo projected his well-practised tricks, savoured by observant children in the controlled arena environment.

In a further zoological discovery, we found a vivarium of venomous snakes, where the banded krait from Thailand was fronted by a message which read 'possibility of recovery remote'. After a flood of excitement we enjoyed the green luxuriance of the tropical botanic gardens in admiration of the labelled and rare specimens in the collection. On a more obviously physical plane we climbed the rocky and harsh slopes of Mount Teide, breathing in the heady, sulphurous fumes as they emanated from the crater.

We became more earthbound as we endured the artificial and conventional atmosphere of the Playas des Americas resort, where we were grounded by touristic realism.

PIGEON MAN IN MONTE CARLO

Conscious of the pristine elegance, the sumptuous and all-pervading wealth, we relished the high life and opulent sophistication of the Monaco principality. Here the rich and famous parked their Rollers and prancing-horse Ferraris with gay abandon. With egos inflated we waltzed into the casino, our eyes transfixed by the ornate ceiling, our hearts lifted by the James Bond ambience.

In feverish and obsessive excitement I lost all my loose money on the gambling machines in euphoric feelings beyond care. We walked through the grand prix tunnel and could almost perceive the ghosts of the greats, men of history, like the charismatic and mystical Ayrton Senna, the legend of Argentinian ace Fangio and the impish playboy James Hunt.

As we drove along the winding corniche, we reflected on the cultural saturation and the sheer aesthetic beauty of our surroundings, against a global backcloth of shanty and human degradation in third-world impoverishment. All that is needed to enter the fantasy world of reality for the neo-riche are a few million little pounds, in ignorance of their acquisition!

PIGEON MAN IN WAGON TRAIN

Upon the intrinsic discomfort of a camel, we wandered slowly in the setting sun along the whispering white sands of the Sahara. The air was pure and fresh and the light crystal as we observed a scorpion, one of the ancient survivors of a landscape where aliens were not tolerated. It was moving and romantic in a peculiarly human way. Later I sat upon a black donkey, and with a spirit as dark as its skin colour he bucked and weaved in a haze of dry dust in the corral. Then with total impudence he left the well-trodden trail to graze on allotment vegetables. To add to the hilarity, a colourful extrovert, complete with sombrero, was tossed off his mount to hit the ground in a chorus of laughter. My finest ride was on an Arab horse as we made our gentle way forward in style and comfort. The most lofty and majestic ride was on an ornate Indian elephant in exotic gardens in Goa, on our return from a jungle where huge tent spiders lived.

PIGEON MAN IN MAJORCA

Magaluf, with its seedy, popular and Blackpool-like character was anathema to my delicate sensibility and we studiously avoided its loud and garish appeal. We enjoyed the initial taste of spiny lobster, created expertly by a courteous Austrian at the Old Vienna in Santa Ponsa. in a state of hyperexcitement, I danced down the evening street in neat white trousers. The aftermath was an allergic reaction to the protein in the fish, accompanied by intense night time nausea. These affects cemented the memories well into the psyche.

More suitable to a soul with Taoist leanings were the open spaces, rugged hills and mountains of Puerto Pollensa. I recall the singular beauty of a hoopoe, and the brilliant ostentation of a male redstart. In Palma was an inbred and unique colony of pure white pigeons, all nicely habituated to man. Clutching one in my practised hands, I observed that the bird was host to the pigeon fly parasite. we found the people to be used to touristic intrusion and largely unthreatening to us naive tourists.

PIGEON MAN IN VENICE

Pigeon was distinctive and original enough for us to explore its aesthetic delights on two occasions. Despite the architectural heritage of the Doge's Palace and St Mark's Square, my singular and urgent need was to feed the dark chequer pigeons in the square, a cemented practice from the little boy in Trafalgar Square, when Prince Honolulu patted my receptive head. Once I was satiated by birds we joined the throng on the Bridge of Sighs, absorbing the unique sights, to lodge them in our memory bank.

Later in the collective voice mode of the archetypal 'One Cornetto', we boated in swish silence under the practised hand of a Gondolier. The great Alan Whicker would not have enjoyed it more, despite the pungent air from the water which tainted our nostrils. In the square we were captivated by a little man who with charming insights said 'for 6 hours the lagoon give and for 6 hours the lagoon take'. Venice in its cultural autonomy is at the dominant mercy of the lagoon.

Our second visit involved a high-speed cat trip from Yugoslavia, culminating in the luminous welcome of the night lights – an image engraved on my memory.

PIGEON MAN IN PORTUGAL

In incredible heat we suffered the deprivations of a hot and crowded coach along the soulless Spanish plains, where my claim to celebrity status was projectile vomiting in a local field, perceived by ghoulish onlookers. The physical appearance of Figuera da Foz in Portugal was one of huge disappointment, with crumbling pathways and monumental derricks on the beach, in gigantic dominance. The negative spell was broken by colourful ethnic dancing in a suspended ring. We were not prepared as an electric storm erupted to consume all others in its sheer intensity. We felt each poignant moment with fork, chain and sheet lightning turning the sky into a luminous glow. I said to Jean, 'Watch that red bulb now', and it shattered. Life was enhanced by cosmic events which made our holiday. On a more homely level we tasted sardines grilled fresh and sweet on the beach with wisps of pungent smoke in the sea air. In pursuit of quality port we tasted the drink from the casks in Porto, a con perhaps as it lacked genuine authenticity. I had got used to sales tricks on my earlier travels!

PIGEON MAN AND THE PECULIAR

There are many occurrences in life that are beyond human comprehension even by the most sophisticated scientist. In my time in Delhi I encountered a celebrated seer. We met on a personal exchange in the grounds of a swish hotel, and he asked me in silence to focus on one word in the world of words. Writing something on a piece of paper, he rolled the paper up in his hand, then asked me if I wished to continue. In quiet and cool anticipation I did. He opened out the paper to reveal the word JEAN written on a piece of paper, the sole word I had my mind focused on. As a former qualified rural science teacher my logical conclusion was that he read my mind.

In India en route to the Himalayas I had a presentiment, observed by my American academic friend Joe Lemak. The impact was so great that I had to lie down. I told Joe that my father had passed away in England – the funeral arrangements were made in my absence. In the 80s I sat bolt upright as a prophetic stream of consciousness showed a whole sequence of images of birds in my pigeon strain that would generate success, and so in 2013 with practical applications and focus, it has proved to be a self-fulfilling prophecy. It is amazing what some humans and animals tune into is it not, believe it or not.

PIGEON MAN IN AFGHANISTAN

In 1979 I reached Kabul via a remote, rugged and epic journey along the seemingly endless and soulless Khyber Pass – swirling heat, arid rocks and military outposts, but nevertheless a popular journey for tribal lords, drugs and every devious shade of humanity. Stepping with eyes open into primitive and ancient Kabul, eyes assaulted by open sewers, shanty and jostling tribesmen, I became aware of my naked and singular strangeness in this ancient and unique capital. Although there were celebrations of the communist rule, armoured vehicles alerted me to the military presence.

My photos taken with locals found them to be friendly, exotic and welcoming - I still have the fox hat to prove it and the raw taste of opium was uplifting in a very cerebral way!

We travelled by ancient bus with no air con, and by the time I had reached the Himalayas my mind, soul and spirit had evolved and morphed into a more enlightened form. The east can teach the west and I try and apply the wisdom gleaned on my worldly travels in the now today - sounds like a Shaolin monk.

PIGEON MAN IN INDIA

We were confronted by the outstanding beauty of the Golden Temple of Amritsar. In sensations that defied human description a shimmering, pure golden light gently reflected on the receptive surface of the lake beneath the physical dome. Seduced by marble columns inlaid with dazzling semi-precious stones, I was lured into the womb of its being. Inside were local musicians absorbed by the resonance of sweet sitar music. With senses intoxicated I gazed into the illusion of a magnificent hall of mirrors depicting far-reaching self-images.

In stark contrast we gazed from a boat at sunrise on the burning bodies, in spiritual purification, from floating observation on the sacred Ganges. The circling, forbidding vultures soared overhead as they swooped down to relish more pickings from the macabre, gothic remains.

As a water buffalo carcass floated by, our credibility was tested by a stunning girl who sold us a perfect lotus blossom for one rupee. The teaming masses of humanity before us were enthralled by the ancient and captivating conquest between mongoose and king cobra. In elegant tropical gardens, as streams of colourful parrots scorched the evening skies, we absorbed these memorable images in silent gratitude.

PIGEON MAN IN KASHMIR

We stayed on the beautiful and exotic houseboats on Lake Dahl in the awe-inspiring, snow-clad foothills of the Himalayas. The lake was populated by four species of flashing and iridescent kingfishers, adorned with water lilies and inhabited by lurking fish. Our local meals were prepared by a turbaned houseboy, a remnant of the Raj. With due and glowing pride he produced a reference book from the British officers he had served, a delightful and charming man.

Over the passing days we took visceral pleasure in a wedding feast including cooked water lily shoots. I confess to enjoying the cool smoke of a hookah pipe, and the consequence was extraordinary in a psychic sense. In Srinagar, the capital, I tried on a wolfskin coat, buying Jean an ornate papier mâché jewellery box. We walked in local gardens amongst native rhododendrons and admired the free spirits of soaring mountain eagles as they wheeled on high thermals. Such enchanting experiences are the canvas of my poetry today.

PIGEON MAN IN LAHORE

A sultry evening, deep in Pakistan, and charged with excited anticipation I summoned a pony and trap driver for a journey that would be life changing. To the clip clop of practised hooves we trotted into the unknown and to an appointment with fear. With life on the edge I sensed an acute and naive vulnerability, at the mercy of an exotic trickster.

After a period of time thick with emotion we stopped at our secret destination. Drawn in by the occasion, we ascended the spiral staircase into what could have been the room of doom. The three men who plied me with hashish were a life threat as they attempted to turn me into a narcotics mule, another innocent victim. Sensing the possible end, I asserted my desire to return safe and legal back to the hotel. This realised, my deep anxiety was suffused by intense relief. With a charmed life I am alive to relate my experience.

PIGEON MAN IN NEPAL

The Pokhara Valley, and what sweet sensations in the scented gardens of the blind. Gently absorbed by gaily coloured blooms I luxuriated in detached reverie, in soulful harmony. In the English style of weather contemplation I peered above at the lofty cumulus clouds, and gasped at the sheer majesty overhead. Moments of reflection then the dawning of reality as I gazed upon Annapurna. Awestruck, I was made to feel tiny at the feet of those snowclad peaks, sensations that morphed my mind. Mingling amongst Tibetan refugees, I enjoyed their strange singularity of exile and the delightful Snowlands gin that they made in finest purity. Now to Kathmandu where a handsome, steely-legged rickshaw cyclist escorted me around the Nepalese capital, a cultural explosion.

THREE

—

CHARACTERS
IN THE SPORT

SOME COLOURFUL PIGEON MEN

We are nothing without our individuality. The sport of pigeon racing is enriched by a magnificent array of characters who add colour and texture to the tapestry of experience.

One of my first encounters was with "Pigeon Percy" of Derby, a well-known local celebrity who made the local press. He could be seen sitting on the park benches in Riverside Gardens. His idiosyncrasy, or nervous mannerism, was to spin his head as if he had spent too much time watching Birmingham Rollers performing.

How can I forget Billy Burdett of Alvaston, Derby? Billy, a feisty, cheerful little character, would encourage young me from his wheelchair. He loved his birds and kept a few rollers and racers. He did not allow his handicap to inhibit his generosity, for he gave me a big blue racer cock, which duly settled and paired to a chequer pied stray. I would take them training in a fishing creel on my motorbike and Billy would utter, "Look at his eye, Jim. Ay'll win Lerwick, ay will, Jim" in a broad Derbyshire accent.

My past holds a myriad of rich memories, but more in keeping with the present I must mention the great Martyn Mitchell, who is outstanding as an individual, now a millionaire in Belgium but who used to live at Wiston, near Selby. At his home, surrounded by Aston Martins and Porsches, was the most amazing pigeon-racing establishment I have seen. Over tea he explained some of the intricacies of his racing methods. No stone was left unturned in the pursuit of excellence, and could he race a pigeon! To be honest, he was in a different league. Do you recall his five birds on the day at MNFC Bergerac, flying 623 miles? An expert at middle-distance racing, Martyn has conquered the racing in Belgium. He is a man ahead of his time and very different.

On the intellectual front we have the great Irish writer Liam O'Comain, MA, who is a lovely, warm man with a romantic and spiritual turn of phrase. In his many writings, especially about marathon racing, he has informed, enthused and enlightened us about the great racing men of the past and present. His body of work secures his place in the future consciousness of the pigeon culture.

Remember Derek Cutcliffe? He was the ex-naval captain who single-mindedly changed the face of how we perceive the hours of darkness, giving the RPRA a model for its calculation. Derek would indulge in some extroverted and heated letter debates in the fancy press and made an impact cultivating and selling his birds, eg Stichelbauts and Van Hees.

As for myself, I have been blessed in meeting paupers, princes and millionaires around the globe on my worldly travels. At 16 years old I met and associated with Kenzie, the wild-goose man, noted poacher, boxer, artist and all-round eccentric and good egg. Yes, there is more than mere pigeon races; there are also the characters, the fabric of the sport. We need more of 'em!

THE PURIST PIGEON FANCIER

Many personalities slot into the role of fancier throughout the world of competitive racing from geniuses to artists to labourers – it is almost all-embracing in its variety of characters. In my personal view there are certain principles and criteria that should be met to make the concept as complete or pure as possible. A person will do well to compete successfully at all levels from club sprint to national and international level to give a total profile and experience. Ideally a particular family or strain of genetically-related birds should be created for this purpose, calling upon the factors of time and patience and severe progeny testing at all levels of racing.

An individual can project his personality into pigeon society via politics, sales, writing and any other activity applicable to the sport of pigeon racing up to global level. In reality it can be an expression of self-reality in the big pigeon world. The secret is to enjoy the journey in pursuit of the self as an individual in the vast sea of humanity. Perfection and purity are relative but in the cold light of truth is it not a noble exercise to pursue them? A few ideas for you to contemplate - and be happy.

CHARACTERS I HAVE MET

In 1965 I stayed with John Shinn, crack shot and big game hunter, in Kenzie the wild goose man's houseboat moored on the Wash saltings. It was a wild, rugged and remote wilderness of tidal creeks, sea lavender and samphire. At high spring tide the boat lifted on its moorings and you were floating on the edge of the North Sea.

At times like this my imagination was fired and intensified - will the moorings break and the boat float out to the eternal sea? Cooking the potatoes from the local fields was done on a paraffin stove with sea water scooped from the depths. A foggy cloud enveloped the boat and the calls of the common seals intensified in the murky dampness. At dawn the great man arrived, Mackenzie Thorpe himself - artist with Sir Peter Scott, ex-jailbird, middleweight boxing champ, poacher and wildfowler par excellence. His eyes were deep with knowledge, face craggy with wind and salt exposure - a unique and solitary figure in this lunar landscape. John and I embraced nature full on as we learned the Wash secrets of the hordes of waders, the ducks and geese, the marsh harriers floating by and the wily marsh pheasants as they tried to evade the gun. We lived the boys' adventure tale and these essential times by the sea, sun and stars framed my life and instincts forever. When old Kenzie passed away in 1976, the houseboat was torched by Romany tradition and John is soon to enjoy the adventure of a wild boar hunt in Turkey, hard case that the man is.

THE ROGUES IN MY LIFE

In my long and colourful journey down the avenue of life I would like to celebrate some of the unconventional characters who have enriched it with their unique personalities.

In 1960 I met John, a rugged hard case whose policeman father was an inveterate poacher in the Derbyshire countryside. One Sunday morning we went in stealth in a 1930s Rover to shoot grouse that adorned the walls of the moors. In a haze of intoxicating excitement I said 'stop the car!' and bowled over an old hare, its ears just above the wheat, with a .22 rifle. Memories of John jumping over a high hedge to retrieve two English partridges from the glare of local farm cottages spring to mind. Old John became a great eccentric wildfowler and African game hunter.

In 1965 we met and experienced the striking, spirited singularity of Kenzie the wild goose man on the remote saltings of the Wash wilderness. Now this man, the son of a Romany, was artist, poacher, TV celebrity and middleweight boxing champ of Lincolnshire. A rugged individualist, I loved our times together in ice, wind and snow in primal pursuit of the pink-footed geese that migrated from Greenland to whiffle down onto the potato fields of the Wash. We narrowly escaped with our skins one day as the tide caught us out.

Later I would meet an old lag called Tony. With facial stubble like Desperate Dan he made a psychopath look like a wimp. He lit up his roll up with a blazing whole newspaper torched by the fiery brazier, feet propped up in hobnail boots. I admired his spirited, brooding and dark masculinity. It is elemental men like these that thrilled me to the bone and switched me on to life itself.

Yes, some people cut a striking path leaving a trail of spirited freedom, and it has been a voyage of self-discovery on my travels to the roof of the world.

MY LEADING CONTRIBUTORS TO THE GREATER GOOD OF PIGEON RACING

1: Zsolt Talaber. A Hungarian scientist and vet, his wonderful books have yielded great insights into pigeon health, diseases and treatments on a global level - a significant and great man.

2: Geoff Kirkland. Geoff is a master racer up to 650 miles, with an honest and gentlemanly manner. His videos and books have been innovative and he has changed the course of modern pigeon racing. A man of great style and charisma, he commands my respect.

3: Chris Gordon. The best long distance UK young bird national flier, as a driven man he is a great all round racer with his own strains of birds. Active on the political/managerial front, he is a serious activist in the North-East Region. A former record holder at NFC Tarbes, his racing record is vast and diverse.

4: Geoff Cooper. A great fancier is this chap and for many reasons with seminal wins up to international level. He has made written contributions on his expertise and mentored the brilliant Mark Gilbert. I like his expert strain building from inbred origins.

5: Jim Jenner. Now Jim from Montana oozes warmth and charm in his epoch making pigeon films of world class distinction. With a huge, erudite and spiritual personality he rules the world in his field.

6: Gareth Watkins. Conscientious to a fault, the man from Wales is a unique reporter on fanciers and their birds via the medium of the BICC. He has popularised the BICC in an impressive way.

7: The Queen's Loft Manager, Mr Farrow. I was a lucky boy to interview this chap as Her Majesty is the premier person in the realm of pigeon racing.

8: John Clements. A serious marathon flier, journalist and author, he makes a real contribution to the cerebral depths and intellectual life of the sport with his thoughtful creativity.

9: Jim Donaldson. An easy choice. He is the greatest marathon flier Scotland has ever produced with persistent greatness racing into Peterhead. Jim is a rugged and dogged man with a host of records behind him.

10: Ronnie Williamson. Ronnie from Ireland is perhaps the greatest racing man on earth, with a singular set of results. A master of technique, he promotes the sport in the media for all to see.

11: Frank Kay of Bolton. This earthy, wise and philosophical man loves the concept of Barcelona International at 869 miles and clocked the Perpignan hen at 798 miles on the second day. A shrewd farmer, flying a small team, he is no fool.

12: Nicholas Harvey of Taunton. I leave my partner until last. Nick is a great diamond of a complex man, and we have enjoyed a rise from humble roots to a place where we can time out of Barcelona International into the very difficult Somerset with opposing west and south-west winds. Our essence is strain building and its free dissemination to others under the umbrella of dedicated sportsmanship.

It has been my duty and pleasure to interview many of the alumni of the sport.

INTERVIEW WITH ROGER LOWE
Elimar Pigeons website, 2015

Roger, how did the fascination with pigeons begin?

I first had fancy pigeons just for something to keep and watch. I then started talking to a neighbour, Bill Huggings, who kept racing pigeons. And after a while that was it, I was hooked. I had a loft with a few racers in and from those humble beginnings I am what I am today.

Did you love and learn from nature as a child?

As a child I guess I was the same as any other kid, no particular fascination in nature just the normal kid things like fishing, watching where the birds nested, finding the odd grass snake etc. All normal kid stuff.

Were family and friends involved with pigeons and livestock?

When I first started racing pigeons my family and friends were not interested in the birds. I have over the years made many good friends in the sport.

You are a colourful character in the sport, do you have an interesting story to tell us?

It's not all serious stuff and I have some colourful friends too, but I'm not sure some of our finest moments could be published! Let's just say we enjoy ourselves at times and I have some very good friends.

How did you climb the ranks, from humble beginnings to be at the top of the National Game - what personal qualities are required to be outstanding?

It took some time for me to climb the ladder of success, if it was easy we would all be at the top. But over the years I have tried to buy from the best, learn from the best, work hard to become one of the best and been dedicated to my birds and the sport. I have changed many things over the years, feeding methods loft design and how the birds are raced, it has all been a learning curve. I would hope after 40-odd years to have achieved the rewards I am now reaping.

Can you tell us any aspects of your methodology which may account for your success?

Methods I believe that have helped in gaining my status of today is keeping birds healthy, good ventilation and no overcrowding in the lofts. Loft design is quite important. Good quality feeds, nice clean corn. Management of the birds, routines and good training, no mollycoddling. The birds are here to do a job. If they cannot return from training tosses that may prove to be a bit difficult, they will not return from a hard race. And of course you need a decent kit of birds that are up to the job, so buy from proven stock. Breed from your best birds only to keep standards high, introducing new blood to keep moving forward.

Do supplements make a difference?

Supplements within the loft are necessary for birds to get all the nutrients required, these are offered at regular times to keep the birds in top condition.

How do you weight the fancier/bird percentage in your many successes?

I believe the fancier to bird ratio for success is a 50/50 match. A top class winning pigeon will not perform if I fail to keep it in top condition. Likewise if I have a no-hope pigeon I cannot make it win races if it's not got it in it.

What are your loves, hates and highlights in pigeons?

Don't get me started on this one, I could go on and on. But in a nutshell, I love the sport of racing pigeons with a passion. I hate it that sometimes we don't move forward, there are solutions and choices in everything in life and it appears at times we are stuck in the past in this sport because fanciers do not see the bigger picture. The highlights for me have been my success at specialist and national club racing these past few years.

What are the responsibilities of a top man within the sport and his impact in the wider field of knowledge, publicity etc?

The responsibility of any fancier at the top of the game is to be level-headed, help others to achieve success, pass on helpful tips and ideas, support young fanciers coming into the sport. Help promote racing pigeons – our membership falls each year. Support your club's federations and specialist clubs in any way you can. Share your knowledge with others through moots or articles, those that want to learn from it can or they can ignore it.

How do you select a bird to value or keep?

Selection of birds to keep is 99% percent proven qualities and abilities to either win or breed winners.

Any comments on the way the game is going, or characters?

I think more fanciers that want to achieve are turning more and more to the specialist racing clubs like NFC, BICC, CSCFC and BBC, I think that's where it's at today.

Do you have a fondest memory, a final hour in your bird life?

My fondest memory is probably Conimix Dream, who won the Lambell BBC National when there were only five home on the mainland on the day out of 2,315 birds in 2005. I had to wait till 12 o'clock the following day to have it confirmed. My other fondest was wining NFC YB National in 2007 with My Little Diamond, having her only race ever.

A happy five-year-old Jim Emerton with
Charlie Fantail and a young pied.

Taken in 1976, M. Descamps-Van Hasten with
Mrs Alois Stichelbaut at the old loft in Lauwe.

The early Emerton Stichelbauts in montage.

Inbred Emerton cock – over 100 times no 1 pair in the breeding.

Direct from g/son Barcelona Dream/Dark Enchantment and No 1 stock hen

Unique breeding g/son of Barcelona Dream and Oddball – g/parents scored at 879 miles and Pau 735 miles against the wind.

Inbred gdt. of twice Barcelona International 710 miles and a dtr. af 3 times Tarbes 671 miles - Emerton/Harvey strain.

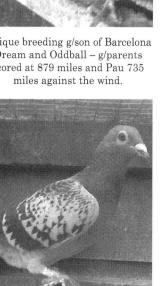

Dam 3 times Barcelona, pure Emerton, Daughter of Musgrove Obsession and Unique inbred gdt. of Oddball, pure Emerton and

A young Harvey/Emerton Barcelona-bred bird.

The No.1 stock cock bred from Iron Man x Iron Hen.

Champion Barcelona Dream, the record distance holder in the BICC

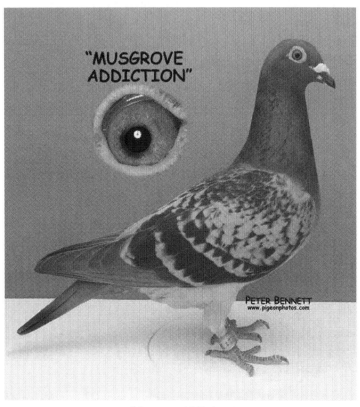

Musgrove Addiction.

FOUR

—

MUSINGS – 2013

UNITY IS IDEAL

Men of imagination and vision aim for the best possible case, to create order out of disharmony and confusion. The old pioneers of long distance/endurance racing sought to stretch the boundaries of possibility with a restless surge, an ardent drive into heady adventure and achievement - a romantic impulse perhaps for hardened men of practical realism. It is this never say die and fiery enthusiasm that creates new levels of accomplishment in any competitive endeavour, and is pertinent with the current movement to International racing in the UK and Ireland.

Now that an infrastructure for race participation is being developed by the BICC, the future is bright for some. I speak with bias and from an optimistic perspective, knowing very well the rigours and hardship of marathon racing, yet success for the few dedicated souls can be sweet. In the final analysis the pleasures and rewards can be great at any level of racing and from the sheer love of our avian companions - I currently feed four species of doves in my garden.

February 2013

CLOCKING BICC BIRDS INTO IRELAND

Now this will be a difficult and onerous task indeed! Power to the people who will attempt it and achieve it. The journalists have sharpened their pencils and the photographers are poised. Birds will home as a result of expert management and loft environments where calm contentment is cultivated by patient and conscientious fanciers with esoteric knowledge of distance/marathon conditioning.

Good pigeons with top levels of stamina and navigation over hours and days will surface on top of the cream and these athletes will be the strain makers. The top men have now got their eye on individual candidates for this demanding purpose - who will they be?

A gradual build up to a conditioner with 10- 12 hours on the wing is required after weeks of high energy and fats feeding as Nic and I do at Barcelona international, with targeted liquid feeding of Mycosan-T CCS and Blitzform. Imagine how a swallow fuels up with maximum reserves before its epic migration across the Sahara deep into Africa - too light, underfed birds will fail!

The good men in Ireland need to believe they can do it, which requires a little culture change in consciousness. It will come, it will evolve in time and with the good will of the BICC and the brave spirits of Ireland.

February 2013

HARNESSING INSTINCTS

Pigeons and their fanciers have inbuilt, innate survival drives and instincts: to breed, avoid predation, find nourishment and keep alive in a sheltered home environment. Nic Harvey and I are part of nature - we aim to work with it and take our place with the birds in harmony with it.

I was observing the wild birds in my garden and was drawn to the brilliant intensity of the life that they generated, and how each individual life becomes part of the pulse of nature itself, a vibrant, beautiful whole.

We like the birds to be aware, pin sharp and on the cutting edge of experience before their long, migratory journeys from France and Spain back to the waiting security of the home loft. If sent super fit and street sharp, we feel they are better prepared and able to cope with risk factors such as variable weather patterns and the need to forage and avoid predation when flying home to us.

It is so pleasing to see the future race candidates radiating vitality and health as they wheel about the sky, free and in the elements. Good birds returning from faraway places often benefit by their experiences and bring joy to the eye of the fancier.

February 2013

ECCENTRIC FANCIERS

Most people, to a degree, conform in a collective way to the thrust and the main standards of society, often called the mainstream. Such individuals may be the backbone and fabric of its structure. Others may plough a singular furrow with obsessive independence at odds with or on the periphery of society, developing creative, original lives, perhaps touched by the hand of genius. With brains and minds functioning in an intuitive, lateral and divergent way they may forge new patterns, systems and ways of expressing themselves in pigeons. Thought of as quirky and cranky initially, their methods after success and the associated publicity, may be inculcated back into the mainstream practice.

These strong-minded folk are stubborn, single-minded and focused, with great impact on targets and objectives. Their life's work is perhaps the monasterial adoption of a system, the creation of a strain, or a complete obsession with a race point. A few people spring into consciousness, and I recall Frank Kay, Nic Harvey and Dave Goddard as examples. In the wider world Lady Gaga is a classic eccentric of high celebrity status. I wonder who you are?

February 2013

THE TIME FACTOR

In racing and breeding we are all under the influence of time. There is the timing of returning birds, the race liberation time, time on the wing, which is an important indicator of quality and future success, and the time we spend preoccupied by birds. In terms of the formation of a family or strain, time expands into years and many of them. It is closely linked with desire, patience, long term focus and dedication.

Just what makes a fancier devote a lifetime to his birds like the inspirational and gentle bird man of Alcatraz? I think it is allied to innate and obsessive curiosity and perfectionism, perhaps suffused by scientific application and experiment. Today we enjoy instant gratification via the media and hypertechnology. Waiting for marathon pigeons over days may be the climax of years of individual preparation of the race candidates for one spectacular race in the prevailing elements where wind direction may dictate time. A loft may hit form when the time is critical to enter the birds.

As you age you tend to reflect on the past to try and revisit the good times in the euphoria of nostalgia - let the good times roll! In preparation of birds for 700 miles plus I like a training race of 10 to 12 hours on the wing 3 to 4 weeks before.

February 2013

SPARROWHAWKS

The female sparrowhawk is a deadly ambush predator of racing pigeons. She is cheeky, cunning and ruthless, in anthropomorphic terms. In the 80s, I used to ponder the cause of pigeon remains in my cottage garden. When Dorothy caught a hen sparrowhawk with her bare hands in the loft, we realised! We would suffer losses of 5-15 birds between late winter and April when the hens would sit in local woods. However we were on a mission and pursued our race targets culminating in the Dax international at 687 miles. I confess it is very hard to watch a hawk strike a favourite down at your feet! Some of the racers became so alert that they were not caught, yet I mourned the loss of Mystical Queen, Delta Lady and Barcelona Dream.

The predators are common even in cities and I filmed recently a male eating a blackbird at eight feet in my garden. We urgently need supportive legislation, yet this is very onerous due to certain humans who instinctively covert, love and admire predators! It is a long, winding and difficult road to success.

March 2013

THE LOFT

I like a nice comfortable refuge for the birds to come home to. It should be nice and cosy with deep, deep litter and lots of nooks and crannies for shelter, security and nesting. In the roof are skylights for the warmth of the sun to penetrate. It is wise to have lots of air space and width for good ventilation and to maintain as even a temperature as possible. The atmosphere should be calming and restful and free from pests and predators. The outside access from the sky should be cat proof as the birds enjoy the open loft system on a daily basis, although the odd crow or sparrowhawk entered over 30 years! I like the birds to mate as they like and where they want in ample boxes. The key word is FREEDOM, which generates contentment in the home and surroundings.

My loft withstood the windy blasts from Holtby fields - an old loft when I bought it for 60 pounds from Tadcaster in 1976. It was extended later, and as the shavings deepened your head got nearer to the skylights. The old structure housed all the race birds together: young and old, with the YBs tending to gather at one end for security. I would be able to watch the racers from an easy chair inside the cottage - I called it PATIENCE.

March 2013

THE TWILIGHT ZONE

Imagine a warm summer's evening. You sit enchanted waiting for your 5 to 700-mile candidates. With the itching of midge bites, the bewitching hour approaches. A sparrowhawk soars on a high thermal as the swifts, barely susceptible in the sky, screech as they stream around the heavens scooping up flies in mid-flight. This is racing at its beautiful best, cloaked in pure magic with the riches of the imagination and the oneness of nature. You ask the ancient question of bygone distance men - will I clock this evening?

And now, in the setting sun, the mystic twilight zone. roosting crows float by to form a murder in the local copse. As night signals the end of day the old cock swoops low over the rose-clad cottage, and with trembling hand is safely clocked in. Birds clocked in the hours of darkness, illuminated by street lamps are special. My Dark

Enchantment was clocked at 10.08pm from Pau 735 miles, 2nd day. Memories are born of such moments.

March 2013

THE NATURAL ELEMENTS

I was walking across fields today in half a gale full of snowflakes, and the sheer force of freedom hit my face. How great it is to be out in nature! I must confess I hate to see and sense racing pigeons cooped up in little stuffy lofts, when they can be on instincts in the rain, snow, sun and wind honing their navigation skills and enriching their muscles with red blood cells.

The central philosophy of Nic's and my Barcelona methodology is centred on fitness, familiarity and contentment with the home environment. They will face gruelling conditions on their long migration back home from Spain, and will not acquire race environmental experience in the loft! What a treat they are to behold swirling around in a snow flurry and then the sun as it reflects off dazzling feathers. I have enjoyed deserts, mountains, woods and seas and remain convinced from my biased perspective that pigeons need to have the freedom of the skies as they were born to fly. Freedom!

March 2013

HUNGER & DESIRE

What are the feelings inside the heads of champion fliers? They have a yearning, a fire that glows from within, to succeed. It motivates them to achieve great things, to attempt the difficult, the complex, the seemingly impossible. The charismatic greats like Warren and Paley were the epitome of these personality traits, and forged new paths through history. A desire that is cemented in the myth and folklore of pigeons, such men are the archetypes of excellence.

In simple practical terms, it means testing all your birds at the top level - good old natural, Darwinian selection in action! I have noticed how many Americans have the juice to excel, yet look at our own sporting stars - the inspiration is there. The results this year will be peppered by those with HUNGER AND DESIRE, and brave young souls who seek to stretch the boundaries of possibility in pigeon racing. Roll on Barcelona International.

March 2013

THE INDIVIDUAL

With the current accent on general names of fanciers used to indicate certain origins of pigeons, eg Busschaerts, let us focus on the individual pigeon and fancier which are what create the results and success - each are unique and singular! We use labels such as 'natural' and 'widowhood' to describe systems, yet each one is peculiar to the person who practises it. Pigeon culture is awash with generalisations, is it not?

Great enjoyment can be derived from focusing on and preparing single birds for chosen events eg for the single bird clubs, which calls for specialisation. This will be a test of the foresight and skill of the fancier in combination with each bird.

We have concluded then that all birds and fanciers are different, even specimens of a common name origin. These factors make the sport diverse and interesting, with all the characters available. In the last analysis then, if you obtain a new family of birds they are all individuals - even if cloned.

March 2013

THE LAID-BACK APPROACH

I found that intense, hard work was in the foundation of a system that would produce birds to perform at a high level. This took me many years of painstaking mind research in books with periods of inspiration. Personal exchanges are fine on a social level, yet I learned most from established experts and academics in the field of pigeon management. After all the complicated goings on an easy method can induce a nice, controlled procedure which induces calm. I often say that a bright 11-year-old girl can do it!

This said, you will be awake during the night during the exciting, big races, particularly those of an international nature. The complexity then is in the thought processes behind the genesis of a simple system. Watch out that you are not asleep on the arrival of your top birds - I used matchsticks to prop up my eyelids for marathon races. May your individuality go with you.

March 2013

HOURS OF DARKNESS

In terms of the environment, it never becomes black dark in the UK and beyond. In racing organisations hours of darkness and thus of non-darkness are introduced as procedural rules for the evaluation of velocities of race birds under race conditions. To my knowledge a bird has no understanding of these matters. They fly when they fly in various conditions and for different reasons. There is something romantic, eerie and wistful when a bird drops as the bats fly and when the black crows have roosted. This can be under the glare of city lights, the twinkling of stars or the gentle rays of the moon itself. I wax lyrical, yet it is a profound experience which echoes deep within the human psyche. The wise old sages of the fancy reflect with fond nostalgia as they tell their colourful stories of late encounters with night fliers, such are the rich colours of pigeon folklore.

April 2013

TRAINING

In my youth and in pursuit of race wins at club and fed level, Jean and I would take a flask and make a nice little trip of it, taking in some beauty spots like Filey, the Humber Bridge and Beverley - all in Yorkshire. Sometimes we would try and beat the birds back, as it became a human race. At home the birds, on open loft, could maximise their local fitness.

We used local collective training facilities laid on by the grand old Ted Booth, whose wife cooked me bacon and egg. We need more of these generous-spirited people today. For sprint repeated tosses eg at 25 miles on the assumed line of flight can do the trick. As I got older and more stamina, distance and marathon orientated, from an open loft I entered hens at 95 miles and cocks at 138 miles. However be careful, as this is for conditioning on maximum feeding for long international races later. Now Nic and I start the old birds at approx 60 miles. The acid test of reality is a condition on the birds suitable for the tasks in hand. Experimentation will show you the way.

April 2013

TO SEND OR NOT TO SEND?

That is the question! For sprint and middle distance specialisms it is wise to exercise caution for the team, especially in inclement weather, north-east winds and temperatures below 50f or 10c. The early races in April in the UK can take the sting out of a team, particularly yearlings. This factor is very relevant for birds that have been confined to the loft during the winter months. The shrewd fanciers will make decisions from race to race in the light of perceived conditions and with foresight. The long-distance men will bring the team into form for June to August events with incremental increases of distance and, crucially, time on the wing. I like 10 to 14 hrs as a fly before big events. The choice is yours, yet I always sent mine to the races with mixed results, having formed a plan earlier. If you have some success in the season then *a priori* your decisions and birds were sound. It is interesting how the same names tend to appear at or near the top with frequency, is it not?

April 2013

TALES FROM THE PIGEON LOFT

At one time I sold pigeons to many pigeon characters. One night I had an excited call from China, a Mr Norris, when Chun Wing from Kowloon was on the phone. He asserted that he wanted some birds pronto. 'Of course Mr Norris' I said, with half-closed eyes. In my keenness I bought an aluminium container, made all the arrangements and set off to Manchester in a rainstorm in the blue Datsun Cherry. Now, all the cars had pulled over apart from a Porsche 911, whose lights I could just make out in the misty, rain-splashed murk. He rang me again to say, 'Your pigeon no lay any egg!' The corollary was that he duly bought some more - a lovely old character, Mr Norris.

I recall when Dr Tim Lovell turned up in his nice Jag in pursuit of children of Barcelona Dream. Acquiring two he indicated, with nonchalance, the figure to write on the cheque. Then, placing them neatly in a tidy two-bird basket, he coolly passed me the fob to the boot of his shiny Jag. A delightful man who has done great hospice work and is an exemplary figure in north-east pigeons.

April 2013

GOOD ALL-ROUND PIGEONS

It is often believed that birds can be differentiated into sprint, middle distance and long distance types, and a whole media and commercial culture is built around this perception. The reality is that this holds water in some cases. The exciting truth is that distance and velocity are very dependent on the efficiency of the system that you devise to create race condition for the race points in question. To illustrate this concept by practical reality, Nic was 1, 2 at 52 miles last weekend with 2 birds that flew Barcelona International at 710 miles in 2012, and the next bird had flown Agen International at over 500 miles as a yearling. Although unusual, these are showing tendencies to be good all-rounders, and they are genetically of mixed origins. with a great deal of focus on externals ie the names of origins of pigeons and the theory of type and phenotype. I like any bird that performs in EXISTENTIAL REALITY in the fireblade of experience.

April 2013

PIGEONS & MONEY

I believe the greatest moments of a man's life in pigeons are priceless. Money may buy you some well-bred birds at inflated prices, although good birds are available as friendly exchanges on gentlemen's terms! To me humanity is greater and of more value than currency in a capitalist society. However if you need money, the Chinese will cater for your every need via shrewd and slick advertising of apparently really good pedigree pigeons.

There are some men of acumen who trade in fashionable names, when the irony is that each pigeon is an individual under the umbrella of a strain name. Old Jack Ross of Holtby used to say 'good pigeons are given Jim', a dictum I have remembered well. However it is wise policy to finance your expenses with a few sales, although I know a man who stands by his kind generosity and gives them away. In the vast infrastructure of modern racing in western society the fanciers blessed with ability and dedication will prevail with their clever management of good birds, and they will all be different.

April 2013

WIDOWHOOD VERSUS NATURAL

Each individual fancier will develop a system to try and be successful, eg from club to international level of racing, and may be skilful with many approaches to flying. Widowhood birds often have controlled exercise periods around the loft, where both sexes are exercised separately, where the desire to mate and nest increases in conjunction with the physiological/psychological changes precipitated at the hormonal level. So-called natural birds are often flown free range and close to nature and the elements, a system that suits my personality.

Nic and I use our own system combining elements of freedom with targeted periods of separation to prepare birds from 31 miles to 710 miles, sometimes (eg with the Marmande cock) scoring from sprint to marathon level. There is a tendency of top fanciers to win with their good birds on various systems. The essence is the expertise and knowledge generated by the focused and dedicated mind of the fancier which may have taken years of research and study to develop. It is a life's work, a grand obsession.

April 2013

THE PHILOSOPHY OF WINNING

We win races, but do we feel like winners? I have witnessed several top prize winners who at the end of the season are tired and stressed and wonder if it was all worth it. It is in the nature of competition to want to win, but why, and what are the human costs? In my little opinion if you feel like a winner then you are - I know a lady with no legs who is a cheery soul to talk to, a fine example of humanity. A clever psychological stratagem is to target a key race point and make an intense study of how to fly it. The Barcelona International, which is THE big race in Europe, has yet to be won in the UK. Can it be done, and who may do it, with what winning bird? The key may be to continue to raise the bar of existential excellence towards the dizzy heights of perfection, an ideal state which is impossible. I find the performances you recall are the ones suffused by euphoria. However in our reflections, do we not recall the nectar taste of our first win? The impact of it can be central in our memory in the cool light of nostalgia.

May 2013

SUCCESS

Just what are the factors and qualities of a successful breeding and racing loft and person? First a comfortable secure loft in surroundings conducive to the adaptation of racing pigeons is required. I loved my loft at the village of Holtby in the Yorkshire countryside, where an open loft - at some risk - could foster the type of condition required for racing from 71 to 879 miles. I reflect on it now with sweet nostalgia, where at times man and bird were contented.

The personality of the fancier is the key element in the success story, requiring total focus and an enduring dedication in pursuit of excellence! Pigeons are the flying instruments of mind - a good fancier will source, breed and evolve good athletes. Recognition by people may be the outcome, but surely personal satisfaction is the central objective. However, whatever lights up your sky is surely the modus vivendi.

May 2013

PIGEON RACING & FAME

There is a huge pigeon media surge for personal recognition, enhanced, hyped and facilitated by journalists in books, magazines and on the internet. The positive impact of it is the global promotion of it in films, TV and so on. Some of the knowledge becomes mainstream and a few fanciers, within generations endure in the psyche of people. These are the charismatic people of popular culture, and the image prevails. Fame is often born out of self-promotion linked with commercial sales of fashionable strain names, with the irony that some top fanciers are known only by an esoteric few. If you want your ego to soar, it is helpful to establish yourself with some quality results. Surely the pure aim is pleasure produced by feelings of satisfaction at your own level and the joy that good birds bring after your work is done.

May 2013

SPORTSMANSHIP & JEALOUSY

Most of us will have experienced these human phenomena, for better and worse. These personality effects pervade the sport of pigeon racing at all levels from club to international level, and the denigration of a winner seems to be cemented in the English psyche. In the fiery heat of competition, especially in close contact with a peer group, emotions run high, especially the green gods of jealousy and resentment! Often these feelings are linked to ego defence mechanisms.

The converse is the selfless and beautiful sportsmanship manifested by some generous souls. Oh yes, being a winner with a good bird is the essence of the game, and to some it is of paramount importance. Nowadays I target a race point, ie Barcelona International, and the motivation is general improvement of man and bird. A well-structured and disciplined system will enable you to have a go in big races from June to August with a steady and gradual build-up of the condition of your charges in the light of the multifarious personalities you will meet.

May 2013

THE CONCEPTUALIST IN PIGEONS

We all have unique approaches to performance thinking. Most competitors aspire to and are excited by the prospect of beating other individuals, especially motivated by the big and charismatic names in the area or UK and international levels of fame and significance, eg Ronnie Williamson and Mark Gilbert. History is cemented by men of high impact, and I believe that this is largely due to publicity in the popular culture, as some of the best are little known - the beautiful irony of it all!

Personally I aimed for the best with perfectionist tendencies, fuelled by naive and youthful assertiveness. Now in the cool light of day, I take an abstract view in my mind's eye and enjoy the passion fired by a race point, the quintessence of racing aspiration, the unique and intoxicating Barcelona International, the zenith of the fancier's wildest dream. It is the only race to spawn poetry from my psyche - a powerful obsession.

May 2013

RACE CONFIDENCE

The young fancier starts out with hopes, dreams and aspirations, and probably some trepidation and a lack of inner confidence. Racing is a deeply psychological chess game for each person. Sprint and middle distances seem a long way to a raw novice and his feathered charges, and so it is. If the system is right success will be achieved with enthusiasm and hard work, since good birds abound in all families - the key is the fancier! Top men will prevail with birds of different origins - notice how the same names reappear on the results time and again.

After this homespun philosophy, confidence may increase as say distances get longer, over years of dedicated time as targets are realised, with the ultimate race in Europe being the Barcelona International up to as far as Poland, Malta and Denmark, a race which calls for obsessive dedication to the point of lunacy and confidence in ultramarathon pigeons. To be honest 879 miles was enough for me!

In tightly competitive areas, eg amongst the top men at York, it is very hard to combine popularity with dominance and is largely a masculine phenomenon, although there are some outstanding lady competitors. Confidence is determined by mood, is felt and may be ephemeral and transient.

I act now as aid and mentor to others in my maturing years and enjoy the people who I count as my friends - and they know who they are in the noble sport of pigeon racing.

May 2013

PIGEON EYES – AND HUMAN EYES

The most significant eye is the human one looking into the eye of the pigeon! Yes, most of the answers lie in the mirror. Each person makes perceptual judgements on colours, shapes, patterns and forms in the eyes of pigeons, and decisions in the mind on beauty, health and condition. Iridologists have made a theoretical study of eyes with practical disease diagnosis implications. As for the divination selection of winners and breeders, this is not humanly possible in every case, since there are too many external environmental variables to make an enlightened, predictive decision. However, certain fanciers have superior judgement when attempting to select the performance bird from overall interaction with the bird on an intuitive level of awareness. With optimal bird management champions are created, taking their place in starry constellations in the pantheon of pigeon racing. I like a nice pretty eye, like those of a young lady!

May 2013

PLANNING TO BE A CHAMPION

The great racing men orchestrate success with their birds in a structured and clinical manner. Having evolved and created a winning system, they target future races with the best of their birds. With insightful judgement the clever fancier will specialise in and cultivate the racing condition of birds with innate potential, whilst producing the team to optimal readiness and suitability to the tasks in hand. If he is fortunate he may hit on a champion performer, ie regarded as being at the top of its class. I have noticed that outbreeding of highly inbred lines sometimes does the trick, and wise men practise this in the stock loft. There is no exact science or art to pigeon racing, yet the champion flyers know the game and often replicate good performances, sometimes at a high level, eg Snydale Express for Chris Gordon. It's all a lot of fun and will engage minds for a lifetime.

May 2013

WEATHER OR NOT?

In my long career in racing pigeons, I never held birds at home due to forecast inclement weather conditions, ie from 71 to 879 miles with my family. In particular I liked northeast winds as a real test of management and bird and mistrusted birds with velocities over 1200 ypm. Many sprint/middle fanciers will disagree liking the birds home sharpish and back under control - purely a matter of subjectivity and personality.

To fly 700 plus miles, a nice warm-up race of 10 to 12 hours was crucial in preparation terms and some birds will go 17 hrs on the wing. We do what suits us as individuals and I like birds to experience a holdover in the systematic preparation for international racing where long periods in the transporter are symptomatic of the race. My strain evolved over hardship. Such is the nature of the beast.

June 2013

THE SUPERSTIMULUS

In anthropomorphic terms pigeons home as they respond to mates and the love of home, food and the fancier. In blissful ignorance we attempt to manipulate these elements to facilitate top race results. With nesting birds, I prefer a hen flown separate and allowed her first chick before the big race, with the added stimulus of sitting five eggs. I believe this can create a physiological/psychological high as subtle internal biochemical changes occur deep within the bird. Dax My Girl flew to her first pure white YB of the year, and with impact in International racing. The concept is a vast sea of esoteric knowledge waiting to be discovered. In the future men with insight will evolve new methods and stimulus tricks - will it be you? The bond between a hen and cock is little understood, now that we accept that animals display emotionality. Fascinating, is it not?

June 2013

LOFTY ASPIRATIONS

Men with vision and imagination dream of triumph over difficulty in the races of significance to them: the only bird on the day, the record flight, the name carved in the foundation stones of historical time. In this way the collective good of the sport is richly enhanced. Such personal traits are the fabric of folklore. It is very human to seek the elusive perfection in sport.

I am delighted that UK success in International racing is the norm, evolving from the original diehards of the great BICC. However, we all seek our own levels and credit is due to each person who engages in the ancient and noble art of pigeon racing. I feel the future of the sport is secure in a world where companion pigeons are cultivated in conjunction with the competitive impulse of man. Like horse and dog racing, powerful groups will cement its survival. It is an insular world where it means all to some people.

June 2013

IT'S BARCELONA TIME

The great pigeon spectacle and race is soon upon us. Hardy men of dedication and courage will send their prime candidates into the unknown with faith, belief, hope and expectation. Years of work will meet the day of destiny, confronting the possibility of meeting the interlopers of fame and glory head on, to forge their name in the steely firmament of history. Will it be an established star who triumphs or a neophyte to be sprinkled in dust? The birds tuned into their essence will face marathon distances and the vagaries of the weather on their swallow-like odysseys to the home of their being - safe and secure in a warm, cosy loft. And so this epic and singular migration will enchant the minds of men who stretch the boundaries of possibility. Long may it dwell in the timeless folklore of international pigeon racing.

June 2013

BARCELONA DUPLICATION UK 2013

United and ideal thinking and decision making has realised this opportunity between the BICC and BBC organisations. May I spur you all on to carry this practice out, and send 'em. Yes, test the quality and speed/endurance of your birds in the world's greatest pigeon race.

Young John Ghent in his obsessive perfectionism and drive has organised Louella Pigeon World as a marking station for this objective. I call upon fanciers from the Midlands to the North to partake of this magnificent opportunity to attain excellence. The press is poised to shower you in just recognition. It has been a hard season, yet one wildest dream of 1st International Barcelona may yet be realised. Faith and belief my friends - even if it is just an academic dream. it is for sure that the good bird returnees will help to be strain makers for old fashioned pigeon men.

June 2013

BLOODLINES & GENES

For many years I have raved on about the personality of individual fanciers as crucial and limiting factors in the racing success equation. This is true – no fancier, no method, no loft, no birds! By the same token, the origin and performance heritage, ie genome, are crucial too. From humble beginnings in 1976 my intensive strain making is evolving after 37 years and continues under the control of some good men. The birds today are all down from the 7 foundation originators, especially Dark Destiny and Daughter of Darkness, the no 1 pair.

One of the yearlings for Nic Harvey and myself has the no 1 pair on numerous occasions in its ancestry, as were our first four birds from the BBC Niort endurance race of 2013. Good birds thrive on extensive inbreeding with occasional infusions of other genes. You can theorise all you wish, yet performance testing is the master of racing/breeding REALITY. This is pedantic, reflecting an academic background but true! In simple terms treasure your good birds, particularly if related - it fosters success. May I wish all good flying at 2013 Barcelona International.

June 2013

GENIUS IN PIGEON FANCIERS

Genius is a relative, cultural phenomenon seen from a human perspective, and can be defined as exceptional intellectual and/or artistic power demonstrated by people. In my biased and loose application to pigeon racing, I use it to celebrate outstanding efforts of racing folk. Others may create another list, since it is all a little fun. In Ireland we have the inimitable Ronnie Williamson, a top class man, in Wales we have the Padfields, in Scotland is marathon master Jim Donaldson, and from Yorkshire we have Neil Bush, Chris Gordon - a peerless all-rounder - and Tarbes specialist Brian Denney. From the south of England Mark Gilbert is still, believe it or not, improving, plus Nic Harvey at Barcelona International. All these men are gifted practitioners in the subtleties of the art and science of breeding and racing and world class in my perception. Their achievements should be showered in praise and glory by the fancy at large, irrespective of their individual personalities.

June 2013

THE DAYS OF DESTINY

Anticipation builds as we enter another momentous and historically vibrant period of long distance and marathon pigeon racing, where iconic men and their charges will change the popular face of the sport. Yes, Agen International, NFC Tarbes and Barcelona International are upon us. It is the threshold of a dream!

Birds that break and win out of the European convoy are rugged individuals to be applauded along with their specialist keepers. Birdage at NFC level has declined dramatically, yet I have a close eye for Gordon, N. Bush and Denney - just who will prevail?

Many people will be engaged on PCs and other media as sources of rapid information and gratification. At Barcelona I shall be fixated on both the BICC and the British Barcelona Club - will Mr Kay, a rare and charismatic character, win my solid silver trophy?

These are races for purists that are the cutting edge, the fireblade of the future! UK racing is poised to maintain a strong presence. Can we yet take it to another level at Barcelona International? We shall see.

June 2013

CAUSES OF FAILURE

As a writer I wax on about elite fanciers and their birds as a celebration of my enthusiasm for the game. In sobering reality many fanciers struggle to find the energy, drive and motivation to fly up to international level, as they attempt to balance busy and demanding lives in a capitalist, mainstream society. The pigeon sport in the world accommodates any personality type in its obsessive grip.

Fanciers with steely determination and organised lives tend to fill the top echelons of the sport up to the zenith of racing aspirations - the Barcelona International. In my biased perception the reasons for negative results are mainly psychological, since the top flight produce good birds for any level of competition! My assertion is – do what you enjoy and derive satisfaction from it, then you are a winner. There is an old adage that there are more good birds than fanciers who keep them - in relative terms this smacks of REALITY.

July 2013

BARCELONA INTO POLAND

It fascinates me that the Polish lads and lasses have mustered over 2 thousand entries into the daddy of all races! There must be a strong belief, becoming a tradition in the collective psyche of rugged individualists over there. I bet they have some hard birds negotiating over 900 miles in race time. Let us see interviews with and features on the outstanding fanciers in the media, since wonderful stories abound for our contemplation and admiration. Surely the Polish initiative is the blueprint for UK and Irish racing? I say this in the conscious realisation that entry numbers have increased with due motivation since the pioneering days of BICC diehards. This upward trend will roll with publicity as we are to witness some seminal performances in the race of 2013 into our islands. Long may this be and please make sure of your verification procedures and be lucky.

July 2013

MY BARCELONA EXPERIENCE 2013

Nic and I had conceived and pre-planned our assault on the unrivalled and peerless race of all races. After a very difficult BBC Niort, we set about the meticulous preparation of our seven candidates, comprising our total old bird team!

They say anticipation is better than realisation, and an intense vigil preceded the final liberation, filmed by young Ghenty - a star for sure. At 710 miles to Taunton, Somerset we needed one on the second day - a problem to the west of England, as the cognoscenti will realise.

In blistering heat and from a north-easterly air flow we timed Musgrove Addiction on the 3rd day to be 11th BBC National - a result we need to improve on. However, in a race of attrition we were pleased to clock another bird to complete our attempt at excellence. As we are fairly new to the scene it is now forged in our psyche. Barcelona is the product of total mental focus and application of scientific techniques with intense underlying breeding of the birds - in fact a mental exercise. Allow me to praise all the hardy souls who chanced a vulnerable arm in the cauldron of Barcelona. We can't wait for the next odyssey when the UK will distinguish itself once more in the execution of the epitome of races.

July 2013

THE MEANING OF COMPETITION

What a combative set of people pigeon fanciers are! Life at or near the top may bring transient and elusive happiness with the joy of a race win or other assorted emotional states. It can be a *modus vivendi*, a way of life. In reality the world of the writer has allowed vent to my self-expression regarding race birds where I am totally hooked. Levels of success are very personality-related in terms of how you react to comment by fellow competitors, which are not always positive. A little pure resolve and single-mindedness should ensure your future participation in the sport at the level you are suited to from club to international levels. The irony is that being regarded as a great competitor is not an automatic formula for success, since life on earth as a human is more complex than that as it encompasses fleeting moments of total fulfilment and oneness - sounds rather Buddhist in influence.

July 2013

YOUNG BIRD LOSSES

These are endemic, and will continue so as long as racing exists. There is a multiplicity of reasons for non-return of young birds. We know about distance of race point, environmental/weather conditions, the English Channel, clashing and unusual atmospheric conditions and combinations of more than one of these variables. Full loft returns over time are a rarity, and so it is and will be a fact of life. Where possible and to offset some of the losses I recommend open loft systems and a feeding/medication and supplementation regime which is optimal as practised by a thoughtful and kind person with empathy - women are often gifted in these criteria. Try over time to improve the base quality of your stock via selective breeding systems. At the end of the day the persistent, clever and talented fanciers will prevail, as the whole sphere of racing is human based.

July 2013

MY LITTLE DARK ENCHANTMENT

Her memory lives long and vibrant in my imagination. A little dark chequer hen and inbred to my no 1 pair Dark Destiny and Daughter of Darkness. She scored twice from Pau NFC at 735 miles to Holtby, Yorks, England and in the hours of darkness at 10.08 pm, hence her name, and was verified at Barce International 879 miles injured. With great affection she served my stock team well for 11 years in true spirit. Paired to a son of Circus Boy and to Barcelona Dream, her genes have flooded the future with excellent offspring for Jim Donaldson and recently Nick Harvey with 11th open BBC Barcelona International 710 miles and Trev Robinson with 2nd north section BICC Barcelona International 854 miles - third time at Barcelona and only two birds in the north in race time (both to Robinson).

Enchantment is a testament to marathon performance inbreeding. Her descendants will continue to excel in the field of endurance competition, and so it will be.

August 2013

THE ROLE OF SCIENCE

Certain fanciers such as Mark Gilbert in the UK are getting close to an ideal, optimal system of management for their birds and will flourish with birds of many origins, irrespective of cost I may add! The key base element is the brain and personality of the fancier - dedication and psychology are always at the core of success. Top level racing, ie international, is enhanced by the application of modern scientific research. There are many ways to create top racing condition without official doping and German boffins have formulated a group of active supplements which for example in the case of liquid feed, will with a good home environment precipitate flying condition, narrowing down and improving performance levels with time up to Barcelona International level. From experience I recommend Chevita and Rohnfried products, since these are not bogus and work for the fanciers' benefit.

August 2013

ARE GOOD BIRDS A RECIPE FOR SUCCESS?

Fortunes are and will be spent in pursuit of success by obtaining birds which by outward appearance, often through sales techniques, are winners or will breed winners at desired levels of competition. In truth the key factor to excellence is the genetic blueprint or genome of the bird's ancestry wherein the racing performance potential lies. Then the onus is on the management expertise of the fancier to produce the bird in optimal condition for the targeted race. Some can do this and we will see the names at or near the top for years - many with birds of different origins, ie genes - be they obtained for nothing or costing loads of money. Shrewd fanciers are careful with their dosh!

There is no one strain or family that is the best, since all are of mixed origins taking the names of the good and great, often for ego/commercial and fame reasons by slick operators in the pigeon culture.

In my long career I put breeding at the top and tried to perfect my overall system with the use of extensive inbreeding to brother times sister with inbred outbreeding from time to time, finding more intense control at the loft compared with all the risks engendered by racing. Success is when you derive personal contentment from the progress made, even though one never reaches perfection.

August 2013

RACING PAST & PRESENT

How knowledge in the pigeon culture has changed, from when many saw Old Hand as the font of esoteric knowledge. The cultivation of a personal strain was paramount, tick beans in hoppers were fed ad lib and the so-called natural open loft system prevailed. We bathed the birds in potassium permanganate water solution and used quack remedies of doubtful efficacy. However records were broken, fanciers became famous and legends evolved in the consciousness of the sport. Today men with ultra-competitive science-based systems are producing entries in almost perfect condition with types of systems developed from classical widowhood/roundabout/celibacy and natural with innovative suffusions of jealousy and other performance enhancing techniques so good at physiological/psychological conditioning as to look like doping!

The future will see yet more improvements with intuitive leaps by visionary men. The benchmark race will be the Barcelona International with gradual improvements in UK and Irish and wider European performances.

August 2013

DISTANCE/MARATHON NETWORK

In pursuit of better and better performances up to Barcelona International level I have established a social and competitive network in the UK, eg from Cornwall to Holy Island. Quality birds are being provided in a common objective of raising standards in breeding and racing with the accent on strain development and the acquisition and application of gleaned knowledge via the medium of science and the art of pigeon racing. This does not have the formality of a club or society and the common ethos is excellence and the development of the racing pigeon. The network is provided on a spontaneous and intuitive personality level. Young John Ghent, an aspirational Barcelona man, is a keen writer and participant in the thriving network.

August 2013

THE WITCHING HOUR

For aeons men hardened by toil and competition, and indeed some women, have sought heightened and mystical sensory awareness in quiet yet vibrant communication with their long distance candidates in long and stamina-sapping endurance races. It is the poignant, spiritual anticipation, the visual significance of the final arrival of the favourite cock or hen which may propel your name into the esteemed collective folklore of pigeon racing. In mindful, zen-like focus you are full of warm euphoria. The rush of adrenaline may offset the anxious fatigue that subsumes the long wait. Time may seem to cease as you unite with the evening crows, the setting sun and the moth-catching bats as the twilight zone absorbs you into the darkness of the night, the normal signal for roosting racing pigeons. My Barcelona clocking at 879 miles was one of soaring transcendence, which I try to capture over time.

September 2013

WHAT MAKES A BARCELONA SPECIALIST TICK?

There is an absolute fact in pigeon racing, and that is that the Barcelona International is the no 1 race. Fanciers often begin with club races and graduate to races of greater and greater personal meaning in pursuit of more satisfaction, perhaps being bored by other races, or attempting to test the speed and endurance of individual pigeons and a strain. A Barcelona specialist may adopt an obsessive, religious preoccupation with Barcelona as the godhead in pursuit of a mental buzz like a mystical and euphoric state.

Responses to clocking vary. Frank Kay, a man from near Bolton of profound and shrewd wisdom, likens it to floating on air. Nicholas Harvey refers to it as a rush of reality, like the drug of realisation. Others dream of conquering the mountain, the zenith of a man's career in marathon racing. In a race of ultimate glamour and prestige, like Monaco in Grand Prix racing, fanciers from the UK and continental Europe engage in the practical preparation of their candidates and, if entered, will fall prey to pre-race anxiety and hype, followed by the heightened awareness of the long wait. Exponents like Wouter Jorna of Holland may clock 2nd day at over 800 miles - a feat yet to be achieved in the UK with the English Channel to endure.

Many continental fanciers are motivated by financial gain out of the Barcelona International, yet here in the UK with a different psyche we tend not to be. Apart from inhabiting dreams, Barcelona International preparation is a lengthy fusion of methodical preparation of quality birds by men who are not afraid to be different. In the final analysis I would describe Barcelona people as enigmatic, fascinating, mysterious folk of imagination and idealism.

September 2013

SELF-CRITICISM & SUCCESS

The old adage 'look in the mirror' is very much needed in

today's society with rampant criticism and denigration of others, especially towards people who have risen up in popular society. In pigeon racing and breeding, although hard for some the way to improve towards the impossible perfection is self-analysis of the essentials of a good fancier, and to persevere in practice until a competitive system, which will include good birds, is created. If you hit on the formula for success, which many do, then it is essential to send and send over many years until you have gained inner satisfaction from your efforts - a psychological phenomenon. The answer lies in the total home environment of which the fancier is crucial - his personality and presence are key.

It is easy to unload negative criticism on others and birds - it may relieve emotions. It is obvious that the good and top fanciers breed and produce good birds for racing by practicing knowledge and sophisticated skills, some without great material cost. I recommend fanciers, if able, to research all aspects of the art and science of pigeon breeding and racing, then have another look. I am like all others - we make errors in our lives.

September 2013

TRICKS OF THE TRADE

There are many ways to pigeon racing success in racing/breeding and sales and personal satisfaction and fame are enjoyed by many in the insular little world of the racing pigeon. A quality and focused plan is the net result of a method and system evolved by the fancier, with some telling tricks of the trade. With intelligence and cunning people, short of official doping, hit on foods, both liquid and solid and supplements that work deep within the being of the bird at the psychological and physiological level.

A sharp mind may have a circle of contacts for the mutual exchange of top genes for the chosen distance, with little cash flow! Some fanciers rely on their partners or pay managers to work the race entrants, acting as directors and mentors. Some folk have an intuitive sense of a bird's value, with others reliant on large numbers sent in good condition and with hope and expectation. When results follow, friends are made of scribes and auctioneers who will promote and sell as far as China, Japan and America - fame being a desire of many! Some have hit on the reality of crossing two inbred strains for a potential boost of hybrid vigour, which is scientific fact.

It is a truism that if you enjoy satisfactory success then you have the job sussed... and many do.

September 2013

THE REALITIES OF PIGEON RACING

With 61 years of accumulated experience with birds and pigeons I have come to realise certain truths in a general outlook on the sport. Weather and environmental conditions will tend to vary with each race and race point liberation, so that it is not wise always to blame the officials, the race controller and the convoyer for relatively slow or low percentage returns. I think more insight can be gained by looking at the overall effectiveness and quality of your system, management and birds. When most people are extra-punitive blaming others and outside influences for poor results, a little mirror searching, ie introspection, can yield dividends as an aid to self-improvement.

The degree of difficulty tends to increase with distance/time on the wing and perceived difficult environmental conditions. The need for fame and wealth and to experience success is very powerful and the media is a melting pot of hungry egos looking for gratification, and some find a modicum of contentment and happiness after their hard work. Races are the cauldron of competition with a biased emphasis on the first place, yet the Barcelona International race has yet to be won in the UK! Some fanciers, partly due to sheer personality, become popular and perhaps icons via results and publicity, yet others who are skilful people shun the limelight, and such is the rich human diversity of fancier folk who keep the humble pigeon in its many forms.

September 2013

THE IMMUNE SYSTEM

Not yet fully understood, the immune system is a complex of biological structures and processes in the bird which protect from and ward off diseases. On this notion a good fancier aims to produce a total home environment conducive to an optimised immune system. In my experience giving pigeons fresh air and freedom in all weathers was good practice. I never kept any birds hungry and fed Chevita supplements which were active at the cellular level, pellets and brewer's yeast etc.

The art/science fusion is well known to maintain good condition in the flock. The corollary is that some birds will become ill due to genetic or other reasons when effective supplements may be of great help in lifting condition. Try and ape or echo the environment that stock doves and wood pigeons enjoy, ie sun/wind/rain/snow and lively air, plus the benefit of enhanced feeding by the hand of man. OK, this concept is not suitable for all people and lofts, yet for natural fliers it can work up to Barcelona International level.

September 2013

ELITISM

In every pigeon club in the land at every level of competition is a human power struggle for the treasured first prize. This may be rewarded by a red card, money or a trophy etc as material rewards or as personal/ego satisfaction for a job well done. Some people and birds may be perceived, especially in the popular media, to be superior to others, becoming famous, iconic or cult figures. Status in pigeons is at the base of contention and dispute and the successful are often negated on one hand and praised on the other. Some of the most outwardly competitive people I have seen are sprinters.

However each person is unique and rest assured most enjoy a win or two, yet chasing the top may make you miserable - such is the irony of elitism. I can see the real value in the Barcelona International as a world event, and take pleasure in writing, strain formation and helping my contacts in the sport. In the great scheme of things our efforts are little ripples in the ocean of humanity.

October 2013

REASONS TO BE CHEERFUL

With the atmosphere of doom and gloom brought on by a mass reaction to global financial mismanagement, let us celebrate some of the more positive aspects of pigeon racing. We are flying high with some seminal International performances from the unique BICC organisation. In addition we are climbing up the ladder of the Barcelona International and this momentum will continue with greater and larger significance. There are endemic problems in many local clubs due to political and personality issues and erosion of membership. Some of these can be resolved by a radical rethink, resolve and effective focus and leadership. People will always specialise in and enjoy sprint and middle-distance racing with its massive continental influence and influx of birds which are deemed to be superior. I see a happy renaissance in long distance and now MARATHON racing where the die-hard oddballs can make an impact in the grand sphere of racing. The sport accommodates many psychological types from pessimists to optimists to realists and fusions of all, and this factor will continue as long as man desires to compete, to excel, and prevail and to conquer the skies with their feathered charges.

October 2013

WHO ARE THE GREATEST?

There is no conclusive or absolute definition of greatness or genius in any human field of endeavour. In pigeons we believe certain fanciers to be of a high order and outstanding. To perceive this is often the product of publicity in the media, where interested parties generate attention and interest. Sometimes men like Neil Bush, who do not court publicity, go relatively unnoticed. Now this man has an exemplary record in the Grand National Pau and Tarbes races over 700 miles since 1982.

Popularity and greatness can be similar, yet I rather admire the quiet resolve and singular dedication of those who steadfastly target a race point in pursuit of perfection. Seeking fame is like a norm in society, yet power to the people who do not embrace it, oddballs or not oddballs!

In the UK and Ireland some leading fanciers are Williamson, Padfields, Arnold, Donaldson, Bush, Harvey,

Gilbert, Cooper, Denney - all big names, and the accolade of the greatest is open to debate and analysis and question.

October 2013

WHY CERTAIN FANCIERS SUCCEED WHEN OTHERS FAIL

Let us analyse and throw some insight on this phenomenon. It is a fact that the top people have the knowledge and capability to source, breed and produce birds in a competitive condition for racing at their chosen distances. The total home environment has to be conducive to good racing performances, and this will depend on your choice of location, your home needs in the first place. For marathon and distance events I prefer a country location. The consistently brilliant fanciers have an organised system and plan of campaign to execute their chosen races then the rest is down to the individual capability of the birds in relation to the race conditions. Over the years, men with a personalised winning system in the total sense of racing and breeding, and who continue to send will tend to do well. They may well specialise in a certain racepoint or organisation. Rest assured, people with long term resolve, focus, dedication and a total winning personality will secure the right birds for the job, bearing in mind that the biggest race in Europe has yet to be won in the UK. Success is a matter of perspective is it not? In the final analysis if you feel like a winner, then existentially you are!

October 2013

NIGHT FLYERS

On many a night out in nature or just in the street I have heard and caught glimpses of night migrations and local movements of many species of birds and not just ducks, geese and crows. This factor means that they can orientate and navigate without the immediate influence of direct sunlight, which has been deemed to be so significant in homing. We know of many recordings of racing pigeons in the UK and Continental Europe in what we refer to as the hours of darkness, do we not? Many types of birds will feed eg catch fish, at night. I find this fascinating in relation to concepts of actual navigation of racing pigeons. What senses are activated in relation to what external phenomena and how does the brain and or mind take a possible role in the homing process? Do pigeons have abilities not common to man which are yet to be discovered or beyond human comprehension? What makes a pigeon tick? Does man have the ability to know? I suspect not.

November 2013

STRAGS

Today's champion maybe tomorrow's straggler. Most of my good birds had time out eg in fields, lofts, barns, towns or in a myriad of locations. If they return fit and well it can be the making of them, and they always got other opportunities to excel - another day, another race. This is of course a distance man's philosophy not an out-and-out sprinter's perception of a good bird. In 2004 a blue strag landed on my loft. I liked it and, duly transferred, it bred a cock to fly Barcelona International at 850-plus miles. What tends to happen with marathon pigeons is the loss of desire, or whatever propels them to return home in the first place. A deep understanding of a pigeon's psyche, assuming it has one, is yet to be realised - only scientific and anthropomorphic attempts at understanding and knowledge! In a shot at strag prevention we try and supply their every need and enter them in races in prime condition for the event.

November 2013

NO FIXED RULES

We look for certainty, for dogma for the definite in the sport. I evolved a system that suits Nic and me on a personal level, which may be applicable to some but not all. The variables in the genetics of breeding make the various forms of breeding hit and miss, and with the best of intentions we try and master it. At best pigeon racing is a fusion of art and science in relation to ever-changing environments. Once we have liberated the birds at the race point, they are free in the prevailing elements. With some control of the home environment, we hope to influence their desire and ability to home.

Some fanciers have a greater impact on their birds than others and tend to prevail in racing and with no fixed families, as good pigeons come from different sources, not just the fashionable name of the day. All the top men have a system capable of competition at a high level, and usually with many pigeon types none of which are absolutely pure in a genetic sense, all being of mixed ancestry. In a society based on instant gratification we look for the quick fix, the formula of success-linked to impatience. Men of old served their apprenticeship in the cauldron of pigeon racing in an atmosphere of learning within no fixed rules. The beauty of the sport is the pleasure in uncertainty.

November 2013

PIGEON REALITY

Men of dreams and of vision contemplate and dwell on how they see their racing ideals translate into actual results and success. After many years of plotting, scheming and thinking, and doing what many do, that is talking, I realised that the true test of value was the results in breeding and racing reality. This is the acid test of what we have achieved after years of painstaking development of the birds and system.

Are you happy with your results? Is more time and work necessary? We operate on different levels of hope and expectation, and believe me, if you are happy with your results then you have cracked it – that is your personal reality. There can be a world of difference between our inner and outer worlds and surely the secret is to closely match the two realms, when our dreams become reality.

November 2013

BARCELONA INTERNATIONAL - WHERE ARE WE NOW?

Rest assured the great race is secure to UK and Ireland in the hands of the BICC stalwarts, who maintain consummate and steadfast dedication to the International cause. I have been asked to highlight the cause of the needy in the British Barcelona – I stress Barcelona – Club whose only love and desire in pigeons is to race from the Barcelona International. It seems worthy of the club's name to continue on a united front with the BICC – the more the merrier in the race of races where men are made and strain makers found. There is no greater challenge in the minds and hearts of men than to conquer Barcelona. The BBC committee need to consider in great detail the future objectives and status of the club in relation to the blue riband racepoint – its prestige, difficulty and worthiness to perpetuate the name of the club.

December 2013

FOCUS ON THE DETAILS

The unified whole of a successful loft and system, including the manager, consists of lots of interconnecting details which must be in place. As the system of racing and breeding evolves via experiment and practice, we note all the little aspects that may give us a competitive edge. It is wise to record all the useful bits of feeding/exercise on a daily basis and all that constitutes the loft management, since you will need to repeat it or modify it on a yearly basis.

Try and make your notes and pedigrees as precise and accurate as possible, as these tend to be breeding grounds for errors - use a pedigree as a rough guide only, even if it looks professional. As you become successful the big picture will become clear, where small benefits can be added after new insights and the acquisition of modern knowledge. The aim is perfection, although gradual improvements will suffice. After years of mental focus you may become a specialist in your chosen discipline of racing and able to make a contribution to further knowledge.

December 2013

THE PIGEON FANCIER'S BOND

A crucial element in pigeon racing success and loft harmony is the sensitive and close relationship between the fancier's personality and the individual being of the birds. I worked on calm kindness and a stable environment where positive feelings were in rich evidence. My mother brought her love of individual birds to enrich the atmosphere within the colony. She is noted for singing to them as they soaked it all in from their perches. This is the sort of attention to detail which encourages marathon birds to face it and return to the home where their wellbeing is cultivated. This sentimentality is part of the objective process so well executed by Nicholas Harvey, who manifests a great deal of warm empathy in his build up to the Barcelona International. Yes, there's more to fanciership than ruthless manipulation of birds to win races. The practiced fancier is like the avian equivalent of a horse or dog whisperer. He knows sufficient of the psychology of his birds to have insight into and real understanding of their individual needs to form the pigeon fancier's bond.

December 2013

PEACE & HARMONY

As mentor to my marathon friends I aim to establish a system and an atmosphere based on positive feelings all round. The essence of this is knowledge, mutual understanding and trust. We all share a common goal in an objective which is greater than ourselves, ie the Barcelona International. All communications, thoughts and feelings are primed in the development of systems and birds which will conquer this noble and great endurance race. The corollary is that it is essential to instil and develop peace and harmony in the loft and local environment, whilst creating a balanced approach to predators and developing the instincts and rugged hardiness of the birds to the natural elements of sun, wind and rain - all that earth offers. These are the sort of birds, with the right genetic blueprint that will persist through races of attrition to get home, to bathe in glory. Such birds of singular quality are the quintessence of the approach to racing Nic and I take.

December 2013

THE FINAL FRONTIER IN PIGEON RACING

This is the time of year when opinions rage, attitudes shift and emotions run high as to the biggest, the greatest, the fastest and all the superlatives in pigeon racing. Clubs and organisations battle for supremacy, led by needy and hungry human egos. Is the NFC or the BICC the greatest of the organisations with exemplary programmes? The contest will continue as long as the competitive spirit of man runs high and people identify and associate with what is popular and perceive to be the best.

In the final analysis it is opinion, biased thinking and lacking in absolute definitive selection criteria. However in my personal, individual and biased judgement the final frontier of contemporary pigeon racing is the Barcelona International - organised in 2014, ostensibly by the BICC and BBC. Take a risk. Be ambitious and chance your arm. Feel the rush of euphoria when you clock.

December 2013

A MATTER OF DEFINITION

There are certain words used in pigeon terminology and in the pigeon media that I will attempt to clarify. My definitions, as opinions, are purely subjective and based on personal experience.

Distance in my mind's eye refers to races of 5 to 700 miles and race birds that have actually flown those distances, ideally in race time. Marathon birds and races I associate with distances over 700 miles, and they are my chosen ones. Sprint races will embrace races and birds up to 250 miles, and middle distance from 250 to 500 miles.

Inbreeding refers to the practice of pairing closely related birds eg generations of brother to sister matings, father to daughter etc. in a family colony in an attempt to produce birds with similar qualities, desired by the fancier, and expressed in the phenotype as feather quality, balance and racing capability etc. Inbreeding depression, via recessive genes may manifest itself in reduced size, fertility, vigour and susceptibility to disease. Outbreeding refers to the introduction in the breeding programme of relatively non-closely related birds, into the population, and I favour experimenting with inbreds for this purpose.

We can go on and on to clarify exactly what we mean by all the terms in the sport, and in the final analysis, will yield an understanding, which will reflect a mere fraction of the full scope of knowledge available for our comprehension. In my experience of racing, a working understanding is needed so that you can create a winning system at your chosen distance, that you are contended with.

December 2013

CULTIVATING BARCELONA PIGEONS

Right from the potential in the egg they are all individuals, which need specialist treatment. In theory the genes are crucial and good birds for Barcelona can be found in any so-called families, all being of mixed origins. I note the popularity of Barcelona performance birds imported into the UK, some of which may leave good birds in the right hands. There is one way to prove a Barcelona pigeon and it is simple - send it to the Barcelona International race and see if it comes home.

I will advise the steady racing of young birds with rich feeding at all times, preferably on open loft to hone the survival instincts around home. Using the same basic principles take the yearlings out to 4 to 500 miles, and 2yr olds to Barcelona around 700 miles, or if Barcelona is over 750 miles use 3yr olds. Each bird is sent to Barcelona, where the results will be self-evident. Nic Harvey aims to send all ours each year, so that eventually we will have birds to achieve 3 times Barcelona International. The race has inbuilt difficulty, yet the UK under the jurisdiction of the BICC and sometimes the BBC will continue to raise the bar of excellence.

December 2013

GAZING AT 2014

Olympic Ric, sadly deceased, crowned a year of glory for UK racing in 2013. I anticipate another great year as we have cemented our distinguished place in International racing, and this trend will continue under the dedicated jurisdiction of the BICC - with help from the BBC - at Barcelona. It has been a lofty aspiration of mine to extend International racing further and further north into Scotland and Ireland. Gradual progress will be made in this onerous and compelling objective. In the short term activity by the Midlands catchment area would be ideal, and create much enthusiastic interest.

In the purist of senses new champions will assert their prowess on the pigeon culture, and the media will give glowing recognition to those who prevail and their feathered charges. The beauty of the sport of pigeon racing is its openness to all, and with a dream, a desire and a will you can join the greats in the rich fabric of pigeon history. I think the secret is to enjoy what you do.

December 2013

BEHIND THE MASK OF A CHAMPION

The great fliers of the past, present and future are gifted with certain personality characteristics that they have utilised on the road to glory town. They will glean sufficient knowledge of the art and science of pigeon racing, and then execute a winning system plan, with enduring focus over many years in the cauldron of competition. A little like the lone wolf archetype, or Lonesome George the tortoise, they will carve out a singular path, perhaps of eccentric excellence, as their identity is realised in the consciousness of the popular pigeon culture. Household names they will become as the sting of publicity is felt and they may evolve as icons, legends and folklore figures, enriching the human fabric of the sport. There is a profound sense, and yearning to know what fires glow behind the masks of these exemplary champions. With the potent passage of time man may celebrate and denigrate the successful in equal measure, yet the flame and fire of the greats burn and smoulder into history, in the celestial hall of fame.

December 2013

FIVE

—

MUSINGS – 2014

THE GREATEST DIFFICULTY IN PIGEONS

The current accent is on win, win, win, performance, performance! This is worthy of a question - just what has been won and at what level of difficulty? We find our own levels of aspiration and success, do we not? For many the target is to maximise the numbers of firsts in club/federation or what is called national racing. In my mind's eye there is a phenomenon which transcends the world of pigeon racing. It is the creation of your OWN family or strain of all related birds. I started mine in 1976 and continue to work on them under the management of good men and lofts. So far related birds have scored from 31 to 879 miles, and attempts are contemplated to extend the concept further, under the general maxim of bigger, better, further. It is all very idealistic, yet keeps good fanciers focused and motivated and rejuvenates the gene base of the good old strain. Practicing the science and art of breeding has been the most profound experience of my pigeon career.

January 2014

THE EXTERNAL APPEARANCE OF PIGEONS

Many fit racing pigeons handle with symmetry, silky feather, balance and eyes that sparkle like diamonds in the perception of the mind of the beholder. The flying world is full of strags like these, which poses the question - are they any good? The short answer is that most of these beauties flatter to deceive and are next to useless as breeders and racers. I like a lovely pigeon to admire in the hand, yet place greater emphasis on my understanding of the genome in the ancestry of the bird - this is where the creation of your own family is valid and saves all that money trying to buy in success. Do the birds in question carry performance genes that can be transmitted into valuable performances at your chosen distance? Nic and I have a simple plan of execution to try and discover good birds. We take late-breds for stock from our best performers which will be related to intensify and maximise racing performance potential. Ask the question, what is the origin of the cracker in your hand, can I trust it? My maxim is look within, is there a positive insight with the pigeon?

January 2014

SOURCING OUR OUTBREEDING PIGEONS

Time for some experimentation with our inbred strain. We have acquired three direct from Padfields Invincible paired to Nellie's Lelly from House of Aarden - a direct daughter of 1st International Barcelona. From gentleman Bert Shepherd we have five direct from his Barcelona national winning genes. The birds inspire confidence with their breeding, price and breeding potential. The practical key is that all two year olds will be destined for Barcelona International into the West Country, which will act as a measure of their true value. Not concerned about looks and phenotype of the offspring, the sole parameter will be breeding and racing performance, before we make value judgements as to the intrinsic quality of the birds - excellent origin or not!

On a psychological note, it stimulates our minds in terms of the future development of the strain. Happy with our race preparation, we hope to further improve the base quality of our birds and reputation. We could have sourced any birds, yet we chose the two origins on analysis and intuitive perceptions of the pigeon men concerned being confident in their genuine intentions and values in the pigeon sport.

January 2014

NFC TARBES versus BICC BARCELONA

Many opinions are polar opposites between the two parent organisations and race points, a fact which will remain as long as birds fly. Tarbes is a domestic race with a popular fan base, with Barcelona International more for the purist marathon or extreme distance flier. Birds of my breeding have flown both, and it is easy to draw a blank from either. Tarbes can be comfortable up to and in excess of the 750 mark, whilst Barcelona with up to 30,000 birds in the main race is noted for its continuous severe degree of difficulty into the UK and Ireland, and birds on the second day are always the exception, with the modern, popular archetype being Padfields Invincible at approx 756 measured miles - a lot further into Wales.

Tarbes followed on from Pau, which I have more affection for at 735 miles to my old loft. Both Barcelona and Tarbes will produce key and influential birds in a strain, IF YOU CAN GET THEM TO FLY IT. My ultimate confidence lies in UK Barcelona International pigeons, and the exponents of this unique race, and we are seeing a wave of confidence in birds tested at this race, hence the purchases by Louella and House of Aarden. The secret is out, the choice is yours, just what are the ultimate pigeons in your opinion, and WHY? Nick and I have chosen Barcelona for the old, and to trial yearlings at Tarbes.

January 2014

THE STEVE WAIN CONNECTION

In 2002 Stephen from Foston, Derbyshire, made contact with me and the birds at Holtby, Yorks. He had serious long-distance aspirations up to NFC Tarbes. I supplied him over the years with top genes from the family - some free and some for a song. Evolving from these was his No 1 pair of directs bred from an inbred son of Diabolos paired to Velvet Destiny, he direct from Mystical Queen and Dark Velvet. The son of this pair became a key producer when paired to a red hen of Dark Enchantment and Circus Boy genes.

Steve has given my friends direct children of the top pair, and children of his three times Tarbes hen - a NFC section winner at Nantes. The latter is the dam of Nick Harvey's current No 1 stock hen - a champion progenitor to BBC Barcelona International level.

Currently taking a break from active racing, we owe a debt of gratitude to the selfless generosity and sportsmanship of the man. The offspring from Mr Wain's birds will ensure the future of his contribution to the complex world of the sport.

January 2014

THE LONG-TERM VIEW

Instant gratification is endemic in popular society and pervades the sport of pigeon racing, supported by rapid turnover of pigeon families and with the march of commercialism. Many of the great and famous fanciers of now and the historical past have adopted a different approach. They visualise a long-term plan with individual preparation of birds against a system that includes years of dedicated work. Birds may be targeted for key distance/marathon races when they mature into 2-4 year olds. This mental approach takes the long-term view with delayed final gratification. On a similar note a fancier may come to specialise in the creation of a sprint to middle distance family by the adoption of an advanced method of flying them. It seems likely that the fanciers who endure have been motivated by an intense and sustained focus, up to fanatical levels. The traits are currently personified by say Geoff Kirkland and Geoff Cooper, and the Bush family, who reap what they sow in the long term view.

February 2014

THE PERSONAL TOUCH

In an age of texting, computers and other electronic devices, are we not in danger of losing that individual, personal touch in our pigeon-related relationships, contacts and communications? I help fanciers in the UK and Ireland, and prefer the telephone where some real thought and emotion can go into the encounters, since you can hide more readily behind many other forms of technology. Texts and emails are a little abstract and objective in style - perhaps good for the shy and for secrets. I like the PC, where deeper thought is called for. In books and magazines for articles and advertisements you can create a certain image. My message is that in every aspect of pigeon society are the individual and unique people, who behind the mask of money and materialism make it happen, and I am blessed to have met some truly great characters who adorn the rich and colourful tapestry of life.

February 2014

PIGEONS - DO THEY HAVE MINDS?

Of the many life forms on Planet Earth, why should man have the monopoly on mind? The collective idea was that humanity was superior, since animals and birds were deemed to be living out their life cycles based on pure instinct - a series of innate patterns of responses and behaviour laid down by years of genetic/evolutionary adaptation to the external world.

Based on study, our senses and intuitive feelings we know that pigeons have an inner being or personality, individual to each bird. The sensitive, perceptive fancier takes note of the subtle interaction between himself and the birds when assessing the condition and behaviour of his birds in relation to form and racing potential. Likewise the birds respond to the fancier - my mother sang to them. I suspect they have a type of consciousness and possibly some emotionality, perhaps a little like that so clearly manifested by elephants. It would be great to probe inside the head of a bird on how it reacted to us. Ironically due to the limitations of our understanding we will never know in full the complexity of a racing pigeon - the challenge is to attempt it, and the insights may illuminate man.

February 2014

LIQUID FEEDING OF RACING PIGEONS

There are ongoing opinion and debate exchanges about the relative merits of hard corn feed mixtures and straights and supplements as magic ingredients of racing pigeon diets for different distances. Often the nature of these is linked to the confidence/belief and success of the fancier, with or without real knowledge of the science and art of pigeon racing.

Fashions change along with publicity and popular knowledge of the sport. There is no exact and definitive formula for feeding, and the essence is to fuel the birds up with sufficient reserves of fat/muscle and energy for sustained flight at variable distances. We need to work on the level of the blood, brain, cell and internal organs of the bird, ie at the total being of the bird on a physiological/psychological level.

The success of this can be perceived by observing the outward behaviour of the birds in correlation with racing performance. A powerful and rapid effect can be made via the liquid feeding of active supplements, which are classed by vets as non-doping, eg Chevita Mycosan-T CCS, Rohnfried Blitzform and Vydex Supersix - all of which are administered as liquid feeds. I hope you find this useful in your search for the optimal feeding regime of a pigeon.

February 2014

PREPARING 800 MILERS

Now this is a specialism for the rare fancier and pigeon. Forget strain names and commercial hype, as the innate potential lies in the individual bird, and a tiny percentage of birds can cope with Barcelona International, hence the paucity of fanciers and birds who chance their arm in the UK and Ireland. It is extreme, and in the top echelon of endurance pigeon racing. However the more the merrier is common into northern Holland. To achieve it I recommend maximum feeding from the egg to the 2 to 4 yr old stage. Every attention is given to the orientation and navigation of each individual bird, and all yearlings need 4 to 500 miles as a stamina test. As old birds give them a 10 to 12 hrs on the wing after rich feeding in the build-up to races of fats/carbs and proteins. Follow this with total loft rest of 3 to 4 weeks say, then a little pipe opener of about 120 miles before basketing day, the birds having been out in all weathers to sharpen and harden them up. I like Chevita, Vydex and Rohnfried supplements as they all are good conditioners. Book a week's holiday, light the blue touch paper and wait, and wait, and wait some more.

February 2014

THE OLDER FANCIER

We all get there if we live long enough. At three and twenty years as a student in London, I never thought I would get past 30 - hard and fast it was. The irony is that I now feel younger at 65! The majority of the fancy are over 50, and it is wise to make pigeons easy to deal with. Is your loft easy to access for water and food supplies? if possible in your area birds on the natural style systems may be all you need. Draw up a chart to highlight the daily needs of the birds, and stick to your system. You may need help to basket and get your birds to the club from an able friend. Pick out, in advance, the main races to compete in. Manage a nice comfortable colony of birds and reduce costs with minimal additives and medications. A nice, quiet, laidback chair in the garden cheers the spirit, a vantage point for observing nature and navel contemplation. It may be possible to sell a few progeny to support your pension. If of literary inclination you may wish to record a life in pigeons, and how the hobby changed and enriched an old man's philosophy.

February 2014

PIGEON NESTS

For nesting racers and breeders, I like cosy little niches where the birds are secure and contented in command of their territory. In my quirky old loft were little shady spots and corners for the breeding colony. I reject regimentation and order in favour of natural, instinctual behaviour, and some of my racers nested at my feet on ancient deep litter in which mealworms thrived!

I prefer the birds when they fly in and out with nesting material gathered in from the wild. This can be supported by the gathering of twigs, dried wild herbaceous plant stalks and wheat straw. Tobacco stalks are expensive and not as good. The lining of nests should be soft, and I like papier mâché bowls like dandy nests, and not clay which tends to crack eggs. With a surgical light, you can check for egg fertility after a few days and reject clear eggs. I treated the family breeders as an egg factory, with the sole objective of producing progeny, as producers have a relatively short life. Right from the egg the keynote for Barcelona flying is FREEDOM.

February 2014

PIGEON EGOS

The essence of the sport is self-gratification in active competition. Behind the mask of champion pigeons, the whole sport down to the writers, the scientists, the politicians and the rich diversity of human kind, is the fulfilment of the hungry needs of individual minds. We may function in organised groups, committees and societies, yet these are there to serve the individual needs of people. What do you covert? Is it money, fame, prestige, personal satisfaction, or an obsessive urge for perfection in your chosen sport? In the rich and colourful tapestry of man, there are some folk who act as ambassadors, patrons, mentors and philanthropists, who generate feelings of sympathy in me. I do like the ego-altruistic approach of those who do obvious practical good. If you accept the premise that we are in the game for self-enhancement, where do you fall in relation to the unique and singular face of pigeon people? I admit that my life has been the expression of my complex needs triggered initially by my father introducing me to pigeons at aged three at 14 Borough Rd, Skegness, a passion that is intoxicating and consuming, and I am acutely aware of my own ego. Are you?

February 2014

GIFTED FANCIERS

These remarkable and singular individuals have and will make a huge impact on the world of pigeons. Noted for their penetrating and persistent long-term focus, they often make a lasting and original contribution to performance levels, the knowledge and intellectual life of the pigeon subculture and leave an indelible mark in the complex web of the sport and hobby. Some of these characters are pure competitors at an advanced level, whilst others may contribute to literature via reports, books and films and interviews. All of them reach out beyond themselves as observers, and in happy connection with birds. Some maintain a private profile, whilst others embrace a little fame in the media, depending on personal style and temperament. We know them and we read about them, as they are the hardcore of the foundations. I have been privileged to encounter some great characters like Jim Jenner, Cameron Stansfield,

Gareth Watkins, John Clements, Ghenty, Liam O'Comain, and recently Dr Graham Dexter from the wonderful world of performance Birmingham Rollers.

March 2014

WHAT IS A GOOD PIGEON?

It is so simple, being fit for purpose. Some folk may have an inkling or sensory awareness of quality on occasions - we call it stock sense. To cut through the complexity of any selection theory criteria, opinions or other human, subjective judgements, allow me to tell you how to find a good bird. In reality a child can do it.

A good racer will perform to your satisfaction in actual races, and testing under each set of race conditions is a sure way of finding out. The purist fancier proves good birds by racing them, hard fact results are the evidence, black, white and beautifully easy. The corollary is that good breeders breed good pigeons. The essence of this simple and practical philosophy is the management skill of the fancier.

There is a system and formula for racing at all levels, and some people have cracked the modus operandi - how to do it. Behind the dreams, myths, imagination and the personalities of folklore, basic racing as an entity is simple. It intrigues me that the big race, ie Barcelona International has never been won in the UK - it is possible, and may be done by men who aspire to conquer the near impossible. The mantra then is SEND 'EM.

March 2014

NEGATIVITY IN PIGEON RACING

You know I accentuate the positive and decline the negative in an optimistic mind mode. However, there is a rampant and insidious malaise in our society, epitomised by the attitudes of some fanciers. I think it lies in the propaganda and negative perceptions of the messages in the media, and is a response to some of the personalities who govern our quasi-democratic society. At the core of the endemic problem in the sport today is an unhappy synthesis of commercialism, jealousy, criticism and a decline in generous, spiritual and moral values due to the unhealthy rise of materialism as the base line entity of out of control capitalism. People demonstrate their instincts and emotions in a diversity of guises, and the obsessive will to win at all costs philosophy is contributing to a sport that has rejected balance, fun and enjoyment, in favour of exaggerated hype, self-delusion and illusion. Bring back the long distance master, poised in vibrant expectation, for the arrival of his old favourites, in beautiful and kind surroundings.

March 2014

THE ROMANCE OF RACING

What motivates people to dedicate themselves to years of specialised hard work with their feathered charges? It helps if you have a dream, a vision of what you desire to achieve, or to win, perhaps against the odds. This may be suffused with an obsessive inclination towards perfectionism. A love of wildlife and birds is often key to the whole process. As you mature in your career, you may be intoxicated by one race as reward for years of effort, and a test of ability of your evolving family of birds. I regard this as the purist approach.

At the setting of the sun the whole scenario is seated in personal satisfaction - a reward in itself.

I still celebrate the traditional philosophy and waking dreams of men who wait in excited anticipation to feel the thrill of arrivals from great races and mind-blowing distances, and now in my little world, the lonely pursuit is priceless. I like the spiritual quality, the lofty idealism of it all. Some of these principles may be inspirational, and are all beyond the material.

March 2014

A WELL-HANDLING PIGEON

It is easy to fall for good looks in a bird: the sparkle in its eye, the balance, the symmetry, the feathering and overall physicality or phenotype. We can be seduced by the oil painting cliché, ie good looks appeal. We theorise, wax lyrical and predict winner after winner, do we not? On occasion we may actually select a good one out of our decisions, expert or not expert. I love attractive birds that breed or race to my satisfaction, and these are rare.

To enjoy the sport we need to make a compromise with perfectionism. In your own family of birds the appeal may be spread across birds of your own evolution. The sobering truth is if the bird in your hand does not contain performance gene potential it will never achieve greatness in racing and/or breeding. This is a reflection of science fused with my personal belief. Be wary of glossy pictures that please the eye and seduce you to part with money! If you can trust a pedigree or the supplier study the performances with great interest. Get a feel for the bird and fancier. My personal favourites are dark chequer and velvet birds with yellow or silky feather, and for years all my strain were of this ilk.

March 2014

THE MIND OF THE SPECIALIST FANCIER

The specialists tend to predominate in racing, and at every level of competition. In theory any fancier can know success with a top bird. In practice the main fanciers, those who become the elite, are people with a winning mentality. Each intricate detail constitutes the blueprint or master plan of the concerted campaign towards the self-fulfilling prophecy of sustained excellence. If it were a matter of just good pigeons it would be easy, since there are plenty.

The specialist then employs a practical, personal and efficient system, of which he is an integral part to achieve his objectives. He endures difficulty in the overall concept, and maintains mental discipline and focus over years or a lifetime in direct association with some aspects of the sport. The international winners are all people of applied intelligence and often advanced and esoteric knowledge.

Ask yourself the question - what do I need to know and do to be a purist, perfectionist and specialist? The central aspect and essence of this philosophical outlook could be self-satisfaction or contentment - whatever lights the flame of your mind. In conclusion, mind is the core of specialism in man and probably bird too.

March 2014

TIME IN THE BASKET

With natural pigeons primed for the distance, there is no need for concern. For NFC marking, my birds were contained in the house front room to be taken for marking next day. The essence is calm relaxation and energy conservation - I want my birds to doze off in the transporter, and not be agitated, fighting and engaging in other stressful behaviour. For Barcelona I boxed up for parcel delivery on Friday to be liberated in the Barcelona International one week later - no problem man. To learn relaxation, take a trip to Jamaica, where the locals make it an art form. Cool birds for marathon racing at all times - then the good ones will fly. The corollary is that the speedsters amongst us will want their projectiles of velocity on the transporter for as little time as possible. The whole philosophy of marathon birds is one of controlled calm, where great feats of speed/endurance are the recipe of greatness - when you can walk this rice paper without leaving a trace you will have learned.

March 2014

THE GENEROSITY OF FANCIERS

In the cynical and cold world of the competitive psyche are some lovely people noted for their simple generosity of spirit. Old Jackie Ross of Holtby said 'good pigeons are given Jim'. His warm sentiment echoes in my mind now. I do not take any money now for birds of my origin, although some are sold. I like the kind feeling generated by the exchange of friendship, do you not? Believe me the commercial waters are shark infested, and great whites too! I sold birds to China in the 80s, and now I face the reality that most birds bred from any source will never succeed as racers or breeders - despite the hype associated with fame. Marathon racing hardens and it is nice to share communion with likeable folk.

I enjoy the people I mentor, which adds an extra human dimension to my life. My writings over the years have been open as to how I created my overall system, which is in capable hands. Modern racing is dominated by specialists, and I like to see genuine generosity in donation of trophies and charity birds, even though it may be free advertising and self-satisfying. Despite my awareness of many negativities of the sport, my overall feeling and perception embraces optimism, and to fly Barcelona International into the UK, dreams maketh the man and results in good birds.

March 2014

WHY OPEN LOFT PERSISTS

The sport is flushed by modern regimes of applied widowhood/celibate/roundabout/darkness and lightness systems, yet the irony remains that most 7 to 800 mile UK Barcelona International birds will have been on types of the natural system, perhaps combined with some controlled separation of the sexes. If you can tolerate the activities of birds of prey with occasional kills, relative to your home area, natural birds may attain optimal race condition. With applied modern nutritional science and working on the total beings of the birds, ie a holistic approach, it is almost perfect preparation for marathon, speed-endurance races. Normally around 10 percent cover themselves with distinction from the Barcelona International, it being the ultimate contemporary test of a pigeon. Study the behaviour of wild doves and pigeons, feel your way around how they survive in the raw elements of nature, on the generations of survival of the species, then apply this lore to your racing management - it works!

March 2014

QUALITY IN A PIGEON

Now this is very simple. A quality bird will race and/or breed to your required standards of excellence. A relative concept to nail, yet if we are satisfied then the objective is realised. As with all aspects of the sport, the essence of it all is PSYCHOLOGICAL. Photos for pigeon marketing are often enhanced to appease the money god, ie for sales purposes. Lookers make a visual impact, and may handle like a dream. Many beautiful pigeons are useless for purpose, eg breeding/racing. A good looking quality bird is the ideal, yet perception tells us that many good birds are plain ugly to perceive with the senses. My Number 2 stock cock manifested recessive traits in the phenotype, yet his genes survive in 2014. We may ask why this should be. So simple: the performance potential and in interaction with the environment is determined by the genome of the bird, INVISIBLE determinants, which are invisible to the naked eye. From a scientific perspective I would favour a gene analysis of champion birds to increase our understanding of the secrets of a quality pigeon - thus all that glisters is not gold.

April 2014

THE COMPLETE FANCIER

There is no such entity, yet we have people who make a great impact on results, knowledge, the collective good and the history of the sport. The archetype will progress through the ranks to international levels of fame and achievement, create a family and act as a charismatic leader/mentor to others. All a matter of perception, his personality in the sport will act as a template or benchmark for others.

Although flying a little short for me, a man who approaches the ideal package is Geoff Cooper, and not just because of his international wins - it is about lore/original insights/knowledge that can be taught as a teacher of the many - good old socialist principles. A book by Cooper would be a lasting tribute to his quest and dedication to perfectionism.

April 2014

WHAT'S IN A WIND?

There is a certain preoccupation with high velocities and win, win, win and speed as arbiters of relevance and quality. I am a little different in my principles. When racing south I like variations of north/nor east and east winds as a test of my skill and intrinsic qualities of the birds' endurance/navigation and desire to home from great distances in velocities from 500 to 1100 ypm. I trust these bods for my family breeding purposes in the stock loft. For 500 miles I like 12 to 16 hrs on the day and 700 miles within 3 days and 879 miles within 4 days. Yes, I am biased to this concept, and for many the mantra is the faster the better - all part of the hardcore of the sport. We all decide on our preferences, yet look at the growth of the BICC as a club worthy of your participation - now huge.

April 2014

SINGLE BIRD NOMINATION FLYING

This is a specialist, demanding and very rewarding activity for the discerning fancier. The Single Bird Greater Distance Nomination Flying Club caters for participants in the main races of the leading race organisations, eg NFC, BBC and

BICC. For the person the foresight and skill is in the selection of an individual bird in advance, where you can be judged on this particular event. It certainly focuses your mind on one bird in an attempt to perfect the management preparation of one performance athlete. Once you are successful you can apply the lessons learned to all your other birds.

I am surprised that this peculiar skill is not practised more widely, as the reports would appeal to continental fliers. It really intensifies the harmony and unity between man and bird and must be good for the collective expertise of the fancy.

April 2014

LATE ARRIVALS

You will get them, and for my purposes they may turn out to be the best. They learn survival behaviour experience, and when reconditioned may bring glory to your loft. When a fit bird is fixated and develops a bearing on your loft it may evolve as a great racer of the future. The kind fancier allows for the recovery! To aid this physiological / psychological process I like peanuts / Hormoform in the mix and Vydex Supersix in the water. The electrolytic balance is restored, and with loft rest the wellbeing of the bird is worked on in a determined fashion. It may be months or years before the bird returns. Experience in nature is critical for marathon birds. A good fancier develops esoteric knowledge of his flock.

May 2014

WIN & WIN AGAIN PHILOSOPHY

All good competitors have a concept or perception in their mind's eye of winning. Small fish are sweet and new starters or initiates into the inner sanctum of the sport yearn for victory as an idea or to surpass their peers and rivals. This is positive psychology and may fire ambition up the sweet ladder of acclaim. After numerous first places, a grander picture and scale of achievement may emerge from the lofty realms of consciousness - how significant was the level of the winning in relation to the sport? If this notion is duly recognised a bigger picture illustrated by national/international racing may loom large - now it is time to aspire to greatness, to make a mark in the historical context of the Barcelona International which is haunted by the ghosts of the greats.

May 2014

FOOD MIXES & MEASURES

Winning from 71 to 879 miles, I have never weighed and measured food ingredients. The birds of all ages had the same food supply before them all day and the hoppers of pellets all night! The key is what total ingredients as solid and liquid nutrition that you use. My birds as individuals peck what they want and most will eat peanuts!

Gradually reducing plumpness by time on the wing I saturate the internals of the bird with fats/carbs and proteins from many ingredients. It works up to the top race – Barcelona International. The yeast is mixed in with the Hormoform/Breedrite and oils and stirred into the hard corn mixes. The essence is fuelling up for speed/endurance – like migratory birds. OK the sprint men use ratios and measures, yet fuelled up fit open loft birds distinguish themselves – hens and cocks. We mixed all the goodies in a tin with a stick – consumed with relish by all. With supplements by Chevita, Yydex and Rohnfried you will target condition.

May 2014

OBTAINING WELL-BRED BIRDS

Yer pays yer money and yer takes yer choice, yet there are many ways to obtain birds of good origin. I will spend money on what appears to be a specimen introduction, and have done so in the past. Now I have a UK/Irish network, where the founding principle is strain development and the exchange of pigeons at carriage cost. All the birds are long distance/marathon genes and with the proper techniques some will sprint too. We do not go to the vendors on the continent, although some of the birds have some Belgian and Dutch ancestry. The fact is that there are great birds/fanciers in the UK - why pay a fortune to line a dealer's pocket? Chris Booth of York is my key person in the supply network and does a great job. It is like an extended brotherhood of dedicated men, where the key is improvement up to Barcelona International level - we all get our kicks from it.

May 2014

PREDICTABILITY

Have you noticed how the same names, like Gilbert and Cooper, tend to be at or near the top of the results on a regular basis, with room, of course for new names to emerge from time to time? This is not down to just a few good birds, and we all breed plenty of inferior birds even from excellent genes and bloodlines. The corollary is that most of what we buy and sell will never make the grade. In reality we are looking at a minority of top fanciers and their birds. There is always an element of uncertainty in racing, since the birds on liberation are out of immediate control by man and in changing environmental conditions and variables. However skilled people can nominate their birds eg in the SBNFC with relative ease. I maintain that the quintessence of it all is the individual genius or personality of the fancier, as they source, breed and develop good birds for racing, and credit to them all. Recall the old adage of distant bygones: LOOK IN THE MIRROR.

May 2014

HOW DO YOU GAUGE SUCCESS?

If you feel successful, then you are. I will say from my biased perspective, that if you have realised your dreams and fulfilled your objectives then you may have a sense of success. At 65 I am still driven and preoccupied to improve my written material, our performances at Barcelona International, and my overall contribution to the sport. Motivated by life itself I still wish to improve, as I set myself near impossible targets of achievement. We are in a society fuelled by fame, money and power and the rise of the individual. To balance the psyche, although I intellectualise and analyse it, I feel an injection of spirituality is needed. It is nice to feel it, in human terms from time to time, as it flows from within. The success of others is evaluated in the media, as we project it on to others. To me if you have lived a full life, doing your best, then this philosophical view appeals to me. The corollary is that many of us make life too complex in the face of all the social pressures to conform.

May 2014

THE OBSESSION WITH CONTINENTAL NAMES

With the accent on sprint/middle distance racing and the number of wins philosophy, the culture of Belgian/German and Dutch names is a persistent craze which invades the psyches of many. Now the Belgians all fly too short for me, although some good birds are available throughout the world. The name can be an indicator of the success of the fancier, the key element being his mind/loft environment and system. Each bird is different, even from the same family, and most are lacking when tested. Fashions will come and go, along with the rise and demise of all the greats, who emerge as iconic/historical figures. In my early days I was hooked on the names of Stichelbaut and Denys, and based my old strain on these imports. It was marathon flying distances to my loft that has evolved them. Today, as an outbreed, the parents must be outstanding Barcelona International birds at over 700 miles, ideally into the UK. In this way I may source the complex genes that I seek. After that it is progeny testing and experimentation. It is wise to consider the options before you buy, yes!

June 2014

LONG-TERM PLANNING

Some folk live for today and in the moment as it were, which suits some personalities. I have always had goals and targets that are years in the making and come to fruition. My academic post school studies matured over 11 years - a great deal of time in educational establishments, with gallons of sweat from the brow. In my specialist marathon racing, I would predict and plan around individual pigeons for years. An example would be to earmark yearlings that have flown in races around 500 miles for later 700-800 mile racing. This type of philosophy takes huge focus and dedication, yet can be very rewarding in national and international racing up to Barcelona. The wisdom is to find out what your ambitions are and pursue them with a relish. A forward-looking fancier will foresee in his mind's eye the long term strategy and potential impact of his efforts. The famous and iconic people are there for a reason it would seem. Having said this, whatever ignites your flame.

June 2014

THE INDIVIDUAL PIGEON

The media and many people label pigeons in various categories eg sprinters, distance and by fanciers' names eg Vandenabeele. This is symptomatic of the popular culture and commercialism. In many cases it implies certain qualities and characteristic performance traits, and let me tell you it's a generalisation. Every pigeon and every person is an individual, and I try hard to treat them as such - even from brother x sister matings. My strain has been family bred for 38 years, and I expect every single bird to perform at differing levels of capability and different distances, with sometimes some similarities. We race ours through to Barcelona International at 710 measured miles, and on the way sprinters/middle distance/distance and marathon birds emerge from the same family. A bird like Musgrove Addiction did the lot, as did Obsession... on one system into Taunton. Think about it.

June 2014

THE PURSUIT OF PERFECTION

A goal towards achieving this would be to win the Barcelona International race. This is a lofty aspiration indeed, and is possible into the UK. The significance would be substantial - potential material wealth and huge fame, and a real injection of enthusiasm into the world of pigeon racing. I dream on, yet the concept of it motivates some fanciers. The way to improve is copious quantities of self-criticism - a shortage exists in the minds of the many - and it is sorely needed. Examine your systems, methods and objectives and mindset, and aim for radical improvements. This applies to the quality of your birds too, and the overall impact over years may be dramatic, as measured by results and satisfaction levels. Instead of blaming the bird, the weather and the race controller take a look in the mirror of truth - a good hard look. This approach does not suit all, with the emphasis on the blame game - it depends on your degree of introspection perhaps. Yes, success is measured by subtlety and overall approach. Personally I constantly seek for improvements overall.

June 2014

SPOTTING A FORM BIRD

This is relatively easy to do if you have the brain for it - your brain is the nucleus of all you do! On a sensory level it boils down to perceptual and intense study of each individual bird. Outwardly look for obvious changes in behavioural dominance of cocks that sparkle and shine with fired up eyes - they glow with vitality and health, and so should you when you see them. It is a two-way process then, and a form bird will give you a buzz!

I like quality hens that sleep in the basket. On externals, balance your decision on the previous results of the candidates - single bird nomination will test your mental powers and clever management of your birds. The process then is a challenge to your sensitivity and gifts as a human. The key is to sensitise your brain in relation to conditioning of quality birds. I relax now and let my racing partner do it. For Barcelona International we have three particular birds in mind - all will be revealed.

June 2014

THE SELFISH FANCIER

In eight solid years of writing on the world of pigeon racing, I have been open and revealed all to the fancy at large, although I see myself as a poet/philosopher! In my youth I was as selfish as it needed to be to realise my objectives in breeding, racing and selling. After a good run, and with age I contemplated the fact that the sport was a greater concept than mere dominance in racing. There is the human and personality side to it, the promotion work and the teaching and intellectual sphere. Writers contribute to the creative and imaginative side of literature. The selfish man keeps his secrets and knowledge of, say, feeding and supplementation to himself, like guarding the Holy Grail or the elixir of life. Beware of shallow little reports in the media and filter what you are told, it may be laced with bovine faeces! I believe only what I prove to myself! Although like a moral imperative I act as a mentor to some friends in the fancy and it fuels me with pleasure - a little compassion goes a long way. It pays to pick your people in life that have a positive feel about them.

June 2014

WHY DO WE SOMETIMES FAIL?

This is a very difficult area to analyse as it implies many negatives. Initially the loft and surroundings must be conducive to healthy and contented birds - I prefer the country for all round racing from sprint to marathon level. If you are a city loft you may have problems with controlled exercise periods. I do not favour shut up birds in stuffy lofts to enable me to go as far as Barcelona International. I feel most city lofts will be adequate up to 500-mile club and fed type racing, and there are some good ones, yet many fail in national and international racing. Cats, neighbours and difficulty with free ranging may induce problems.

On a psychological note a real lack of dedication/focus/persistence and other personality traits may seriously handicap the fancier, particularly regarding ambition/desire and work ethic. Fanciers in clubs compete ego to ego for status and supremacy, mainly male behaviours and mental processes which are fiercely contested on housing estates etc. In relation to the quality of the birds, good birds abound in most families of birds and some people fail to condition them optimally, or do not enter the races where results speak volumes.

On a positive note, if we give intense study to gradual and consistent improvement then if we are right, in an effective system we will do so. I started racing in 1976 and am still trying to improve our Barcelona performances, motivated by love and obsession to strain perfection.

June 2014

COUNTDOWN TO GLORY

The greatest pigeon racing odyssey and spectacle supreme

is poised to deliver its radiant magic. It will enthral us, entertain us, test us and near break us. I speak of the unsurpassed greatest race on planet earth, the wonderful, the frighteningly beautiful **BARCELONA INTERNATIONAL**. Little men will be poised in silent, intense and moving anticipation of a possible arrival from this epic peregrination on wings. It is the encapsulation of the wildest dream suffused by raw and sometimes painful reality. Are you the one to join the majestic icons of human history? A race for mere mortals, it transcends the sport, raising it to the lofty pinnacle of excellence. Cherish the moment, feel it and nurture it as you would no other.

July 2014

THE WEEKEND OF TRUTH

Nic Harvey and I have emptied the loft, with all the 15 yearlings at Tarbes NFC, and the six old birds at Barcelona International. We fly into Taunton, where the birds often have greater than the measured distance to fly of 710 miles due to the prevailing south-west and west winds bringing the birds into England in central and eastern England perhaps - a tracking device may reveal the truth, which I would welcome.

My basic philosophy is to ignore theorising and speculation and await the arrival or non-arrival of the birds to the loft. We send with confidence, belief and expectation born of experience and maturation. It is a practice that has reaped rich dividends, and is not the philosophy of chickens. We aim to prove our breeding and husbandry in the two blue riband races, where the race point and conditions are the final arbiter - the acid test of realism. Of course we fly our birds on the wings of ambition and propelled by dreams. We are both purist, romantic idealists in pursuit of another champion like Musgrove Addiction.

I hope my words inspire more dedicated souls to take a giant leap of faith into the unknown, to return full of satisfaction.

July 2014

SPORTSMANSHIP AND GIVING CREDIT

In the last analysis it is how you feel about yourself and your results that counts. There will be some genuine and not so genuine praise and credit afforded at this year's Barcelona and Tarbes races. It's simple to me - all the birds clocked will have some intrinsic quality in both races irrespective of the wind, location and overall race conditions. Decisions are biased, relative and products of the ego of the judge. Some folk motivated by jealousy and negative emotions will always criticise others in an extra punitive way. A little self-analysis may enlighten the individual to their own inadequacies, Grasshopper! Rest assured, I am guilty of all these failings - I must aim for a more balanced perspective on life. Credit given freely and in a pure spirit of intention may help oil the wheels of society, and may lessen the impact of cold, jaded cynicism. Excuse my moralising, yet unhappiness is the malaise of competition - a 'well done' will suffice. Amen.

July 2014

SOME OF OUR BEST 700 MILERS

A marathon distance is fairly difficult to nail in racing. It normally takes a specialist with advanced skill and knowledge and a few quality speed/endurance birds. In my mind's eye I favour the 757 miles birds into the west, ie Wales of the Padfields at the potentially most difficult Barcelona International - try it and see for yourself the arduous mind-bending difficulty. The NFC would tend to increase its power and testing power if it went 700 mile International.

Having said this, Neil Bush has open results in every Grand National from 1982 to 2014 and is a largely unpublicised supreme master of his monasterial pursuit of perfection with the Neil Bush strain. Check out the evolution and history of this singular man who does not pursue ego-led publicity - what do you think?

Denney has grown into a fancier with a great modern record at Tarbes culminating in Northern Lady, 3rd open - a shrewd and charming man! From my personal experience of Barcelona, Pau, Tarbes and San Sebastian, all at marathon distances, I favour the Barce performances of the Padfields and have some children of Invincible as an outcross with our marathon pigeons, along with five from Bert Shepherd who is a little-explored distance king.

July 2014

YOU CAN BUY THE MAN'S BIRDS BUT NOT THE MAN

This concept, in particular, applies to the longer and marathon distances. With clever reporting and sales publicity of a man's results his birds may become in short supply and in great demand. A fancier may accumulate wealth in the process, if this is what he covets.

Having played around with different intros since 1976, I find very few top birds in any family, using children of champions. The key is to create an overall management system strategy that produces some good birds for you in race reality. Having said this, top producer birds may be good for you and be key breeders of performance capability and the genes are never homozygous or totally pure, yet I like my nice inbred based strain that I have put 38 years' work into, in an attempt to produce some good ones.

Have you noticed that the race time returns from Barcelona International do not usually go much above 10 percent? The chief reason why a man becomes a champion lies in his brain for the successful management overall system that he adopts is peculiar to him - old Eric Gibson said that all pigeons were mongrels and by Jove he was bang on! I would advise that you learn all that you can from the champion flyer - what makes him tick? How does he do it? My friends and I supply pigeons for nowt or a small token amount in the interests of the sport and friendship, and to perpetuate the strain, which is the main objective. Have a think.

July 2014

DO STRAGGLERS BECOME GOOD PIGEONS?

I love birds which in their early career have long periods away from the loft and out of race time. If of the right inner potential, they may gain a great deal of survival and navigational skills via being in alien lands, in parks, cities, fields and lofts and tested to the inner core of being of existence, of life itself - sounds like my youth!!

Most of my top birds which are the ancestors of my strain today were part time strags, eg Barcelona Dream, Mystical Queen, Oddball, Dark Velvet, Dax My Girl etc. Given nurture these all became key birds in my ambitions as a marathon man. Some birds always came in good time eg Dark Enchantment, Dot's Delight, Diabolos, Dark

Expected, Dorothy's Courage, Delta Lady, Dedication, Sister Damien and The Dutchman. All these birds were of one family from my foundation birds, and 38 years later I am using them at Barcelona International with all the lines represented in the strain formation.

The moral of the anecdote is value your birds, dig in with a vengeance and persevere against all odds. It is a truism that hardship maketh the man and his birds.

July 2014

YOUNG BIRD SICKNESS

Many talk of young bird sickness, but in reality it is a vague term and a bit of a myth. Young pigeons may be prone to or succumb to a number of pests and diseases. After an infection by virus/bacteria combinant, eg adeno type 11, circo, or herpes, with E. coli or salmonella, the immune system may collapse and the pathogens may overwhelm the bird and kill it. Stress at home due to overcrowding and excessive heat and humidity, and too much basket training and tossing to try and induce speed, may reduce base condition and precipitate invasion by the alien organisms. The usual outcome is that the illness runs its course, often with a percentage of mortality.

I advise as much open fresh air as possible and administer Vydex Supersix in the water as a solution to improve resistance responses. Baytril may have a positive impact on some of the invasive bacteria. Fresh air, rest and cull the terminally-ill birds is a wise practice, and aim to induce appetite with tit bits. An anxious time that should be faced and it will harden you eventually. A tough old game, pigeon racing.

July 2014

ARE MARATHON MEN BARKING?

Barking, a popular word these days, has caught on to mean quirky or of an oddball nature, and is socially encouraged and acceptable in certain levels of society. I am noted for my eccentricity, and it helps with the Barcelona dream. I have some nice dedicated marathon friends, rugged individualists and a fascinating collection of nutters - I must be a magnet to them. The crux of the matter is the focus on, build up to and wait for the arrival of the 1 in 10 from Barcelona. Hyped up, losing sleep and buzzing for days, racked by stress induced hormones eg cortisol, you may well crash with exhaustion - be careful of burnout. I endured it as a country boy who sought gold in London. Watch for the joys of a breakdown! All my pals who I associate with in marathon internationals are both fascinating for their character traits, some a psychiatrist's dream and fall nicely under the general umbrella of barking - absolutely an essential requirement for the job.

July 2014

POLISH & OTHER PIGEONS

Birds with the right fancier will do some wonderful things. I note the modern influx into the studs of Dutch Barcelona birds, for the commercial dissemination of the offspring for keen enthusiasts who want a taste of big time racing. International racing, based and organised from Belgium, is de rigueur for us in the UK and Ireland. You can certainly form a strain on some of these imports if you do it right! The House of Aarden is dedicated to quality of origins in its selections for breeding purposes.

We need to step outside the conventional countries of

origin, and import some of the Polish Barcelona International birds which fly mammoth distances and in great numbers between 900 and 1000 miles, which is a rugged, sporting religion to the tough guys of Poland. Let's see a stud establish these birds for sale to develop the pioneering work of the Poles. Other potential countries of source are Russia, Denmark, Sweden and New Zealand. At the setting of the sun the fancier makes the pigeon and there are some top men in Poland.

July 2014

THE BLAME GAME

When things are not right in our society, many people will defend their position by casting the onus of responsibility onto any person or entity outside of themselves: the weather, the birds, the convoyer, anything but themselves. You are responsible for the quality of your birds, the system and the choice of loft location. The old distance boys said look in the mirror - the glass of truth. Yes, if you want to improve a little introspection goes a long way. Nick and I now have five Tarbes yearlings and three Barcelona arrivals – I maintain the faith that more will return. We do not set out to denigrate or negate anything connected with the racing, it is as it is - my philosophical approach, and I am being critical of certain people in an abstract manner.

July 2014

THE OBSESSION WITH SPEED

I can tell by the patter of a pigeon man if he is sprint or distance orientated - in very little time. The true marathon man tends to be a little relaxed and laid back in presentation of his psyche. The sprint men tend to be of competitive, rapid responses echoing the widowhood cocks they may race, and most fanciers like a quick fix on a race up to say 300 miles. This tends to be a metaphor of the instant gratification aspects of society - computers/texting/games etc – it's like we are all hyped up on stress and amphetamines! I prefer the Jamaican style of cool, and some of the spirituality of the Nepalese who I met on my exotic sojourns.

When I was young win win-win was all, with high velocities and competition with the key fanciers of the day - with sayings like 'they beat me back', and 'I had the first four'. The cock crowed in those days and the ego played the solitary trumpet. Now with the wisdom of age, I like endurance events with a sprinkling of speed epitomised by the Barcelona international, although our yearling at Tarbes in D and G sections did us proud with reference to its breeding. In my mind's eye the perfection of the origin ie breeding is always first on the agenda of significance. It's up to you and my ideas are purely subjective.

July 2014

REACTING TO DIFFICULT RACES

I take it on the chin, and aim to improve my own system and attitudes towards the race conditions. With due respect we can but guess at the actual conditions faced over the total race distance by the birds - we are not the birds and do not necessarily know. I hate the idea of automatic blame of the externals ie the birds/holdover/transporter/convoyer/race point etc. I have had some humdingers in my time, and they are what they are in race reality. Why get extra punitive and blame everyone else? Future races will entail some difficulty and that is the essence of the sport. Having said this, sometimes there are human errors in forecasting or liberations, all down to pressure/responsibility and judgement. We now have seven yearlings from Tarbes NFC 2014 and that will do for us.

July 2014

TIMES HAVE CHANGED

In the 60s hoppers of tic beans were the diet, and birds bathed in water suffused by potassium permanganate crystals. Old George stood, corn tin in hand in the garden by the old bow top loft, in poignant anticipation of the old red cock. He told excited tales in sweet nostalgia of past victories - the only bird on the day in the 500-mile syndrome. He was a respected and revered old character. The 20 YBs were raced through the moult in the club programme to 200 miles. He would spend his pool money on a round of drinks, in an atmosphere of colourful stories and tall tales. The pigeon sub-culture thrived in the local community. Now the superdominant, wealthy big hitters are launched into international celebrity status. At the core of modern competition can be the ugly mask of commercialism - the money god. Personally, based on the fact that a good one is blessed by innate abilities I am happy to toss YBs at 60 miles, then let them grow and mature. With rampant outbreeding, inbred strain development is a rarity and the ancient lore of family breeding is in retreat. I enjoy an expansive view of the sport and keep my ideals alive with a nice little network of characters who I value as greatly as the finest of birds. More and more folk are enjoying true international sport, yet the archetype survives - the little character in his rose clad garden, pipe in hand.

August 2014

LATE-BREDS FOR STOCK

My policy is to take YBs direct from the best performance birds of each year. My no 1 and 2 stock cocks were siblings hatched in September. Late-breds will be bred July onwards in the UK. These need rearing to perfection as they are the future of your family. All mine are genetically related and will be paired together the following spring to try and create that elusive champion. It does not matter if they retain some feathers in the moult - it is their inner potential that is significant. I like a nice looker, yet ancestry is all in the racing game. Breed your own then you know some of it. The YBs need plenty of exercise, baths and no training - stock them. After a while you will have the nucleus of your own strain, and that is the final frontier of a fancier.

August 2014

WAYS TO IMPROVE THE SPORT

If each person did one positive thing directed at improving the sport, then changes would be radical. Negative emotions and jealousy towards others are endemic - we need to look in the mirror over this. The resurrection of some nice sporting values would be effective - the shake of the hand, the well done, the round of drinks - even if they are not genuine, the ritual is significant. Help a network of novices with free advice and birds - I have a network of mad mates who exchange birds for fun. If you make a few quid, donate a trophy to a racing organisation that you favour. The base line is to send your birds as far as you can - be ambitious, since you can be famous with 1 really good result. You may wish to write articles or a book for international circulation. Finally take a look at the wider implications of the sport and be less aggressively political. The final wise note is to enjoy it as hard racing is punishing to man, beast and soul

August 2014

THERE'S NO FAST TRACK TO THE TOP

In a world hell bent on instant gratification, many seek instant success. I started with pigeons 62 years ago and now feel accomplished in my efforts with them. It has been a tour de force of prolonged dedication, with a great deal of research and study, and when hard information was scarce or did not exist. It pays to start with local clubs and earn your stripes through hardship. With the right personality you will do well and develop some expertise and acclaim in the cauldron of fame. The game is psychological and decision based - the good fliers make some right choices of system and original stock. Help from a mentor may reduce your learning time by years, and a great deal of knowledge is in the right books and the media - how you apply the wisdom will determine your future.

August 2014

MODERN TRENDS IN PIGEON RACING

The sport and hobby are in a state of flux. A huge rise in the popularity of the BICC is evident with a firm accentuation of international racing. The Barcelona International, as the premier race in the UK and Ireland, is gathering more momentum, due to its lofty prestige and inherent difficulty. The icons of racing in the UK are becoming international stars via publicity in their own field. Money in the mainstream culture is at the core of many people's ambitions and modus operandi. The consequence is that the archetype of racing, the little man with garden loft and corn tin, is an endangered species. I want to see a return of a love for the birds, a true understanding of our joint connections and part of nature, both philosophically and as an insight into marathon preparation and conditioning.

The whole question of doping and performance enhancement is complex, dynamic and ever expanding and changing with no obvious and clear total knowledge, understanding and direction. It will have a global impact and there will be changes to controls and directives by the rule-making organisations. Supplements are endemic in the sport, yet which are truly tested and safe in today's competition? Specialist fliers with slick professional outfits are dominating the sporting arena.

The purists with generous and sporting values with the accent on strain building still have a role to perform, and it is nice to witness a revival of international aspirations into Ireland exemplified by Michael Feeney and friends. We will be on the threshold of many more changes as the sport in its rich diversity evolves.

September 2014

NEGATIVE ASPECTS OF THE SPORT

My comments are subjective and may or may not be shared by others. Rampant commercialism is detracting from the sporting essence of pigeon racing, and every conceivable device is used to accumulate money - I say this with some sales experience myself. Some aspects of the hobby are a little too high-powered and aggressively competitive, inducing resentment, negative criticism and jealousy. The competitive nature is highly personalised, and I would like to see a return to the honour and desire to conquer the longest race points in a conceptual, idealistic and romantic way. The pursuit of multiple sprint and middle-distance wins is not necessarily conducive to finding individual birds of sustained long distance and speed/endurance capabilities. The archetype of the good-natured character with generous sporting motives is being eroded - he has been the standard bearer in the evolution of the sport. There is the race-to-win ethos, and the irony is that the Barcelona International has yet to be won in the UK, for many and obvious reasons. In a small way my little network of like-minded marathonists aims to exchange quality bred birds in the spirit of mutual sporting objectives. I think a little introspection is timely in today's hot competition.

September 2014

DO BIRDS OF GOOD BREEDING ENSURE SUCCESS?

It is very simple – well-bred birds sent to races in poor condition will almost never be champions. Good genes are freely available, yet elite fanciers by definition are rare. The key to success at all levels is sustained good or optimal management. The top fanciers manage to get the best out of birds of mixed and many origins - not just expensive strain names. It is a truism that all racers are of mixed origins and genomes, and each one is an individual. A great racer in terms of results is well bred, and so are the breeders. Expensive birds or ones given generously are proven by testing in breeding and racing.

A good method and system in your individual style is the acid test of reality. Dreams make men, and empirical reality is the realisation of them. You will find that certain particular good birds will respond better than others to your way of racing, and these should be bred from for testing in the future. I am trying to cut to the quick of practical racing, and continuous racing sustained over many years will produce the type that you require, and then, a priori, they will be of good breeding. Many good men exchange birds from the good ones, a virtue which is the quintessence of sportsmanship.

September 2014

THE MAIN MOULT

Ecdysis is a natural process in healthy pigeons. Some feathers may fall at intervals through the year. The main moulting period is stressful to a racing pigeon and it requires support. In September and October in the UK, birds - often late-breds - may succumb to invasive diseases, since the immune system is threatened and compromised. I advocate baths with salts to ease the situation, and highly nutritious foods rich in fats and proteins to around 16 percent protein level. Make the diet varied and composite and use supplements like Hormoform and extra G10 pellets.

It is an art/science fusion, with no definitive or exact formula for success, as birds may thrive on various diets. Extra vitamins/probiotics and amino acids like methionine will help optimise the feeding regime. To raise natural immunity levels in the flock, reduce environmental stress, and allow free exercise in the big outdoors to echo the superb condition attained by wild doves and pigeons. An experienced distance pigeon may shed its end flights in the

January of the following year. By November the birds should pulse and shine with energy and vitality. Any late breeding will delay the moult - we always take late-breds from the key racers. A perfect moult may be conducive to good results in the following season. On a psychological note I like quiet, contented rest for the birds in harmonious surroundings.

September 2014

SIZE OF THE TEAM

One real quality racer can make the season. As many as possible is the way forward to compete in multiple national and international races. Bird numbers in the loft tend to decline with the severity of the races and distance. On my open loft system I could muster between 20 to 30 old birds at the start of the season and 60 plus young birds to have a go at. The big lofts do not always prevail, yet big teams of quality birds are competitive, when prepared properly. The little man with the good small team, eg under 20, often commands respect. Many fanciers like to overwinter relatively large teams eg 40 plus birds. The acid test in race reality is the speed/endurance and navigational abilities of each individual bird.

Most fanciers produce a paucity of champions in their racing career - you will know them when and if they appear. The ones you recall become old favourites and it is nice to reflect on the few with due sentiment and nostalgia. In practice the team size tends to match your ambitions/space and affordability.

September 2014

SIMPLE TRUTHS OF PIGEON RACING

There are some plain facts which the discerning fancier will spot. First, sound physical appearance alone does not a champion make, since the genes and inner constitution must be of exceptional quality. The eye, other than an indicator of near ancestry, health and vigour is not an automatic organ of race-winning prediction, although we might think so. Race wins are the product of good management under the total prevailing conditions.

Inbred birds up to brother x sister levels may or may not be good breeders or racers. A good bird can be any colour, even though I like a dark chequer. Late returnees in short races, ie up to 250 miles, may be the distance/marathon birds of the future. Good birds at any distance may arise from racers of any human name origin, as they are mixtures anyway - heterozygous origins.

Birds will thrive on many individual systems and diets. Some of the UK birds are as talented as any. Bird losses tend to increase along with the distance of the race point. A breeding bird may produce a good bird as long as it is fertile. Seemingly optimal to good weather forecasts do not necessarily indicate maximum returns. All my points are mere generalisations as general tendencies from experience and not intended as dogma set in stone.

September 2014

INTERNATIONAL RACING INTO CORNWALL

We are on the cusp of this possibility, due to the sterling efforts of the BICC, The House of Aarden and other luminaries. The potential is large for some dedicated enthusiasts to rise to the occasion. It will need a great deal of planned logistics to secure the facility initially. To ensure the future of this novel and brave idea a change in racing philosophy at grass roots level is crucial, with methods adapted to clocking birds in west and south-west winds from long distance French and Spanish racepoints. I hope it materialises and new champion birds and fanciers evolve to take their place in the public eye. Will it happen? Who will they be? What recent origin of birds will they be? I feel that a great deal of practical effort can meet the needs of this objective, and like the moves in Ireland it will excite the fancy if realised. I see that the sport needs creative ideas and innovation to propel it into the future.

September 2014

SOME TIPS

If you obtain birds from a top man, try to adapt and adopt his system and methods in detail as these are keys to his success. Decide on your chosen race distances and then specialise. Keep away from the club power game unless you need to be a politician. For marathon races fly open loft if you can. Be single-minded and set your targets high. Be prepared to come last and lose your favourite birds. The late comers may be your winners of the future. If gregarious you should volunteer for a club position. Make a few quid, yet 'good pigeons are given' is a good maxim to live by. Learn from the experts, the net and books until you are comfortable with knowledge. Progeny test and race every bird in the loft to demonstrate their intrinsic value. Keep producer birds together and close breed to relatives to form a family. Try not to be overawed by the top fliers, as you may be one yourself. Form a long-term plan for the future, and learn and learn.

October 2014

LEADERS & FOLLOWERS

In a flock of pigeons, individuals with stamina and keen navigational abilities may take the lead in flight. There is a subtle and dynamic connection between the members of the group which we only guess at from a human perspective, yet it exists. We are deluded and arrogant if we pretend to understand it. Perhaps in long marathon races it is these leader pigeons which persist and make the arduous journey home. I suspect that genes are fundamental to leadership. Similarly people with recognised leadership qualities are on the edge in all walks of life, as a result of personal qualities. The irony is that leaders and followers are interconnected and mutually dependent for the roles they perform. Your outstanding and consistent racers are likely to be leaders. We could do with an ethologist to study a racing flock of pigeons all fitted with tracking devices to monitor them.

October 2014

A GRADUAL BUILD UP TO NEXT YEAR'S MARATHONS

The work is in progress, and hens and cocks are out on alternate days, to arouse and stimulate themselves in harmony with and as a response to the natural elements - the rain/mist/sun and all that the earth gives. After the main moult the toughness and immune systems will be at a premium. The diet is all they can eat to appetite of a nutritious moulting mix and supplements that we formulate, for bodily growth of tissue and feather, and to supply all the physiological needs of a non-racing pigeon, eg pellets/Hormoform/a protein mix/oils/Matrix etc. The view is long term and focused ahead to produce targeted race condition for the following year. Psychologically it requires mental discipline and a long fuse. The modus operandi is long-term gratification and gradual improvement within the limits of our capabilities. The final goal is the evolution of a hardy and reliable family of marathon birds, some of which have speed/endurance capability.

October 2014

MODERN CONVENTIONS IN PIGEON RACING

The main thrust is still sprint to middle distances up to 500 miles on the day of toss, and many are hooked on this. We have some great exponents of the practice in the UK and Ireland with quality birds, yet many are drawn to Belgium, Holland and Germany, where it is conventional to spend money on the purchase of pigeons, when race reality dictates that very few birds really make the grade - they have a Ferrari-like desirability. It remains a fact that there are some clever racing men on the continent with specialist systems and a professional approach to the game. If I need any intros - a rare practice - my convention is to find them in the UK. The corollary is that for distance aspirations, Barcelona-bred birds from the studs are becoming the norm, along with the BICC, which is seen as the premier club of choice by many - it used to be an unconventional minority group.

Times change, and where widowhood/roundabout systems, personal to the individual, are conventional, some traditionalists are modernising open loft systems with up to date supplements and nutrition, where bird of prey predation can be dealt with and tolerated. Things will change and evolve now that we have collective high expectations in international events, yet Barcelona International remains the yardstick and measure of marathon prowess and maintains its conventional appeal to the pioneers of speed/endurance pigeon racing.

October 2014

ALL YEAR ROUND CONDITION

The year can be seen as a series of seasons and significant periods in the lives of fanciers and their racing pigeons. We have winter/breeding/racing and moulting times, which are in a sense outstanding and important periods to us. In my mind's eye, the year flows into one interesting whole, as a pigeon will have a different series of responses to chronological time. On this premise I like our birds to be in good physiological and psychological condition every day of the year, and we aim to meet their needs on a security/comfort/nutrition and instinctual level - we try to empathise with the birds on a deep level of understanding. With the goal being selection via marathon events, I like a year-long build up in condition, aimed at peaking it for the one big race in July. The thought pattern is long fuse, long term, specialist, and gratification is enduring. Birds in the wild will lose their lives to predators/the gun and the natural elements if not in condition - our aim is to replicate nature in a domestic loft environment. The skill of the fancier manifests itself with the almost perfect conditioning of the bird for the selected race, and I feel our unorthodox approach aids our success.

October 2014

SEASONAL POLITICS IN THE SPORT

With the climax of the competitive racing season, there is a power shift, which is expressed in rules, procedures and committees. These are hierarchical where personalities and egos prevail - fascinating from a psychological perspective! Personally I like the truth to prevail and some ordered objectivity, and it is not always possible to get what you want, and that is why I no longer belong to any parties or ideological groups, although I am recorded as an advisor to British MENSA on various subjects. Pigeon organisations like the BICC are fine where the main thrust is the provision of a fantastic international race programme. I try and keep geared towards the actual racing which is at the heart of the sport as a purist approach rather than any negative personal aspects which may cloud that objective, although the whole sport is personality based. Sound politics are fine, providing that the effects result in the positive impact on the actual essence of the sport, which are improvements in racing standards. I take a rather idealistic and purist stance on this factor - I go to bed with Johnny Walker and wake up with Will Power!

October 2014

THE PALAMOS/BARCELONA INTERNATIONAL DEBATE ROARS ON

Both points are immersed in tradition, history and prejudice. Palamos as a domestic race by the BBC liberates a relatively small contingent from the Spanish point and is difficult for the birds into the UK, yet an 800-mile plus bird was recorded on the second day by Mr Wales of Malton, Yorkshire. The Barcelona International race is a global spectacle in pigeon racing, with glamour, prestige and lots of kudos and money involved. UK studs are clamouring for the bloodlines of the key birds in the race and their sales and marketing is a modern craze. From my own perspective I feel the Barcelona performance of Marco Wilson was the highlight of English racing in 2014 - you can read his interview on the Elimar website. As a matter of belief/desire and choice we enter the Barcelona International, and look forward in this race to a UK fancier making history by recording an International bird at 800 miles on the second day. It should be noted that 800-plus mile birds out of the Barcelona International have been clocked on the second day into Holland and an analysis of this would be interesting. I feel that an expansion of this debate on Elimar would be a revealing stimulus to the fancy - please forward your ideas to Elimar.

October 2014

A HUMANITARIAN APPROACH TO THE SPORT

In my view, the people, the personalities and human values that pervade the sport are at the centre of it all. We race for personal satisfaction, attainment and achievement. At the heart of all the good birds and race results are the individual folk who make it happen - no man, no birds in lofts, simple. It's a fact that livings are made, fortunes spent and reputations cemented through the medium of the humble pigeon. The corollary is that when politics rule and the ruthless vote is cast, we should consider the personal impact on others - will it have a positive effect? My approach is both a little soft and a tad moral, yet is touched by some compassion, and is a reaction to arch materialism. I am sure it is wise to enjoy as many aspects of the sport as possible, and the exchange of well-bred birds at carriage costs, amongst associates is nice, with an aim to improve the birds. Naturally, hardcore pigeon men are not saints, yet a little spirituality goes a long way.

October 2014

CORNWALL RACING IN THE BICC

There is a will for actual birds to be sent from Cornwall in some BICC races. Interested people need to take practical steps to realise this, for example by forming a specialist club to compete if membership of individuals is accepted by the BICC, or a suitably-worded proposition for the AGM for the membership to vote on the initiation of a Cornish section. Over 40 people have demonstrated their interest in joining the expansion of the BICC. I am keen to promote the availability of further distance racing for Cornwall and have donated a trophy for the highest velocity into Cornwall from BICC Barcelona International on a perpetual basis. It is a lovely piece and will take an awful lot of winning. Why not be a modern pioneer of marathon excellence and go for it?

The BICC is in growth mode, and some top-class birds are the result of the national/international programme of races. The essence is to provide via effective organisation and leadership the facilities and means to have a go. With generosity and good will all round, any basic problems can be resolved - an open, responsive and broadminded, personal approach is key to the future success of this exciting venture.

October 2014

LESSONS LEARNED

Our sport is a continuous learning experience from start to finish. It is a heady encapsulation of nature/art/science and humanity under the competitive umbrella of sport. To produce a versatile performance strain of racers is a lifetime's dedication, with an obsessive desire for perfection. The humble pigeon teaches you about life and death in the face of raw nature, and attempts to manage and control it. A racer in prime form is a life form of great beauty and gratifying to the eye, especially for nature-starved urban children, as an educational tool. You will become aware of human emotions expressed in the form of politics and perhaps some jealousy, since the essence is the hierarchical organisation of competitive events. Reaping what you sow it may be life enhancing, or a difficult journey to the winner's enclosure - have a go, see how far you can make them fly.

October 2014

GOOD LOOKING & HANDLING PIGEONS

The perception of a good pigeon in the hand is individual and subjective to the fancier. You may be right or wrong as to whether it is a good racer or breeder. In my personal judgement a silky-feathered small to medium balanced bird with a shiny eye and well developed muscles inspires confidence, yet the reality is that it may be poor as a breeder/racer. The old cliché 'beauty is in the eye of the beholder' may apply. Often in a family of good lookers there may be some decent racers. The simple reality is that good racers do just that and the same with breeders.

On a mental note they often appear to be the right type when they do so, and I have seen good ones that were great and small, and variable types in the hand. Is it not so easy to be impressed by good looks that look nice to the human eye, when it is the inner invisible qualities that really count, especially the genes? The discerning fancier tests all the racers and breeders to establish the TRUTH. I call it race reality.

November 2014

VISIONARY STRAIN MAKERS

There are men who become famous for their singular dedication to the perpetuation and perfection of a recognisable strain of pigeons. With a narrow focus and pedantic attention to detail, they lovingly line and inbreed to key birds, with an intense eye on progeny testing, performance and dissemination of the strain to others. Material gain and commercial profit are often subordinated to the overall mental concept of the evolution of a line of birds with distinct hereditary characteristics. In my mind's eye they demonstrate an idealist and purist approach and with esoteric knowledge of the strain. A huge store and reservoir of personal knowledge is gone when these great men expire, to be but icons and memories in the fading mists of time. Most of these men are intelligent people, unique and possibly intellectual in a pedantic way. Two of these exemplars who have kept the Alois Stichelbaut strain alive into 2014 from 1946 are Michel Descamps Van Hasten from Belgium and Gerhard Schlepphorst from Germany.

November 2014

THE FAR-SIGHTED FANCIER

These are people who look to the future with a discerning eye. Plans are made to peak the performance of individual birds in specialist races, and they set achievement goals for themselves. There may be family creation objectives and some have commercial and fame interests. Why follow sales trends and fashions in pigeons when you may have good birds at home? Success in the sport is deemed to be a long term objective, rather than a short term, quick result recipe, and may develop over a lifetime. This type of person will see the innovative and creative ways forward that individuals show, eg the Irish and possible Scottish attempts in BICC races - although on the edge of difficulty, such feats are possible. Some folk encourage and gather others around them with shared interests and attempts to break boundaries. A few of these visionaries emerge in a generation to change the popular face of the popular sporting culture.

November 2014

IRIS COLOUR

Each eye of every pigeon is unique in itself. Certain colours may prevail eg in related, family birds such as red, brown, orange or bluish. I can see the possibility of a genetic link with performance factors in family birds, yet I have no evidence for this. Perhaps repeated, large scale experiments may or may not confirm this hypothesis. Across the pigeon population able racers and breeders can be found in many iris colour types, due in part to the genetic diversity of the ancestors. In my own birds I did like to see pretty, brightly-coloured eyes, in particular reds and oranges - an aesthetic preference. Many fanciers like a contrasting eye colour in the parents, and frown upon similar eye colours together, yet the main consequence of the eye is vision, and I would favour pure performance criteria for selection eg of the immediate parents and beyond. I would never use a bright pretty eye as the sole selection criterion.

November 2014

A QUESTION OF TEMPERAMENT

Good looks are nice to behold in man and pigeon - glossy,

shiny specimen birds. In my experience the personality or temperament, if you can read it, is crucial. Marathon birds and fanciers tend to be quieter, conserve energy, are more laid back, patient and outwardly tolerant of stress. Sprint birds and fanciers are often overtly excitable, fiery, impulsive and energetic and do not like extended periods of prolonged stress. A Barcelona bird may endure days of endurance flying and a sprinter perhaps two hours on the wing. These are generalisations, since each bird and fancier is a unique individual. Logically a quiet bird is not necessarily of any racing value, as it is the sum total of internal and external traits that comprises the whole package. Waiting day after day for returning birds is the domain of the patient, yet some men can race right through to all levels with a degree of calm. I think the truth is that racing is stressful for all concerned.

November 2014

CONCENTRATED BREEDING

When breeding your own family of related pigeons, some line breeding to a common ancestor may be the case, and inbreeding to relatives. In my strain common ancestors figure many times in the pedigree. The objective is to concentrate performance potential, determined to a degree by the genes in the offspring. Now pigeon genetics in respect of performance is not an exact science as much as theorists write about inbreeding and line breeding and outbreeding. The birds you pair will all be of mixed origins from way back, and beyond particular pigeons that are familiar to you. A clever racing system will discover the performance curve of each bird in race reality. I concentrate on the hard evidence of actual race performance, which may be indicative of some ancient ancestor, rather than say the parents, and the apples often fall a long way from the tree. There are some birds at stock which have all my performance birds in their breeding, yet the irony is that they may or may not produce good offspring pure or outbred.

No matter what mind-set you take with any birds, very few will cut the mustard in marathon racing. I was very fortunate to get three from six at 879 miles from which grandchildren are still breeding. The whole area is a continuous practical experiment to prove both your ideas and birds and is the area where some expertise may result from your toil.

November 2014

THE BUZZ

I refer to this fairly modern word for what is described as a high. If you receive a mental mood lift in your efforts to win races and enjoyment in association with the birds, then the tasks have been worthwhile. The secret in life is to keep doing what you enjoy, and making the complex simple - in this philosophy is the essence of genius. Many folk are given a buzz by prescribed drugs in today's society. Walks in nature, my writing and my oddball friends give me mine. Many fanciers get a weekly buzz, and a manly feeling of dominance from racing up to 500 miles - therein lie the majority of fanciers. I promise you that a good bird out of Barcelona International will keep you buzzing for years, as the brain/mind synthesis will go into overdrive. The corollary is that some fanciers are stressed to the point of burn out, and when this happens you need rest and withdrawal and to hell with it all.

November 2014

USING THE NATURAL BEHAVIOUR OF PIGEONS

Having made a study of birds for 63 years, there are essential needs and survival behaviours in the flock, which are observable by the human eye. Some empathy with and understanding of these may inform you as to the everyday practical needs of the birds, which can be inculcated into a winning racing system. Birds need a warm, safe and comfortable roost, free of the threat of predation, where they can live out a life cycle of birth, reproduction and death. Pigeons are gregarious, with individual personalities and dominance/submission behaviours exhibited in a hierarchy or pecking order. As sentient creatures that respond inwardly to the presence of humans, see the joint reaction and learn from it. This unity will cement your feelings and sentiments towards the birds - the old masters loved their pigeons, my mother sang to them. If you get the home environment right, then birds with stamina and navigation skills will reward you in races of great difficulty for man and beast. My feeling for nature reinforces my belief that we are all part of the cosmic whole, a concert or synchrony of life.

December 2014

STEPPING STONES TO SPECIALISM

In 1977 I started racing on what I perceived as the initial stages or bottom rung of the racing career ladder. Then the prestige and role model race was to aspire to 500 miles on the day, and in those days it took some doing with feeding systems as they were at that time. Old characters in the local clubs were celebrated heroes, men of power and distinction. My inexperienced, naive philosophy was to do my best, focus and progress with all my birds going over the

Channel as a basic test principle. After a long struggle, and in a learning curve my birds mastered greater and greater distances and degrees of hardship, and how wonderful my first clocking on the day at Nantes NFC was with Damien at 466 miles, and then to repeat it many times with yearlings and older birds. I looked at the future and raised the bar of distance - a stepping stone - to Saintes at 569 miles on the day.

At this time Pau at 735 miles seemed like an impossible dream, yet ambition took me with a leap of blind faith across another stone on the arduous journey to specialism. Then in July 1995 I did something that was a little crazy and wondrous, verifying 3 from 6 birds at 879 miles from Barcelona International. Thus followed a heady cocktail of awe, exhaustion and marvel at the stamina and will of the birds to home to my little old loft. Now as I write with poignant reflection, I see all my races and experiences in the sport as stepping stones in a rich and rewarding life, where dreams became REALITY.

December 2014

THE REALISATION OF A DREAM

Pigeon racing fires the imagination in its converts, as dreams and wonder are ignited from the fires within. The motivation and desire generate enthusiasm to go out there, to do it, to succeed. Focus on a long-term goal may be the genesis of the dream, often based on the competitive spirit and inner impulse. Practicalities in the external world, ie methods, knowledge and systems, are the engine of success born out of the creative process. As a writer and poet, I turn my subjective dreams into tangible realty, in objective publication. It is a perpetual source of continuous and reflective dreams, which are at the heart of life itself.

December 2014

EXPERIMENTATION

My early career in pigeons involved years of research, practical testing and trial and error with methods, systems, feeding, supplements, racing and breeding. From collective knowledge which is out there in the media, in conjunction with my own insights and creativity, we can now produce a well-bred pigeon in good condition for the Barcelona International marathon. It has been a huge task to achieve reasonable targets, and is one we replicate with confidence. Our results now depend on the total race conditions in relation to the innate performance potential of each bird. Experiments are the nucleus of good science, although pigeon racing is as much applied intuition and art - a very human activity, as the birds are so dependent on man for many needs. A nice early bird for us is always a good one as it has demonstrated that it is in practical RACE REALITY - a test that proves or disproves all preconceived dreams, ideas and theories about the qualities of a good one. The objective is to test our ideas in the cauldron of race experience, which smacks of truth to me, although dreams maketh man. Innovations and new goals are realised in the spirit of adventure!

December 2014

REARING BEAUTIFUL YOUNGSTERS

With good practice management with the parent birds it is easy. Housing in a warm, clean, dry spacious environment is conducive to good condition, and an outdoor aviary for exposure to the elements is nice. Before pairing I aim to reduce the count of worms, trichomonads and coccidia, after a good health check, using modern drugs which should be alternated over time in an attempt to reduce the resistance of the pest and disease organisms. You can research the information in the Zsolt Talaber and Colin Walker books as they are seriously factual.

We feed a high protein ratio mix, with G10 pellets, Hormoform, Matrix, and Breedrite and peanuts - a rich mixture supplying optimal nutrition, and occasional Blitzform or Supersix in the water. A strong, healthy YB is crucial if you are to manifest its true potential in race reality. Diets may vary as long as you supply all the nutritious needs of the stock birds and a good pellet is fine as a feeding basis. The squeakers should be big and fat, feather early and thrive. If not, then analyse the situation for a solution.

December 2014

RACES THAT STIR PASSIONS & EMOTIONS

To me the feelings generated by the many aspects of racing are the essence and motivation, the *raison d'être* of the sport. Behind the world of facts and knowledge, personal responses are the pulse of it all. It occurred to me that the idea and impact of the famed Barcelona International race is so large that it transcends the sport in the world of pigeon racing. See for yourself how the leading studs are competing to buy and sell from the champions. It has become a collective, cultural phenomenon, and excites the emotions, dreams and aspirations of the many, and *sans doute* the race, a magnificent spectacle inspires awe and wonder. The racepoint is the culmination of a man's dream - have a go!

The fabled Pau in the NFC has been replaced by Tarbes, which still inspires devotion, and is as far as many want to go and can be testing. My little Dark Enchantment was recorded twice at Pau 735 miles and once at Barcelona 879 miles and she lived out her days in the stock loft. A bird I recall with great affection - a real old-fashioned marathon pigeon.

If the feeling at the end of the season is happiness, then you have cracked it.

December 2014

A NOSTALGIC LOOK AT THE PAST

Nearly 40 years after my original introductions, I reflect on many of the key pigeons that were characters in the evolution of a strain. They become the central foci of a man's contemplation and imagination. This is one of the joys of an obsessive fixation on a related group of individual pigeons. You always remember the fruits of your labour, since they are like extensions of your hopes, dreams and desires. This is the beauty of the singular act of a close breeding programme, devoid of commercial motives, and it takes on a purist, almost religious connotation. It is like a monk attending to his bees in a monastery garden. The nature of the beast is both heritage and legacy, the past, present and the future. As I mark my moments in sport with birds of favour, breeding is a pursuit that inhabits a lofty place beyond the push and shove, the collective craze of day-to-day racing. It is the work of idealists, perfectionists, thinkers and dreamers - try it for yourself.

December 2014

SIX

—

MUSINGS – 2015

EARLY YOUNGSTERS

Have a go, there may be a good one from November to February. All very interesting, and the more from certain pairings the merrier. Really early birds obviate the need for darkening and may be raced up to September. A consequence is the need to train the birds in May of their birth. Early-bred natural birds are often lazy and go down like flies if left untrained, and often will not hold a candle to April hatched ones. Early bred cocks may do well on darkness and lightness systems later, especially widowhood cocks paired to old hens. A clever bird could well do 400 miles on the day of lib with skilful management. All birds of any age are as good as the innate potential in response to the environment. Breed as many as you can afford to keep. I do love late-breds for my stock, but not for racing.

January 2015

NORTHERN EXPANSION OF THE BICC

In time, I see this as a logical consequence of the roaring success of the BICC members, the birds and the momentum of the club. Encouragement of fliers in the Midlands and further north, into Scotland to join the club, could give impetus to consideration of a marking station to serve the Midlands and the north. There is a backcloth of interest to meet the needs of this objective, and interest in participation in many races of the BICC programme. I feel that with real interest and resolve by the committee and its members, then a marking station could result to serve the fanciers' needs eg that fly over 750 miles from Barcelona International. Due attention needs to be afforded to the finance, logistics and need for such a station, and the political process involved, with associated publicity.

January 2015

THE CULT OF THE PERSONALITY

Celebrity culture is endemic in the consciousness of pigeon racing, where recognition assumes mammoth proportions. Yes, who you are perceived to be in the media and in the minds of men is an obsessive preoccupation of the many. Our status in the thoughts of our fellow fanciers becomes a craving and a yearning. Sometimes the love and joy of a good bird are relegated to a handshake or the name in print. This type of urge is seated in the ego aspect of personality and may be linked to money and materialism.

Some purists dedicate themselves to a racepoint or strain creation, and more power to their elbow. Articles, books, videos and the net bring icons and stars to the public eye, and a few shine like diamonds and transcend the sport - it is the same at all levels of sport, and on a global level. I am in favour of the genuine fancier who seeks happiness in the sport, and love it when they nurture those who made them the cult personalities they became eg some writers, philanthropists and all those who plough the furrow of generosity. The quintessence is that the sport is about PIGEON PEOPLE.

January 2015

FOCUSING ON BLACKPOOL

In the madding crowd will be characters, and bargains induced to detach you from your money. If I went again, after meeting the great Emiel Denys in 1977, I would concentrate on a few distance men and study some of the birds with great intent. The integrity of the breeder is paramount, before analysing and trusting a paper pedigree - some of these are highly creative. In my simple philosophy, do what you enjoy and repeat it - a recipe for happiness.

Bound to be some good ones at the Gordon and Wilcox sales, and don't be mesmerised by good looks, since the inherent quality of a pigeon is internal and genetically determined - you can guess at that one. Blackpool is deeply embedded as a phenomenon in the popular and collective consciousness of pigeon folk - an enduring institution. Yes, my memories have been enriched by my rare sojourns to that intense theatre of excitement which is Blackpool.

January 2015

TARGETS & OBJECTIVES

The execution of your aims and aspirations in the sport is crucial to future success and that elusive happiness. With 12 years in college education, I learned the art of dedication to task completion. I applied this self-discipline to my racing and my writing, and to a degree it works on a satisfactory level. It is crucial to sort out and clarify clear goals that may be attained over time. Starting on the bottom rung of the ladder, you can engage in most difficult challenges, until a little reflection rewards your years of concerted effort. Time flows into one and a way of life is established. My approach to tasks is to analyse them into component parts and adopt a systematic approach to their completion. As a Mensan I have more projects than I can complete at any one time, and it keeps me busy to see a little progress. The key traits are desire, enthusiasm, persistence and a little talent.

Humanity is a vast reservoir of great diversity, beyond our total comprehension.

January 2015

PREDICTIONS FOR TARBES & BARCELONA 2015

Both races will be exciting and create an enormous buzz in the psyche of the fancy. Tarbes NFC will have a spattering of the old stalwart names like Gilbert / Shepherd / Cooper / Bush and perhaps Denney in the result, since these are specialists who can execute the race with individuals from the families they have created. However, time evolves change and new names will be spotlighted as they master this onerous race point, like Winters and Adshead - there is ample room at the top if you muscle into it. It will be a stiff race, with plenty timed in over race time up to 800 miles.

The peerless and epic BICC Barcelona International will be a race for marathon specialists and expect no more than around 10 per cent clockings over the duration of the race, and both my trophies will be won over 750 miles, with an increased BICC entry. We will be short on entries as the BBC opted for Palamos - a difficult little spectacle.

All these races are a sporting test of man and bird, and Nic and I hope to land a good one at Barcelona. As usual UK birds will struggle to navigate the Barcelona huge/diverse entry, and facing the vagaries of the English Channel, velocities relative to Europe will fall - how it is and will be in the future. This factor will not deter our lads who one day will crack the top 50 open - done in modern times with over 20 thousand pigeons in the race. Clocking into Scotland and Ireland is a crystal gaze into the future.

January 2015

FACTORS INFLUENCING UK TARBES &
BARCELONA OUTCOMES

A monitored tracking device on the birds may reveal valid, objective information and may put some speculative, seemingly logical rationales to bed. The fancier and innate race quality of the birds are worthy of consideration - how do we perceive or quantify these variables?

It is thought that navigational leaders and followers exist and that the convoy splits into smaller and smaller flocks, with some solo fliers as time and distance increase. Do some Barcelona birds attempt to navigate the Pyrenees? I suspect so. Are the routes taken from both race points dictated by wind, drag and other environmental factors, and the country of destination eg Poland or Denmark? It would appear that the east of England, eg Dover, is an early landing place for some entries, as opposed to Scotland and Ireland, where terrain and time on the wing and distance would tend to magnify the difficulty. With Tarbes a helping wind flow to fanciers flying over 650 miles may increase the chances of a marathon open win or key position in the race - all very exciting.

Now the race entry into the UK is often a mixture of British/Dutch/Belgian and other origins, although Nigel Lane won Barcelona UK with a bird of continental breeding. It is a fact that all racers have diverse ancestral origins, and most will not tackle Barcelona International into the UK and Ireland.

A large influence is the skill and expertise of the fancier - applied knowledge counts. The same old guard continue to excel, and therein lies a story and perhaps a mystery.

My advice is to have a go, dream it, and think about it for yourself. The arrival or non-arrival of a good bird will be your personal race reality - big inner buzz time.

January 2015

LOFT LOCATIONS & NAVIGATION

Let us consider how pigeons may perceive and interpret signals from magnetic fields or other energy forces, applicable to certain loft locations, which may assist some of the quality birds of say Jim Donaldson at Peterhead or Neil Bush at Amcotts, or the Coopers, under their expert management. Will we crack the code, the final enigma of racing pigeon navigation?

With the limited mind of man, I do not believe it is possible to unravel absolute, total knowledge, although a discipline like science may yield a little human truth on the great question. I believe the great, cosmic questions to be beyond humanity, and I rest in sublime ignorance. I take a philosophical stance on all major aspects of life. The fact that many folk do not repeat the glories of the great fanciers on acquisition of their birds I feel is down to individual systems of management, since I have done well with birds from Denney and Donaldson for example - all being of mixed ancestral origins and not genetically pure or true to type. Each pigeon is an individual from any person. I do suspect that some geographical, global areas are more conducive to racing or solo navigation of pigeons, and to think that ferals fly to the fields in snow and fog - what are the bearings of instinct and memory on this? Is the basis of navigation in the brain/mind of the bird? Over to you!

January 2015

DISTRACTIONS TO YOUR AMBITIONS IN THE SPORT

In a world full of wonder pigeons, stars and celebrities, temptations to change course and direction are the demons that lurk, in the media and round every corner. The other man's grass may look greener, to cloud our long-term focus, and we can listen to too many quasi experts and change clubs and pigeons before really testing our birds and systems and methodology. Much of this can be psychological indicating withering hope and knowledge and belief.

Trends and fashions in names of birds and the who's who rise and fall like the sun and rain. The men who endure over time, evolve a system and a strain, perhaps in the whole expanse of a lifetime. In the ephemeral, transient nature of the sport, the old boys were the sages of the past, who may occupy the pages of the future. To create a team of genuine performance birds is an onerous task.

January 2015

THE TRUE NATURE OF A MARATHON PIGEON

The marathon pigeon is a singular, wonderful and beautiful creature and quite rare. Its innate potential, under clever conditioning, has conspired to endure and navigate over 700 miles to its home loft. Many of these peculiar individuals face adverse terrain, weather and other environmental challenges to split from the flock, flying solo over new ground, drawn by mysterious forces beyond the understanding of humanity, to the roost of their birthplace. Men of curiosity, vision and dreams and fuelled by wonder devote competitive lives to the cultivation of avian miracles. Physically such birds may project beauty or common looks, yet the uniting factor of them all is guts and tenacity to survive against great odds in the fireblade of competitive racing. This fact unites and cements the icons of the sport in true brotherhood - long may this be true.

January 2015

THE IMPACT ON PHYSICAL TYPE OF BREEDING & RACING BY THE FANCIER

It is well documented that I used 4 DVH Stichelbaut-based birds bred from the 1970s base of Michel Descamps, regarded as the premier nucleus of the inbred strain, since he kept novel intros to a minimum. Taking my birds out to 879 miles, I bred many small/medium dark chequers and some velvets - influenced to a degree by the phenotype of my originals, the genome, and the severe progeny testing I subjected them to. A few stood the evolutionary test of time and survive today in strain form, many generations later. Recently I have, via PJLOFTS, introduced my pals to many direct DVH based birds from SCHLEPPHORST in Germany. Both our families have a few intros, yet many of the ancestors are the same DVH base eg Ware Yzeren/Yzeren Kennedy/Remi of 54 - see *The History of the Belgian Strains* Vol 11. Now these birds, raced for years in hot competition over shorter distances are as a rule much larger and bolder looking physical specimens, and a work of great beauty from a master breeder. The test will be to blend some in and experiment out to Barcelona International, pure and fixed in with mine. I think that the fancier, with selection, has a huge bearing, with the environment, on the mental/physical type of the pigeon.

February 2015

THE OLD SYSTEM COMBINED WITH THE NEW

Elements of ancient flying techniques of conditioning distance pigeons ie 5 to 700 miles are alive today. Records of the lives of the old boys, poised with their corn tins, show the love and devotion to open loft methodology of the 20th century. The true optimal race condition can be modernised with scientific applications of special feeding, both liquid and solid and supplementation, and medication where applicable. The immune system of birds close to their instincts in nature can be sky high, supported by routine treatments against pests and diseases. With upwards of 11 birds out of Barcelona International into England, our modus operandi is improvement of the birds we evolve over time. We see no need for widowhood or roundabout, yet do fly the sexes separated from time to time. The policy is late-breds out of the key performers, and any that approach champion status eg at least twice in the clock at Barcelona International. The birds and us respond well to the free and easy system.

February 2015

WHAT PIGEONS LOOK LIKE

The handling and looks of the pigeon, of its phenotype, makes judgement of it relative to the individual person, and is entirely subjective like all things. On a sensory/perceptual level I do like a feeling of beauty, class, grace and harmony induced by the bird. However, when I study one of my strain I reflect on the 39 years in its creation and origin in my care. I can now breed to all the key ancestors in one pigeon squeaker, since my original seven foundation pigeons. This is a fact over which I contemplate for many hours as a fixed idea that remains stubborn in the mind. The whole concept of a personal strain is a design of great beauty and induces a Zen-like state. So when you look at a pigeon in a glossy advert or in the sales pen what do YOU see in YOUR mind's eye? Beware the slick sales operator out to buy his new car or house at your expense, since most birds are not fit for purpose.

February 2015

EVOLVING SPRINTERS INTO MARATHON PIGEONS

This may sound unusual and paradoxical, yet I have achieved it with my seven original foundation pigeons. With much hard work and dedication I won through from 71 to 879 miles.

If your management is correct, with optimal nutrition, the key is to race at all available distances, as each bird is unique in its performance value from any family, since the genetic ancestry is diverse-thus no two pigeons are the same.

The experiment takes time and many birds will fail in the process of attempting to produce versatile pigeons.

I like a good looker, particularly the Alois Stichelbaut-based birds of Michel Descamps Van Hasten origin - my birds are inbred back to those genes.

Nowadays we concentrate on Barcelona genes - from these a percentage of birds with sprinting ability will emerge, since it is a sweeping generalisation to assume distance levels from any named pigeons.

The limiting factor remains, and that is to send all your birds at intervals right through the programme.

The genius lies in this simple race reality or the old clichés 'the proof of the pudding is in the eating' and 'beauty is in the eye of the beholder'. Hope you like my existential approach to the sport.

March 2015

MY HOPES AND DREAMS IN THE SPORT

At certain levels, the sport is vibrant and alive and growing. There is a distinct trend for international/national racing via the medium of the BICC. We now know that great birds come out of the Barcelona race.

Young Michael Feeney is leading the push for a great bird into Ireland and is planning to do something truly great. I hope all fanciers rally round him to support the sheer audacity of it all. It will put us all on the map of excellence. It will not happen, yet I would approve of greater goodwill and sportsmanship - the final frontiers of idealism. The heat of competition will galvanise every emotion known to man and it is the essential human aspect of the sport.

The secret is to find a level that induces comfort and some personal satisfaction be it sprint or marathon racing. It is a hard old game, yet good birds are to be enjoyed as long as the sport survives and we learn and read about the noble men who pursue their hopes and dreams.

March 2015

COMMERCIAL CORN MIXES

The keys are the composition, nature and quality of the ingredients that are fed to the birds. We supplement a mix of Versele Laga Gerry Plus and Superstar Plus with peanuts, sunflower hearts, condition seed, hemp, yeast, Hormoform and oils. As supplements, we give Vydex products in the water and on the corn, viz Supersix and Breedite and G10 pellets. Our flock is never kept hungry and some of our birds will score from 31 to 710 miles Barcelona International. Our mineral grit supplement is Matrix and we fly on a personalised open-loft system in harmony with the natural environment.

The Emerton pigeons are used as the base strain, having evolved over 39 years of rigorous selection, breeding and racing. A few modern Barcelona-based birds form the outbreeding experiment - best of The House of Aarden, Bert Shepherd and Schlepphorst Stichelbaut-based birds, acquired using performance criteria alone. The diet suits our system of management with around 11 birds home in modern Barcelona International racing into Taunton Somerset.

I do not believe in much possible improvement in the condition of our birds. The key variable is the continued development of the strain into modern times by extreme distance tests.

March 2015

PRACTICAL THINKING ABOUT PIGEONS

We can theorise about pigeons until the cows come home, and yet this cerebral work out does not reveal any absolute truth and is largely ego-led opinion - I see evidence of it all the time and it may be male power orientated.

If the objective is to do well in breeding and racing at different distances and moreover racepoints, it is important to take a pragmatic approach to pigeons. The main criterion is to evolve a system that is personal to you and that works - mine has from 71 to 879 miles!

If possible take a scientific approach to nutrition, pests, diseases, inbreeding, outbreeding and line breeding.

I have read all the books I need to and the vets and academics were very useful - it helped that I qualified as a science teacher. The great fanciers have leaked excellent tips and insights in interviews and in the media, less so by word of mouth which tends to be wide of fact!!

With intense focus on how we do things, and with a good bird, we are confident of a decent clocking out of Barcelona.

As a Mensan I can often see the loopholes of criticism in any theory or dogma and choose my way when breeding and racing birds. I owe a debt of gratitude to the great minds: men like Talaber, Schraag, Walker, Dexter and all the other influential souls in sporting history - especially Ayrton Senna.

April 2015

HURDLES TO OVERCOME ON THE WAY TO THE TOP

Win nothing, be the popular nice guy and, other than likeability, you will achieve little. Aspire to the position of, say, club top prize winner and hackles will rise and jealousy will rear its ugly head along with various ego-defence mechanisms in other people in your competitive circle. At this stage, although difficult, perhaps it is time to desist or strengthen resolve to try and master marathon racepoints at the far end of difficulty.

I am best motivated by extreme events, with an eye on strain-building and its application to other fanciers in my network.

With some good performances under your belt, a contribution as a writer and overall personality in the sport can be made from the essential enthusiasm generated by the total concept of pigeons.

Critics always surface in the pigeon cultural consciousness - best to continue with your interests and beliefs in the face of adversity. One life, one obsession, one focus on objectives.

March 2015

YOUNG BIRDS ON THE OPEN LOFT SYSTEM

We have all our birds out together, young and old, and it is the easiest system in the world. The old show the young the way and some of the old range off with the young and in all weathers. The knowledge and sophistication comes in the feeding composition which is original and unique to us. We give a little toss before the first club training flight, yet free ranging young birds do not require it, as they are in condition from hours of free ranging - hundreds of miles under the belt.

All birds in the loft are fed the same and are one colony with an established pecking order, as they would be in the wild.

All this environmental seasoning brings contentment and sharpness of instinctual awareness, good preparation for marathon events later and the birds will race home from great distances if they are bred with the inner potential to do so.

The essence is to sit outside in an easy chair and study them as an ethologist would IE in tune with the observable natural behaviour of the individuals in the flock.

The controls on the pigeons are the loft type/feeding/and basketing for the races – at all other times the birds rule the roost and the overall system rewards immunity levels. Cognisant of modern methodology we have no reason to change, yet to evolve a little.

April 2015

ARE HENS BETTER THAN COCKS FOR DISTANCE/MARATHON EVENTS?

I define long distance as 500 to 700 miles and marathon in

excess of 700 miles. Starting at lesser distances in the club programme, I worked up to 879 miles.

Some great birds are on types of specialist widowhood or other systems where separation induces hormonal and other physiological and psychological changes conducive to form.

On my little open loft system, in spite of losses due to nature eg predation, most of my better results at Pau, 735 miles, San Sebastien, 737 miles and Barcelona Int, 879 miles, were executed by hens - I found them more tenacious with regard to the nest and to have high survivability.

Our recent best Barce bird was a hen. Having said this, as a hens specialist, I love them on types of natural racing systems, where you capitalise on tuning the instincts to the free and natural environment - all nice and free and easy.

Specialist celibate and widowhood fanciers can race them well up to, say, Tarbes NFC AT 800 miles. I do like 'close to nature' methods for birds timed up to the 10th day after liberation, as the birds need to fend for themselves en route in order to reach the loft on day 2 onwards.

I hope this little insight provokes some thought and discussion.

April 2015

ALL OR NOTHING

The s**t or bust principle of racing has appealed always to me.

In 1977 I sent my first team in a very first Falaise channel race and was 3rd with a Jack Ross from Holtby bird. It was a baptism of fire and led me on a tortuous path in the sport. Learning that all birds must be tested we send the team to each preparatory race in the BICC/BBC and

NFC before Barce Int. This gives the benefits of variables like race points, transportation, geography and type of birds in each convoy. The weekend of our big race we empty the loft of all fit birds. Although anxiety-inducing, it has been rewarding over time and sure finds out the good birds and the elusive champion.

The psychological approach is bold and risky, yet the 'faint heart never won fair lady' cliché is applicable to the philosophy.

April 2015

THE NEED TO SPECIALISE

From basic club, win, win, win flying to endurance international events where a win is rare, there is a need for specialist methods, knowledge and techniques.

Total focus is given to the breeding and racing preparation of individual birds in the team, since like humans, each one is a unique personality. Take heed from and be influenced by peers and competitors and critics, and find a niche where you can function with a modicum of success.

It is a ruthlessly and tenaciously-fought battle, yet the premier race in Europe has yet to be won in the UK, which sure puts all the egos into race reality perspective. The irony is that a novice may feel like a king with the euphoria of a win.

My central thesis in all my articles is the satisfaction of the inner man on a personal and deeply subjective level and may your birds fly long and hard.

If not, look in the MIRROR OF TRUTH.

April 2015

WHAT'S IN A NAME?

Good birds and the rare champion are assigned creative names. Some of these are imaginative and appealing to the intellect and celebrate the fancier and bird in history, legend and folklore.

In years to come, readers of books and diverse pigeon literature will study and reflect on the leading birds of the past, within the insular world of pigeon culture.

As a poet, I would say some of these are romantic and idealistic in tone and have a beautiful or mysterious connotation to them.

In my youth I was inspired and moved by birds like Woodsider, Lancashire Rose, Storm Queen and Misty Lady. From the more modern era we have Mystical Queen, Circus Boy and Twilight. I like these names as they are indicative of a mood, of a place, personal emotions and the atmospheric conditions of the race. Perhaps you can contemplate a personal series of old favourites too?

April 2015

DO WE NEED TO TRAIN YOUNG BIRDS?

A pigeon is born with a genetic code enabling it to navigate and race or not. Yes, the fancier nurtures this ability by the manipulation of the total environment made available to the bird-nature/nurture cliché.

In my youth, winning races was the be all and end all, and a great deal of work was devoted to road miles training. Now with the insight of age I believe most of this was surplus to need, although open races were won in true competitive spirit. Our sole target now is marathons and on open loft exercise the training by road/tossing requirement is zero.

At the latter end of my racing career YBs were sent off open loft into 95 or 138 miles with plenty of returnees for the future. We adopt a more cautious/less risky approach now with the accent on quality and condition.

April 2015

OUTBREEDING INBRED RACING PIGEONS

Our experiments are going well. From a highly inbred Emerton-based cock paired to an inbred daughter of Pad's Invincible/Nellie's Lelly, we bred four young. All survived as young birds and the first race as yearlings in the West of England South ROAD Combine.

For vigour and possible racing ability I aim to continue monitoring the empirical results of the programme throughout the season. With a shrewd and discerning eye you can source some inbred birds to Barce Int performers at Steve/Lesley Wrights who are perfectionists in the competitive, commercial world.

With 39 years of family back breeding to my original magnificent seven, we hope to produce another champion. There is good scientific and other evidence around to support the theory of the F1 hybrid-first filial generation phenomenon – heterozygocity or hybrid vigour – and scaling down this factor to practical pigeon breeding has helped me in my pursuits.

Initially then, acquire inbred birds for potential performance in the race point/distance of choice and pair them together. Many of my better birds were derived in this way

April 2015

SECRETS AND OPENNESS WITH SYSTEMS

There are logical reasons why people hit the ceiling in pigeon racing, and some of those reasons may not reach the public domain in the form of hard factual information, which compounds the mystery and enigma of the elite fliers.

If within the rules, revealing the truth must promote and enhance fullness of the collective knowledge of the sport. I would like to see many more probing reviews and reports into the results and the facts behind champions' success.

Unorthodox and eccentric as my system seems to be, I have been transparent with publication of my methodology, rationale and overall philosophy and flying system. It suits us and a few more who see the intrinsic wisdom in the unconventional. If asked I can communicate the clarity and nature of my simple approach to racing from 31 to 879 miles.

April 2015

A WAY FORWARD WITH THE SPORT

There are simple paybacks to the sport that can be done with ease. Donation of a trophy is a generous gesture to a club or organisation, as can be giving birds to the novices and/or to charity. Many individuals sacrifice time to help in many ways - they are not all bad!

I think my contribution has been writing, mentoring, donation of trophies and strain building. I do not belong to committees. My primary motivation these days is enjoyment and cerebral stimulation. We do enjoy breeding/racing and aim for a little improvement, knowing that the big race win remains elusive and on a far horizon - in this sense participation is all, and all that we need.

I would like to see a rise in sportsmanship values and an emphasis on distance being the arbiter of excellence - marathon racing is a true test of the SPIRIT of man and bird.

April 2015

TEAM FLYING

With a single racepoint in mind, we send the whole team to preparatory races. This plan is easy and we always empty the loft. In race reality this discovers the capability of each bird in different winds - and all the external forces that constitute a race.

After a while the quality birds emerge at different distances, even though they are all related via the ancestry. Nominations on observations and perceptions can be made to add spice to the equation. I like the Single Bird Club for that experience.

Big hitters sending big teams, eg 100 at a time, will succeed with a quality team in condition - it is planned domination and can make a great impact on the fancier. To obtain new blood I prefer the small team man who is a racing purist or from sources of champion birds at BARCE.

Good genes are often given by friends in the sport. With testing, expect some radical reductions in the size of your team by the end of the season. The basic concept is the individuals within the team - these will emerge from actual racing and breeding.

Lucky are those who develop producer pairs to form a strain.

April 2015

GROUP BEHAVIOUR OF PIGEONS

A colony of pigeons can be perceived as one interactive, harmonious whole. In a strict hierarchical order the birds live out their instincts and life cycle as lifeforms in nature -

we are part of their external environment. In response to other birds and animals they assume a group identity, possibly rooted in the evolution of survival strategies.

The corollary is to focus on each individual bird and study it as a separate unit: a piece in the whole cake. Observe changes in behaviour with the rise and fall in condition or form before and after a race and to supplement and nutritional changes laid on by the boss. Notice the responses to your presence and the appearance of survival threat predators.

I first studied the work of the scientists Pavlov, Lorenz and Tinbergen - all brilliant men in the field of ornithology. Perhaps the way to insight is to imagine yourself as a pigeon? We are but on the threshold of real knowledge or radical new insights.

April 2015

FORAGING FOR FOOD

In one international race and others lasting up to ten days, depending on loft distance, returning birds will need to find food and water, grit, minerals and other nutritive sources. In order to encourage this natural survival behaviour my birds at Holtby were allowed to roam the fields with the wild birds for barley, wheat, peas and drank from the local pond or sat on wires.

Neil Bush, a great NFC man, encourages this natural flock, and free behaviour to induce contentment and form in his distance/marathon birds and with unprecedented success since 1982.

Nic and I scatter condition seed/peanuts etc on the lawn in front of the loft for young and old, all out together. This method is recommended in certain areas only. It is a truly beautiful way to keep birds and good ones give their all to fly home to the boss and loft, as doves have done to their home roost since time immemorial.

Many top racers will have spent weeks out on the edge of survival, as wild birds, lessons well learned. In certain areas there is a return to the old free spirit system, where old Jack sat on his deck chair with pipe in mouth, corn tin in hand, and joy in his heart.

April 2015

SPRINTING ON THE NATURAL SYSTEM

If applicable to your area, open loft birds will win the sprints and go through to Barcelona. Nic and I have done it regularly. Good management with a versatile strain of birds is essential – down to the brain of the boss. We pair in March, give two tosses and the race and rest, race and rest with organisation of the nest cycle and some periods of separation of the birds to raise hormonal drives in the brain.

Our feeding and supplements have been published. The whole philosophy is based on preparation, condition and contentment, inbreeding/outbreeding and sending the team every time we enter.

The breeding side is experimental around a racing blueprint which is effective. Twice in the clock at 710 miles Barcelona would be classed as a good bird in our thoughts.

We aim to enjoy the mental stimulus of the process

April 2015

LOFT UPDATE

With two little tosses of around 30 miles the birds did well in the combine 7, 11 open 5k plus birds. They are on our unique diet and open loft-young and old together, and all flitting and coming and going amongst the ferals, crows, hawks – alive and elemental.

The 29 racers that are left are destined for BICC Falaise, then separated and rested for two weeks, in a method aimed at Barce Int for old and Saintes NFCFC for all yearlings, emptying the loft in every race.

On the breeding side our top, champion producer hen is with a highly inbred cock of my strain in a marriage made in heaven. Later all the birds of close breeding to my originals will be paired for stock and distribution to the network of fellow fanciers at no charge, to revive the strain.

April 2015

RACING PIGEONS AS INDIVIDUALS

With an inherent tendency to form flocks or colonies, the great racing pigeons demonstrate individual flying and survival behaviour. All my main marathon/distance birds will have flown solo for relatively large distances - I love these birds.

The first ten in the sprint-middle distance race will demonstrate sound management methods on the part of fanciers, and pretty easy flying conditions for souped-up well-motivated birds - this is an expression of psychological dominance and may have commercial connotations!

The fabric of history is punctuated by iconic fanciers and their elitist champions -individuals all. I speak of birds like Lancashire Rose, Riley's Duchess, Storm Queen, Woodsider, Barcelona Dream - pioneer pigeons.

In race migration mode the good birds will manifest keen navigational ability, survivability and rugged tenacity. These are the birds for traditional idealists and racing romantics and they inhabit dreams and fantasy, folklore and legend. Make one your RACE REALITY!

April 2015

THE IMPORTANCE OF REST

We race on a 'race then rest' regime. The whole practice involves the gradual build-up towards the marathon races, not the repeated winning of sprint to middle-distance races weekly - quick buzz psychology!

One good performance a year to test our family breeding skill suits us fine. The birds are never kept hungry at home - light birds motivated by the corn tin are not suitable for endurance flights over 500 miles.

I want my birds to be capable of sustained speed/endurance navigation over many days on their odyssey from Barcelona International, splitting from a convoy of, say, 25 thousand birds flying to Poland and North Holland. In simple terms, after a ten to twelve-hour fly, 3-4 weeks' loft rest will prepare the birds for 7 to 900 miles, if they have the ability to crack it.

The quiet contentment of the birds resting in the home environment is nice to see and is key for the fancier, as too much hype and anxiety leads to early burn out or depression - a persistent laid-back approach to the sport pays dividends, like the racing mode of Denney.

April 2015

LOFT SURPRISES

Racing is not totally predictable and the anticipated arrivals may not appear. Slow and plodding birds may find form, find a line and do well.

I never cull able race birds, always retesting them in the races. Birds may come alive and race with distinction - the main factors are persistence and patience on the part of the fancier: race down to the last bird and always empty the loft.

Over long and difficult years this realistic philosophy has served me well in the creation of a strain.

A fact is certain - all birds will meet their destiny if raced on and on, with distance being the final selection criterion. If the outcome of racing was a known fact, I would not entertain racing any longer. What captures my imagination is the excitement of the total and beautiful mystery of pigeon racing and the finding of champion producers to augment the strain.

April 2015

RACING CONFIDENCE

Confidence closely correlates with belief, and to be a great fancier you will need lots of it. It is hard to endure the realities of a full season's racing as we all tried to do many years ago. For some, times have changed with Continental-style sprinting and young bird systems.

We are confident in our breeding/racing systems and keep focused on our race specialisms, cognisant of the condition of the birds as we go along towards the objective race.

A bright young man is full of dreams and naïve aspirations. These can be realised, and may, with sustained enthusiasm evolve into solid belief and wisdom as the clock of time clicks by inexorably. I am never put off by weather, distance or potential difficulty. These create a genus of masochistic hardship, a few good pigeons and a rare champion.

May 2015

LOFT UPDATE

Falaise BICC was a nice race for many people in different parts of the country up to 450 miles plus. Some good decisions were made by the reliable BICC people. We sent 25 with 19 on the day. With all the yearlings being unraced as young birds, they had ranged well. Some stock birds have bred multiple arrivals and show potential for the future.

We have now separated the birds and will repair two days before the scheduled NFC Fougères race, with hopper feeding at all times to maintain and provide reserves for July. The essence is gradual increases of time on the wing duration, rather than raw speed at this stage. The plan is for the residual birds all to go to Barcelona International next year.

On arrival today the birds were given peanuts and Supersix in the water as a restorative. I do believe that the main interest is strain building via the medium of racing, rather than just winning races per se. Another champion is a main objective. I am looking for birds over 700 miles as usual.

May 2015

CONTRIBUTION TO THE SPORT

Some individuals have done great things for the overall welfare of people and the collective good of the sport. Much work can be achieved in terms of articles, interviews, the dissemination of a racing strain and generous support of the total concept and our understanding of modern pigeon racing.

There are book writers, film makers, benefactors, who express their personalities in a relatively selfless way and are perhaps not primarily money orientated. Or innovations in systems, nutrition and bird science may be the hallmark of excellence. Then we have the folk with the genius touch in actual racing results .A few personifications of my ideals are Gareth Watkins, Jim Jenner, Geoff Kirkland, John Clements, Liam Ocomain and Zsolt Talaber.

May 2015

FAULTS I FIND WITH PIGEON RACING

I adopt a positive approach to racing, yet feel the following criticisms. Negative jealousy and resentment can be widespread and damaging to the sensibilities of fanciers, especially the successful in racing and other spheres of activity. This element has driven many folk from the sport in the world of pigeons, and will continue to do so.

In harsh reality, you can expect stick upfront or in the background. The stalwarts become a little hardened to this human emotion element and persist with their objective dedications. Maintaining a winning loft yourself is very hard work and many elite resultists have people working for them - loft managers.

Adopting a cerebral approach, my strain is in the hands of some clever men with high aspirations. Some corns and supplements, and the prices of birds are well inflated for maximum profit - I would put the shrewd hat on in these circumstances. An ongoing kudos battle exists between sprint and distance men and the bird/fancier debate.

Like all questions in the sport there are no absolute, definitive answers and thus the popular perceptions and ideas will rumble on as long as the sport exists. However I am expecting an Irishman to receive universal acclaim with a new champion – a matter for the future.

May 2015

THE OBSESSION WITH SPEED

The whole ethos of marathon pigeon racing is a gradual build-up of time on the wing, progressing from the shorter race points to the maximum distances we can muster. I like a nice 10-hr fly 3 to 4 weeks before a marathon migration. To be honest I like birds to be doing below 1200 ypm, as that is what they will be doing in the targeted race.

The mindset, expectation and reward differs from the winning sprint buzz which is popular with specialist training/feeding and motivation systems and the cultivation of aggressive power birds - often on the large size and blue in colour. Naturally velocity over distance is crucial to the position in the race and the Continentals so far have beaten us at Barce Int. Logically, as a raw novice you must have the highest velocity to be top of the pops in the club and then the responses will come.

I study the late arrivals in the early season races with interest and apply caution to the speedy early arrivals. Marathon birds may be welcomed over 10 days' race duration into Ireland in the future - time will tell the tale.

May 2015

LESSONS I HAVE LEARNED THE HARD WAY

In my long career I have realised many things.

- You will breed few really good birds and champions are rare, even if the parents are very expensive on the pocket.

■ Sustained inbreeding does work if you have the right birds and know how to do it.

■ The person or entity to put faith and belief into is yourself, not the rest of humanity.

■ A racer that comes good or is consistent may fail to return.

■ Some versatile pigeons will score right through the prog. A strain of pure sprinters or distance performers is an illusion or commercial device - they are all mixed.

■ Marathon races over 700 miles are usually much more challenging than sprints.

■ The most rewarding aspects of the sport are teaching/writing and the creation of a strain.

■ Never put total belief in the weather or another in relation to the sport.

■ Some of the world's top men and birds are on home ground, but there are as well some good Continental birds.

■ Race day is the real test of my management, birds and conditions.

■ I believe in giving good birds away to help others and the strain.

■ As good as we think we are, we are but specks of dust within the vastness of the cosmos and there are no pure strains of birds.

May 2015

RACE REALITY AND PROOF

I have been interested in the thought processes behind the numerous theories relating to the apparent or predictable qualities or racers and breeders at different distances – feet, feather, eye, balance, name of origin and other products of the mind and convention. Nice to think, talk, write and pontificate and theorise about the intrinsic traits of birds.

Today in the twilight of my career in birds I am drawn to a conclusion and that is that the proof of your mental efforts is the acid test of your birds results in race reality: this smacks of TRUTH.

The purist looks at the empirical evidence with enthusiasm, before placing a value on both man and bird looks sensible to my biased eye.

May 2015

FIELDING

A factor often frowned upon by many on controlled exercise systems and welcomed by a few is fielding. My birds fielded old and young together for 30 years. The fields adjacent to the cottage were conducive to this. There were losses to sparrowhawks – very few were shot as there had been pigeons at Holtby for donkeys' years. The birds were fit, sharp and keen and you could lift them into the races with no road training. Birds bathed at the local pond, sat on buildings and wires and had the life of Riley.

We hopper-fed on an excellent diet and like the great Neil Bush pigeons came and went to walk and forage the fields, as they often would in the long and marathon races between 5 and 900 miles. The concept is old fashioned and unsuitable for most people, yet my bird still holds the BICC distance record having been timed in race time from 879 miles.

We now fly 710 miles and yes, on the open loft - with success. The birds and we love the laissez faire, easy going system.

I like contented birds at the home end, since they will rough it in racing at some time in their career - down to base instincts, I call it. The quintessential word is freedom!

May 2015

COUNTDOWN TO BARCELONA

The future is July with the liberation of birds in the race of your life, when to time is an honour and a milestone.

In preparation all our birds are with the NFC at Fougères in a nice head wind fly over the water-yearlings and older birds. On arrival we feed peanuts with Super Six in the water. After loft rest and a fattening-up process they will go to BICC Poitiers and the older birds jumped into Barcelona International to see if a good one comes with fastidious preparation – it's race reality time. The idea will be to execute a similar plan next year until we create another champion to breed around. The ethos is to enjoy each race as it happens and to suck it and see.

All the birds are on our original food and liquid feeding preparation, which works fine from 31 to 710 measured miles.

Have a go in the greatest race on Planet Earth.

May 2015

A NIGHT OUT

All birds that go to repeated distance/marathon races will have nights away from the loft and may be strags for a while. I encourage this from an early age and sometimes fit, young birds will fly round at night in summertime. It can be the making of a good bird, as the survival mode kicks in, teaching foraging and roosting behaviour away from the immediate home environment.

Good ones seem to wake up and come alive, as wild doves and pigeons are. At times there are ample food supplies in nature, and they may associate with ferals, woodies, stock doves and collared doves. I write this from a countryman's perspective, having spent years in the wilds as a rough shooter and wildfowler on the Wash estuary.

The corollary is that pigeons flying under 500 miles are often home on the day, yet may night out at very short distances. We pick them up with peanuts and Supersix in the water.

In relation to the hours of darkness rules, racers that fly during the night fascinate me, say, in Holland or Scotland.

May 2015

BICC/NFC RACING INTO NORTH EAST ENGLAND

I welcome the surge in interest in this phenomenon and there are some great performances with more to follow. This fact must inspire the lofty ambitions of 5 to 800-mile fliers in the far north with some great birds, offering recognition and publicity. A unified huge national/international race would be the ideal and would reveal who's who and what's what.

Nice to see valid praise of distance men and their birds. We can all get the distance by sending to the Barce Int, where speed/endurance and navigational traits are essential alongside the appropriate mindset of the fancier.

The Sportsman FC is a club in expansion mode and I admire its founders and objectives on principle.

We always look and wait for the long fliers in any race - do we not?

May 2015

JEAN'S IMPACT ON MY PIGEON CAREER

We met in '78 at a social club. I sent her to sleep with incessant chatter about pigeons and myself and thus it has been for 37 years, in 36 countries and islands in the world – I have been to over 50.

Pigeons are the grand obsession and in that sense Jean knows more than most men about the common sense intricacies of the daily lives of racing pigeons. We chatter, sometimes merrily and quirkily, all day long in a sea of verbal communication. It is evident that my life has been enriched by her presence and some ladies are wonderful in their empathy and kindness with birds - the sensitive touch.

Jean has a great, earthy understanding of daily practicalities which balance my lofty intellectualism; the relationship works, and she laughs at my absurd jokes. In the early days we enjoyed outings to train birds and Mum and we two enjoyed sitting outside in wait of birds over many years sharing in the triumphs and disasters in the idyllic surroundings of the sweet cottage garden at Holtby village.

It is no secret that I owe these two ladies everything; they have been the nucleus and the soul of my brilliant career in racing pigeons, and the essence of my existence.

May 2015

AN INTIMATE KNOWLEDGE OF EACH PIGEON

A discerning fancier has in-depth awareness of the origin and personality of each bird. Without resource to records or loft book, detailed knowledge of each arrival from the race should spring to mind, eg its name, parents and grandparents - then you have focused on each individual bird in your care.

Some people can do this, particularly those who can nominate and pool. Try sitting in a chair and meditating on an image of your birds in the mind's eye. From this inner contemplation may spring insights and ideas that you can put into practice.

I reflect on my birds some 39 years later, often looking at the images of the key birds in the strain. It is a most enlightening, yet cerebral process. It is probable that you will retain a perception of a champion, if and when it arrives.

May 2015

HOW TO THINK LIKE A DISTANCE MAN

Races of 5 to 700 miles need a different psychological approach. Long-term planning comes into play, perhaps years ahead, and you spread enthusiasm over weeks and months with great patience.

It is a very individual thing to do and all the marathon men I know are individualists, some introverted loners, and often bright and creative people with unusual ideas. It is a minority activity, yet the greats in the field are icons of the fancy and much revered.

How did you get the slow-burning fuse of dedication to sit for hours and days, just in the possibility of returns in all weathers? Men of old were noted for their devotion to the task right through the season, reflecting the slower pace of life, especially to rural lofts. Now much focus is on the instant gratification of the must-win mental attitude and drive to be instantly dominant.

There is a demand and supply of Barcelona performance-based birds, yet the sobering irony is that few birds and fanciers will tackle marathon races over 700 miles. Ask the question - why should this be?

June 2015

WEIGHING AND MEASURING FOOD RATIONS

In my long career from 71 to 879 miles, I never gave a fixed ration, as the birds had food before them at all daylight hours. A gradual build-up in race distances produced the reserves of fat and muscular condition for the longest of races. The secret here is to build and keep the body on, not to fine it down by dieting to try and snatch a few early races.

The leading competitor in the area was Denney - a super race man at all distances to 748 miles and hard to lead in racing. With restricted exercise regimes controlled feeding is often practised and can be an art/science fusion in practice. I had hoppers of pellets down, with birds coming and going by natural behaviour and instinct into the stubble fields at will - great for confidence and contentment around home, if you are in the right spot, free of too many predators and shooting.

The stock birds had hoppers of pellets and all birds were on solid and liquid feeding. My strain was built on this regime and I have flown on widowhood hens and cocks with natural elements as well. All systems are individual to the fancier, yet good contented birds will all have to forage and fend for themselves in races of serious distance over 500 miles and many days away. The basic concept is the adaptation of a system to suit your needs.

June 2015

ALL-WEATHER PIGEONS

We have race plans for the birds which we adhere to in spite of any inclement weather predictions. All the birds have to fly Barcelona International at 710 measured miles into the West - a loft rule. Let us be sensible in long races; the birds will meet variable weather conditions, where the good ones often come through. Today there seems to be a more protective approach to birds, which are very capable of living wild and free in nature - we fly on the open loft to acclimatise the birds to all weathers, using nature as our teacher.

My philosophy of racing works for us. I worked outdoors in all seasons and weather conditions and was a country lad who made a study of wild doves and pigeons. I embrace the Continental systems, yet have evolved my own from 71 to 879 miles. Good yearlings are very capable up to 600 miles and great old birds up to 900 miles in racing and of facing the vagaries of climate and weather and, thus, a strain is created.

June 2015

LOFT UPDATE

Today we trained our team of 22 birds in the BICC Poitiers race and had 12 on the day up to around 14 hrs on the wing. They arrived to peanuts and Supersix by Vydex in the water to restore them. There were 7 yearlings at the 344 miles distance. We hope now to improve at Barcelona International, scheduled in July.

It tends to be a real test into the West Country and we are pleased to get them home on a fairly difficult day. We do like the organisation of the BICC and its excellent programme. We timed 2 today with 2 more just behind, then a steady stream of birds arrived between 8.5 and 14 hrs on the wing. The reason for racing is fun and the personalities involved in the game.

June 2015

A SOFTENING OF ATTITUDES

Since my glory days in racing, when we raced right through the season and in many weathers with a small team, attitudes towards the job have evolved.

Marathon racing is a minority activity pursued by oddballs and the popular consciousness revolves around speed, velocity and fair-weather flying. Let's be honest, we race for pleasure, selfish and possibly commercial reasons. Once liberated the birds are free in the sky to come home or not and are exposed to all kinds of weather, as ours are round home. I find many people are quick to blame the officials when it is they who have decided to enter the race or not.

I think the way forward is to practise SELF-CRITICISM in an attempt to perfect your quality and the race management of your birds. I have practised self-analysis and introspection and adopt a hardened, philosophical approach to racing and I would detach myself from automatic blame of officials, unless they were glaringly at fault.

I do believe we should all toughen up and stop criticising the system - once liberated the weather is in the lap of the Gods and beyond our control.

June 2015

FINAL PREPARATIONS

The race training is done as a gradual build-up to Barcelona International. We have put the muscle on them and now we are working on the physiology and psychology with rich feeding, liquid and solids, baths and rest.

The candidates are nesting where they wish and on open loft are free to fly with the young birds which are ranging. Peace and harmony are the order of the day in the normal dynamics of the colony. The race will be very difficult, yet we hope to get good returns from the 7 candidates and a good timing. It is the one test of the year for us and it is great to watch the race as it unfolds with a small minority of birds on the second day into the UK.

I shall be fascinated to see who wins my four trophies in the BICC, which cost an arm and a leg. The best of British to all the brave souls who will enter their gallant birds in the GREATEST RACE ON PLANET EARTH. Let's see a top 50 open UK performance and the making of modern history!

June 2015

OBJECTIVES IN PIGEON RACING

In order to transcend human emotional elements, I set abstract targets to be realised in practical pigeon racing. These have included racepoints to conquer, with a gradual evolution to the zenith, which is the Barcelona International and the sole motivation of us and birds is geared to the race of awe.

The irony is that we will never win the race and to us this is a purist perversion from the usual treadmill of win, win, win. It is certain that the practice of this degree of difficulty strengthens a strain over many years of persistence in race reality. My advice is to avoid egos and politics like the plague and set your own personal standards, motivated by the will to succeed.

Except when I do interviews of other people in the sport I take this personal stance in my time in the sport - a self-fulfilling prophecy. I place great emphasis on individuals - both fanciers and birds - these are the icons, legends and history-makers.

June 2015

BEHIND THE RACING SCENES

We are overwhelmed by publicity and images of the powerful and famous in pigeon racing, the popular names on the lips of sycophants and critics alike. In reality, our wives, helpful staff and other types of people doing the loft chores often go unnoticed by the public eye.

In many cases the image of the racing icon conceals a gifted fancier behind closed doors. I have been candid that my father started me off with pigeons in 1952 and that my mother helped with the open loft system from 1977 to 2004 when she was 91 years old, while Jean has been a constant companion in my obsessions for 37 years and we have seen a gradual rise in enjoyment and satisfaction, as I pursued relentlessly my dreams and ambitions.

This sentimental feature is to balance out the impact of the egos who crave fame and commercial success and sheds light onto the goings on behind the image of outward race reality.

June 2015

SUPER STIMULUS

Before big races there are some motivational devices that may stimulate the inner being of the birds. Today our Barcelona cock's hen was slipped three shiny white eggs to stop The Optimist from driving before marking - the hen sat them very quickly, thus resting the lad.

I like a hen in July on a nice big fat WHITE yb - use the idea of the visual stimulus to activate the dormant instincts. It sounds cranky, yet I always work on the total being of the bird, its psyche and physiology and harness hormonal responses from within to effect changes in outward behaviour and perhaps form.

There is more than meets the eye behind good race results do you not think? Many believe buying good birds will bring success. Consider this.

June 2015

THE LURE AND MAGIC OF DISTANCE

Alone in the garden, as the crows loom large in twilight skies, I breathe deep on the pipe of dream, my trusty briar. The midges bite, as the moths evade capture and instant doom brought by hunting bats that have emerged from ancient roosts. It is the haunt of patient and visionary men in a silent quest to realise dreams when the air will come alive with pure moments of magic.

I am alerted from my trance when a single old pigeon zooms in from distant lands to turn the old man into a folklore hero and sporting legend. Once more history is made in secret gardens of racing men who come alive in the magical hours of twilight.

June 2015

WHAT TO ADMIRE IN A GOOD BIRD

There are factors about a good one that are praised and admired universally. Birds that shine in adverse conditions, in rain, heat, fog and against the wind, especially over long distances are revered and may become celebrated champions in the popular pigeon consciousness of the day. We still reflect on the great names of the past like King of Rome, Woodsider and Lancashire Rose, as they stirred the heart and soul of the fancy and were much-publicised.

I always recall my 569 to 879 mile birds and the successful progeny they left behind for today in the Barcelona International races and at great distances. I look for hardiness, gameness, survivability and navigational abilities from France and Spain and the ability to fly solo - it is individuals I seek. These are to be found in the lofts of men of great purpose and character.

June 2015

BARCELONA INTERNATIONAL - THE RACE GOES ON

Now day 4 and we are yet to clock. The race has been fairly difficult, as predicted, yet doable, especially for the 6 to 700 milers.

I note the predominance of birds in the eastern and central sections of England, yet the exemplary three of the Padfields of Wales have given us a master class in racing prowess. These lads have superior management and a top-class system in their own environment which the birds respond well to. I have a perception that Vince Padfield is a quiet man and a genius! Interesting that many of their birds are of mixed origins and/or outbred.

Let's see who records birds over 800 miles to test my 20-

year-old record of 3 verifications at 879 measured miles with some facing winds!

I have donated 3.5k for 4 trophies to be presented by the BICC if won this year and claims should go into the BICC. A most interesting race with the usual percentage range of returns in race time - approx. 10 per cent.

Soulful and hearty praise to all the bold and brave people and tenacious birds who entered the world's top race. Here's to 2016 for another shot in the dark.

July 2015

THE BENEFITS OF PARTNERSHIP

If people relate well to each other and have a common resolve and purpose, then things can go well. Take the Padfields with Vince the aloof genius and the ebullient, charming extroversive Dave. The unity of these 2 individuals has created an awesome racing package, flying into a difficult area.

At the end of the day, the plans have to be made and executed and dedicated partners can be very effective. Often, relatives and wives are subsumed by men who take the credit from unseen heroes. Some famous racing relationships are the Denneys, Chris Gordon and pals, and the Wilsons.

My parents and Jean helped me with my efforts and it is tough for the lone wolf lofts to have a real go at the top level. I recommend a combination of brains and brawn and a common purpose.

July 2015

THE POLISH PERSPECTIVE

The 2015 Barcelona International revealed some great and stellar performances by man and bird in Europe. One in particular has ignited my fire and is truly wonderful. Can someone please publish a full report/interview on Szewczyk Ryszard? Now this marathon hero timed the Polish National Winner on day 4 at around 1035 miles. Sending over 1200 birds to the top race, it is surely time that a UK stud imported some of these proper pigeons for extensive breeding of the speed/endurance traits that they possess.

I feel we have a surfeit of 700-plus milers in the UK and Ireland. My personal favourite over recent years has been the champion dark cock of Marco and Cath Wilson at 844 miles in 2014. Birds beyond 800 miles manifest great stamina and endurance traits in their genes and phenotype, do they not?

The Irish are chancing their arm. It will be fascinating if the Scottish return to traditional marathon values like the good old days.

July 2015

HOW TO RECOVER IF YOU FAIL AT THE DISTANCE

It hurts if you do not time at the longer distances, a misfortune that befalls most of us from time to time. Pride and reputation and, in a man, ego may be dented. Now, champions, when floored get up and fight again. I suggest a holiday to calm down and refresh the spirit, followed by clear plans to have another go.

Barcelona 2015 was a stinker, with birds still homing. My basic precept is that you need one good one to make your name. When the going gets tough cliché applies to the pigeon sport. Keep at it and create a system that gives good condition to your entries, then with dogged persistence you may succeed.

Always prepare a late arrival for the same racepoint the following year. Good recovery is largely psychological and with reputations at stake and critics about, your resolve will be tested - have another go.

July 2015

LATE ARRIVALS

The birds that drift in from the longer race need tender loving care. First of all, some peanuts to replace energy level and amino acids for protein/muscle restoration. Some of these birds will have flown hundreds of miles off course to reach, eventually, the sanctuary of their home. Let them rear a young bird, then offer plenty of loft rest, baths and rich food to initiate a good moulting experience for them - they may be good performers next year at the same race point.

We have a hen 3 times Barcelona International at 710 miles - and may send her again if fit. Sometimes the late arrivals are homers - always nice to see them. Often a bird switches on with time and age and may surprise you with its performance level.

We do not cull racing pigeons as their purpose is to race, is it not? Take a gentle approach to the sport and exercise patience - it rewards you.

July 2015

REPORTING ON LONGER FLYING MEMBERS AND BIRDS

In the pressure, haste and urgency to please the majority thrust of clubs and to complete the articles for the fancy press, some marathon men and birds can go underreported or play catch-up in the media. This is one motivation for my donation of four trophies to the BICC - an attempt to balance the reporting effort, since we all like recognition for focus and dedication.

It may be pertinent to delay some reporting, say, on Barcelona International and NFC Tarbes with fanciers flying serious distances in excess of 800 miles.

Years ago I had to manage most of my own publicity. Lucky is the person with a willing writer to stroke his ego in the press, often with commercial consequences! We live in the imperfect world of people, yet improvements can always be made.

July 2015

ACTUAL FLYING DISTANCE AND PERCEIVED DISTANCE

Believe me, your birds are often flying many miles above the measured distance, which may or may not be accurate in the first place. Tired birds may be clocked at 600 to 700 miles in the south, yet imagine 200 miles or so on the top of this for the northern fliers.

Therein lies prejudice, belief and opinion in what could be classed as an outstanding performance. Argument and debate roll on and I have a bias towards marathon birds in excess of 800 miles or 700 miles against the wind. In the UK, Barcelona International at 800 miles plus has NEVER been done on the second day - I value birds on the 3rd and 4th days, with all those around 700 on the second day being good ones, along with the fanciers themselves.

The most difficult is 800 plus Barcelona International into Ireland - yet to be done in race time! Now that will be something left to accomplish - it will transcend the world of pigeon racing.

I dislike races with lots of birds close together at similar distances - individuals are what I look for. How well you have done then is personal, yet I do like the difficulty inherent in many West Country races of England from Spain.

Have a think.

July 2015

REDUCING YOUNG BIRD LOSSES

The best way of reducing losses is to keep well-bred, fit birds on the open loft system if you can manage it in your particular location. Ours are fed on the same food as the international birds, exercised with them and all are bred from marathon genes and all are related in the main to one proven strain.

Frequent short tosses say up to 20 miles will overstress your birds and precipitate the onset of young bird sicknesses as the immune system is compromised. Some losses are inevitable and normal practice on the build-up of the young bird to Barcelona.

On arrival from a toss we have Vydex Supersix in the water and feed in with peanuts. We never ration or reduce the feed to try and gain speed and the birds are out in all weathers on the natural system – a practice I have embraced for close on 40 years.

The fancier is a key element in the total home environment which must be secure and pigeon-friendly.

To create good old birds it is not necessary to race young birds at all, although the novice should cut his teeth on this practice for fun, experience and results.

In my youth I trained young birds in all direction and up to 140 miles with good effect. The keys then are exercise, health, fitness, origin and the fancier and the total conditions.

July 2015

PIGEON KEEPERS AND COLLECTORS

Some people, by virtue of their contacts, influence and persuasive power, obtain good birds from many and variable sources in a near-frenzy of excitement. Ironically, few of these folk race with consistency at the higher echelons of the sport. The cliché 'the other man's grass is always greener' tends to apply here.

There was a chap who collected jewels, with 140 of my strain and never raced a pigeon. To my biased mind's eye, the very soul of pigeon racing is in the constant testing of all birds at the highest level to produce your own strain - a personal and egocentric mission to accomplish.

The corollary is that the world affords ample room for all types, although I prefer dedicated, purist individuals who push the boundaries of excellence - the back garden perfectionist! Where do you sit in the categorisation of fanciers?

July 2015

YOUNG BIRD TRAINING UPDATE

Our team of 70 were on open loft since weaning, in all weathers, flying on and off the loft and flying at will. They had flown out with all the old birds and a few stock and amongst local ferals and passing race birds.

Hunting hen sparrowhawks are infrequent in the area and all our birds take their chances, which is an echo of actual race reality conditions. With confidence and expectation the birds were given a first toss from the loft at approx. 40 miles into a head wind today. 63 birds are now back in the safety of the loft ready for their second toss of 60-plus miles.

Pigeon racing is simple with a good basic system, yet the realist tells me that few of these pigeons will cut the mustard as champions!

We have proven to ourselves that YB racing is not necessary in the great scheme of marathon and distance racing. In closed-up loft, with limited exercise, it is the clever fancier who races well and gets good returns. Nature will put super condition on your birds - check out the wild doves and pigeons in the countryside for yourselves.

Do not follow my ideas if you are really hard hit by aerial predators.

July 2015

IF I COULD TURN BACK TIME

You live and you learn the hard way by sifting through the myths and false beliefs that are built on folk tales until you form a valid, winning system that works for you. With hindsight I would have raced when younger and specialised in international events. Many films are entertaining, yet teach you little because of the shallow nature of the spoken word. I was wise to read all the top books and now internet articles. I have been caught out on buying birds in the past and learned who was who with some difficulty.

You can but try and put old heads on young shoulders and, on reflection, I am pleased with my efforts over the years, yet there is much to learn in the cold light of day.

I was fortunate to have met and lived near a racing mentor, Jack Ross, in 1976, who lit the flame of a nice little career in pigeons. On a humorous note I would have kept awake when racing birds from Pau and Dax as they arrived when I was oblivious.

Nostalgia will not change the realities of the past.

August 2015

TIME ON THE WING TRAINING

The whole thought process to develop distance/marathon birds is not the sprint home philosophy. In fact, it is the opposite. Starting training at say 40 miles, I like the birds to take as long as possible to build both muscle and navigational experience - 3 tosses 40, 60 and 100 miles in head winds if possible where the line of flight is not critical. This will sort the young birds. I want to avoid corridor flying.

A nice 5 to 7-hour fly is good for a young bird and they do not need to be raced. Yearlings I like out to, say, 450 miles with 10 hours plus on the wing. As two-year-olds and over the birds will have 18 hours plus flies and up to, say, 15 hours on the day - an 800-miler in less than 5 days is a good one. A minority will tackle over 800 at Barcelona, where to time in northern England/Ireland or Scotland will involve just that.

These are the races of die-hard enthusiasts, pioneers and oddballs with lashings of patience. The corollary is that for sprint racing you need the fastest route home where dominant wins are key.

August 2015

COPING WITH STRESSED PIGEONS

Birds arriving by courier transit that are apparently fit and healthy will nevertheless be stressed up to the eyeballs. Many younger ones may fall victim to disease organisms in the new bug flora of your loft – just when you thought they looked so well. All that return –young and old – from races are stressed: it is the nature of the beast.

We can take remedial steps to relax the birds and raise their immunity levels. We dilute Vydex Supersix, a well-researched product, in the water and feed some condition seed/TOVO/Hormoform/peanuts and pellets to get some quality nutrition into them. The loft should be airy, calm, cool and well ventilated. Monitor the condition of the birds and use an antibiotic as a last resort like Doxy T or Baytril - these may or may not be effective. New intros will need to adjust to the profile of organisms (bacteria / viruses / parasites) in the loft.

August 2015

SINGULAR INDIVIDUALISM

Far from the common herd, in a world of the absurd, a genius is born. With a singular eye, this creative individual leaves his footprint in what is different, noble and beautiful. He hears a different tune and answers to the beat of his own drum. Why conform when you relish an alternative reality?

Time will judge this misfit or eccentric and may embrace him in the popular culture of the day. It is enough to know that trends are set, discoveries made and new insights forged by the singular individualist with the power of his unique perception and imagination in glorious demonstration of originality.

August 2015

IN THE RIGHT HANDS

The commercial world of named strains is awash with money, trading on the performances of a few top racing pigeons. You buy into a dream, a hope and an expectation.

In reality there are very few real champions and in pigeons – they are a rarity. The tricks of the publicity machine lure us all in – 'the other man's grass is always greener', 'the sun shines brighter on the other side' syndromes.

I am shrewd with pigeons and have an eye for a nicely-bred one and I do not put good looks and handling first: genes first for me from a man of real integrity. It is crucial to condition your birds on a good individual system that cultivates the best in them or you will constantly seek new birds in your winning attempts.

I feel that more attention should be given to the person than to the buying and selling bandwagon. The key behind the top men is the practical application of KNOWLEDGE.

Pigeons have limits and will not match many other birds like Artic terns for endurance flights and few can tackle over 1ooo miles. We try to extend the boundaries of capability with rare positive results.

August 2015

OUR FINAL TRAINING TOSS

We set out to cover 100 road miles in an easterly direction and liberated the young birds on their own. It was to be a calculated third and final toss for the birds in pleasant flying conditions, although over some towns and cities with tempting ferals and racers to zoom into.

After four hours we had four birds and on 10 hours 16

birds. Today a further 17 have returned after a night on the tiles –marathon, old birds always have time out.

Racers fly on their brain/mind synthesis - a mysterious phenomenon not understood by humanity. This trainer has set the good ones with navigation and stamina up for the future. Soon the birds will be treated and allowed to moult and grow for the rest of the year. The jump from 60 to 100 miles approx. disproves the theory of orientation/navigation by perceived or known landmarks!

Every modern hypothesis is applied to racing pigeon homing and set by the limits of scientific and human consciousness and knowledge. The facts remain unknown to me in a sea of speculation. I love the mystique engendered by the humble racing pigeon. If the game was totally predictable I would lose interest. It is the arrogance and delusion of man that feigns omniscience.

You can have a perception of what you think is a good bird, yet the only absolute test is the liberation at the race point - a purist approach.

August 2015

ORGANISATION

Many are very disorganised in their whole approach to the sport. There are some factors which will help if you have a mind for the job.

I like a copy, accurate or not, of every new introduction to the squad. This will give archive background to your strain if you build one. To me identifying every bird is important without access to records ie by perception and sight. Can you bring the name of your race points to mind and distances? How to sex your birds will test your sensory powers and perception. A breeding/racing plan needs to be formed and carried out with efficiency and do not be deterred in your intentions and objectives. The fanatic lives and dreams his birds which are afforded priority. Keep your daily tasks simple, easy and let the birds do the work. Records and any writing can be made concise, precise and pointed - this will take a sharp intellect. I find it helps to target a race point, after you have been competitive against others.

The whole essence of the job is organised mindfulness.

August 2015

THE EFFECTS OF INBREEDING IN MY STRAIN

During thirty-nine years of racing and observation, the foundation birds have experienced concentrated breeding around performance individuals. The pick of the best lookers are stocked for further inbreeding and a little out. Some beautiful, small, refined birds are bred and any inbreeding depression due to homozygous recessive genes is raced out of the progeny.

I like nice delicate-looking little birds, far removed from the big bold, sprint archetype. I have noted a minority of barren hens, frills and crests, yet some lovely smooth feather and light balance in the dark chequers and velvets and we do not countenance a bird that will not go 700 miles. Even so, champions are rare enough to keep us motivated. I think strict racing in the early days was most helpful and Brian Denney made us all try very hard to do well.

Inbred birds may increase your chances of a good one, especially if you mate them with an unrelated inbred for hybrid vigour. The methodology is best suited to individualists who wish to make a stand and concentrate in an introverted way on birds that are the subject of their own intensive breeding programme.

The corollary is that most Continental champions are of mixed origins and a right assorted bunch. Have a look at the pedigrees: there are more outbred than inbred champions. The secret has to be in the racing of all the progeny irrespective of breeding system.

August 2015

BASIC NUTRITION OF THE RACER

There is no definitive mixture for birds, and mixtures are made up of many ingredients. I like to supply all the needs of the birds in the form of our own mixture of grains and supplements and having won from 31 to 879 miles, the feeding must have been adequate on these races.

I like to create the health and condition I have seen on wild doves and pigeons and in this sense will give some animal protein to the birds such as TOVO, for example in order to replicate nature. A good pellet like a G10 is a superior food source to a standard race mixture. Starving pigeons in an attempt to gain control or speed is not good for the stamina, longevity and endurance of the bird and they may well drop in the fields on their way home.

We feed the young birds exactly the same as the old racers and they fly the skies out on open loft. The stock can be fed the same with an increase in the protein concentration of 16 to 18 percent.

Like the pigeons of many natural men my birds worked the fields, just as they do on many marathon races, as, once liberated, they are free to obey instincts, no matter how much control man exercises at home.

August 2015

BASIC OUTBREEDING OF THE RACER

I do not believe in constant outbreeding for the sake of it with birds from here, there and everywhere, although all racers are of mixed origins at some stage and from different sources. A look at the pedigrees will normally substantiate that fact.

I think we can assume many errors exist in many written pedigrees and I will have made some myself. For outbreeding introductions I look for inbred introductions from outstanding performance pigeons at my chosen distances. Paired into the strain you may hit on a bird of hybrid vigour that performs really well, due to the way the genes have combined. It is a well proven process with plants and livestock and the proof of the pudding is in the results.

Outbreeding is not an exact science and each bird will be different. The key to good outbreeding is the inbreeding that has been carried out already.

August 2015

BASIC MOTIVATION OF THE FANCIER

It is wise to maintain a steady flow of stimulus and interest from one year to the next. I have seen some people get overhyped and get fed up mid-season, since racing to win can be a stressful thing to do, as you are aiming to transcend others.

It may pay to target a race point and maintain an objective approach. However you cannot enjoy the hobby in a vacuum and there are certain human relationships I enjoy.

It is enough to realise that you have done your best and improved in ability, knowledge and contribution to the sport. We have a network of contacts where good results are recognised and marathon strains cultivated, a little like monks serving their time. At the highest conscious level there is a spiritual consequence of good long distance birds which can be felt.

August 2015

BASIC TRAINING OF THE YOUNG RACER

Few will make leading old birds - it is the sobering nature of race reality. On open loft a 40-mile first toss may be fine, assuming the young birds have ranged for miles. New starters should start them off at, say, five miles and build up the birds and their own confidence. If they come fit and well, then you are on the right track with loft and management.

To win young bird races I like some nice long tosses, enough to swell the bodies yet not to overstress them or make them vulnerable to young bird sicknesses, of which there are plenty, and they may knock you for six.

I now realise the benefits of individual private training. A lot can happen in flight and en route, yet it pays to focus on the ones that return. I like breeders that produce multiple returns from any tosses.

Contentment at home is of great importance. Some specialists train the birds from all poles on the compass to maximise their experience, and I can see the wisdom in this practice. I do like all the birds to have returned singly where possible, yet speed is often a consequence of group flying. I never starve the young birds, ever.

August 2015

Printed in Great Britain
by Amazon